Positive Organ   avior

Positive Organizational Behavior

Edited by
Debra L. Nelson and Cary L. Cooper

SAGE Publications
London ● Thousand Oaks ● New Delhi

SAGE Publications Ltd
1 Oliver's Yard
55 City Road
London EC1Y ISP

SAGE Publications Inc.
2455 Teller Road
Thousand Oaks, California 91320

SAGE Publications India Pvt Ltd
B-42, Panchsheel Enclave
Post Box 4109
New Delhi 110 017

British Library Cataloguing in Publication data

A catalogue record for this book is available
from the British Library

ISBN 978-1-4129-1212-9
ISBN 978-1-4129-1213-6 (pbk)

Library of Congress Control Number: 2006925019

Typeset by C&M Digitals (P) Ltd, Chennai, India
Printed and bound in India by Gopsons Papers Ltd.
Printed on paper from sustainable resources

Contents

Preface

Positive Organizational Behavior has a broad reach, from past organizational research streams buried deep by business school ideology, through the present with its pressing needs and emergent opportunities, to the positive institutions that the future can hold – if we act upon POB's principles.

POB reanimates a substratum of organizational research's ancient history. A long time ago, before business schools were the primary producers of social science research on organizations, personal growth, interpersonal connection, and worker–employer mutuality were some of organizational research's central themes. Consider Harry Levinson's notion of the psychological contract, as a mutual arrangement meeting deep-seated individual and collective needs; Chris Argyris's focus on authenticity and learning in developing functional interpersonal and organizational relationships; and Douglas McGregor's constructive view of leadership as partnership between managers and workers. To these three scholars, and many of their contemporaries, human growth and betterment were *de rigueur* in an effective organization. The ensuing years witnessed a change in the implicit model of effective organizations guiding scholarly thinking. Recent organizational research has reflected its business school context, falling more closely in line with traditional economic and financial notions of firm performance. The positive psychology movement, of which this book is a part, provides impetus for organizational behavior to revitalize the concern for human growth and relational mutuality as a mainstay of effective organizing.

Growth and mutuality are human needs of special import in our own times. The re-emergence of this line of inquiry is a healing reaction to the averse, often traumatic experiences to which global organizations have exposed many employees and their families. Individual growth, compelling future, and a just and supportive workplace are the anchors of a positive organization, features which contrast with those typically found in firms focused narrowly on stock holder interests at the expense of other constituents. Principles for designing positive workplaces may be especially valuable in helping to rehabilitate contemporary firms whose erstwhile strategies have left the workforce physically, emotionally, and economically depleted.

POB may also be about the future, leading to the design of new ways of organizing. As the colleagues who joined forces to write this book make clear, POB points the way for designing work settings that play to people's strengths, where people can be both their best selves and at their best with each other. By combining positive psychology with an organizational perspective, this book helps make the principles of positive psychology actionable.

Denise M. Rousseau

Contributors

Neal M. Ashkanasy, Ph.D., is Director of Research in the Faculty of Business, Economics and Law at the University of Queensland in Australia, and Professor of Management in the UQ Business School. His current research interests are in emotions at work, leadership, organizational culture, and business ethics.

Claire Ashton-James is a visiting scholar at Duke University's Fuqua School of Business and a Ph.D. candidate at the University of New South Wales. Her current research interests include mood and non-conscious cognitive and interpersonal processes.

Bruce J. Avolio, Ph.D. is the Clifton Chair in Leadership in the College of Business Administration, University of Nebraska-Lincoln. His current research interest is authentic leadership development.

Thomas W. Britt, Ph.D. is an associate professor in the Department of Psychology at Clemson University. His research interests include determinants and consequences of self engagement at work and other locations, the stigma of psychological problems in the workplace, and organizational stress and motivation as predictors of well-being and performance.

Robyn L. Brouer is a Ph.D. candidate in Management at Florida State University. She has research interests in the areas of the leadership, social effectiveness, multiple dimensions of person-environment fit, work stress, and social influence processes, including impression management and politics.

Michael E. Brown, Ph.D. is Assistant Professor of Management in the Sam and Irene Black School of Business at Penn State-Erie. His research interests are positive approaches to leadership with a focus on ethical leadership.

Kim S. Cameron, Ph.D., is Professor of Management and Organization in the Ross School of Business and Professor of Higher Education in the School of Education at the University of Michigan. His current research focuses on the virtuousness of and in organizations and their relationships to organizational success.

Cary L. Cooper, CBE, is Professor of Organizational Psychology and Health and Pro Vice Chancellor of the University of Lancaster, UK. His current research interests are in the fields of workplace stress/eustress, work-life balance and the personal/coping factors that create healthy individuals and organizations.

James M. (Jim) Dickinson is the Strategic Initiatives Coordinator for the Association of Baltimore Area Grantmakers and part-time Director of Planning and Research for the Marion I. & Henry J. Knott Foundation. His current interests include successful reentry of ex-offenders and collaborations among philanthropic organizations.

Gerald R. Ferris, Ph.D., is the Francis Eppes Professor of Management and Professor of Psychology at Florida State University. He has research interests in the areas of social influence and effectiveness processes in organizations, and the role of reputation in organizations.

Janaki Gooty is a Ph.D. candidate in Organizational Behavior in the Spears School of Business, Oklahoma State University. Her primary research interests are in the areas of leadership, emotion and trust.

Tiffany M. Greene-Shortridge, M.S., is an I-O doctoral candidate in the Department of Psychology at Clemson University. Her current research interests include the stigma of admitting psychological problems, determinants and consequences of positive organizational behavior, the influence of individual differences on person-environment fit, organizational health, and work-family issues.

Charlice Hurst is a Ph.D. student in Management at the University of Florida. Her interests include the relationships among personality, workplace social interaction, diversity, and job attitudes and behaviors.

Timothy A. Judge, Ph.D., is the Matherly-McKethan Eminent Scholar of Management at the University of Florida. His research interests are in the areas of personality, mood and emotions, job attitudes, staffing, careers, and leadership.

Laura M. Little is a Ph.D. candidate in Organizational Behavior in the Spears School of Business at Oklahoma State University. Her primary research interests include the areas of affect and emotional labor.

Fred Luthans, Ph.D., is Distinguished University Professor at the University of Nebraska and a senior scientist with Gallup. His current research interests include positive organizational behavior, the development and performance impact of psychological capital, and global mindset.

Marilyn Macik-Frey is the E.F. Faust/Goolsby Doctoral Fellow at the University of Texas at Arlington. Her research interests are in leadership and communication competence, occupational health and positive organizational behavior.

Eric S. McKibben, BA, is a graduate student in the Department of Psychology at Clemson University. His research interests include determinants and consequences of self engagement at work, aspects of emotional labor, and positive psychological states at work.

Debra L. Nelson, Ph.D., is Spears School of Business Associates' Professor of Management at Oklahoma State University. Her current research interests are positive organizational behavior, emotions at work, and occupational health.

Pamela L. Perrewé, Ph.D., is the Distinguished Research Professor and Jim Moran Professor of Management in the College of Business at Florida State University. Dr. Perrewé's current research interests are in job stress, coping, organizational politics, emotion and personality.

James Campbell (Jim) Quick, Ph.D., is John and Judy Goolsby Distinguished Professor at The University of Texas at Arlington and Visiting Professor, Lancaster University Management School, UK. His current research interests are leadership development, emotional competence, and executive coaching.

Arie Shirom, Ph.D., is Professor of Organizational Behavior in the Graduate Program of Organizational Behavior of the Faculty of Management, Tel-Aviv University. His current research interests include the effects of vigor on physical health, the impact of work-related stress and burnout on employees' health, and stress and performance.

Bret L. Simmons, Ph.D., is Assistant Professor of Management in the College of Business Administration at The University of Nevada, Reno. His research currently focuses on eustress, hope, positive psychology and employee health and performance.

Gretchen M. Spreitzer, Ph.D., is Professor of Management and Organizations at the Stephen M. Ross School of Business at the University of Michigan. Her research has focused on employee empowerment and leadership development, particularly during times of change.

Jason S. Stoner is a Ph.D. candidate in the Department of Management at Florida State University. His primary research interests are identification, stress and coping, and the interactive influence of dispositional and situational factors on workplace behaviors.

Kathleen M. Sutcliffe, Ph.D., is professor of Management & Organizations at the Ross School of Business at the University of Michigan. Her current research interests include team and organizational learning and resilience, high-reliability organizing, and the social and organizational underpinnings of medical mishaps.

Linda Klebe Treviño, Ph.D., is Professor of Organizational Behavior, Cook Fellow in Business Ethics, and Director of the Shoemaker Program in Business Ethics in the Smeal College of Business at The Pennsylvania State University. Her recent research focuses on managing for ethical conduct in organizations.

Thomas A. Wright, Ph.D., is a Professor of Organizational Behavior at the University of Nevada, Reno. His current research interests include: optimizing employee performance, sustaining employee commitment, enhancing employee health and well-being, and business ethics.

Carolyn M. Youssef, Ph.D., is Assistant Professor of Management at Bellevue University. Her current research interests include positive organizational behavior and psychological capital.

PART ONE

INTRODUCTION AND FRAMEWORKS

1

Positive Organizational Behavior: An Inclusive View

Debra L. Nelson and Cary L. Cooper

The real voyage of discovery consists not in seeking new landscapes
but in having new eyes.

Marcel Proust (1871–1922)

Moving away from a disease and dysfunction model to a new look at the
world of work with a focus on positive attributes of people and organizations means looking at organizational behavior in a new light. Martin
Seligman and his colleagues (cf. Seligman and Csikszentmihalyi, 2000)
called for positive psychology, defined as a science of positive subjective
experience. They acknowledged that psychology's early emphasis on the
negative was a product of history, and was appropriate for its time. Still,
they noted that individuals rose to challenges in traumatic times and that
they retained their integrity and purpose. Characteristics such as courage
and optimism seemed to buffer individuals from the negative consequences
of traumatic experiences. Seligman and Csikszentmihalyi included in positive psychology's mission the need to focus on both human strengths and
positive institutions.

Fred Luthans (Luthans, 2002a, 2000b) pioneered the positive approach
in organizational behavior by mapping out positive organizational behavior (POB), with its focus on building human strengths at work rather than
only managing weaknesses. Luthans recommended that POB researchers
study psychological states that could be validly measured, and that are
malleable in terms of interventions in organizations to improve work performance. Luthans proposed that states such as hope, confidence and
resiliency meet these criteria.

Kim Cameron and his colleagues (Cameron et al., 2003) championed the
emerging area of positive organizational scholarship (POS), which calls for
the study of what goes right in organizations, including an emphasis on
identifying human strengths, producing resilience and restoration, fostering vitality, and cultivating extraordinary individuals. The POS movement

seeks to understand human excellence and exceptional organizational performance. 'Positive deviance', defined as the process by which individuals and organizations flourish and prosper in extraordinary ways, is encompassed within POS.

This collection represents the best work of many travelers on the voyage toward a more positive view of organizational life. In reviewing the contributions to this volume, we were struck by the variance in the many perspectives and points of view, and the many agendas within the field. Some chapters use positive psychology as their point of departure; some use Luthans' perspective on POB; and still others use POS. We welcome this variance and strongly believe that it enriches the whole domain of positive organizational research. We see no need for a fixed or narrow identity for POB. There is room for a host of players and contributors who can elevate the study of the positive to its rightful place in organizational behavior. In fact, like Diener (2003), we hope that sometime in the future POB will be fully developed and absorbed within organizational behavior (OB) such that both positive and negative are studied in a balanced way.

Meanwhile, challenges await us. Foremost among these is determining what is positive. We take an inclusive view, and believe that there is room for the study of positive states, traits and processes within POB. Another issue is this: should we limit ourselves to the study of only positive outcomes? Although positive outcomes have been understudied and deserve emphasis, we call for a balanced view. Positive states, traits and processes should be studied in their own right, but again, not at the expense of the negative (Lazarus, 2003). Some positive states, for example, taken to the extreme, could result in negative consequences. In addition, the role of valence must be explored. What is positive to one person may be experienced as negative by another individual. Inseparable from valence is the importance of the social context, which shapes the individual's experiences, both positive and negative. We also need to know more about the simultaneous existence of some positive and negative variables, and their interplay. Positive states, traits and processes that prevent or buffer negative outcomes should legitimately be a part of POB research. Are we advocating abandonment of the study of dysfunction and suffering at work? Absolutely not. It's a necessary and vital part of OB to understand, resolve and prevent negative outcomes. We are merely suggesting that the positive side be given equal time, which is essential for a more fully integrated domain of organizational behavior.

In this pursuit, concerns about scientific rigor become paramount. These concerns are not unique to POB; however, they warrant careful attention. Measurement issues must be attended to. Although the above-mentioned variance in the field is positive, it brings with it a caution. We need to ensure that we are defining and measuring these variables appropriately and consistently so that we all may understand the impact of our results. Multiple levels of analysis are essential as we endeavor to stake out the domain of optimal individual, group and organizational functioning. Processes take place over time and demand that we employ longitudinal designs.

The contributions to this volume represent the variance in POB and speak to the challenges that POB researchers face. The first section of this book, consisting of this chapter along with three others, presents broad and over-arching works that show the breadth of applications from the positive movement.

- Fred Luthans, Carolyn Youssef and Bruce Avolio put forth their description of psychological capital (PsyCap), which consists of the states confidence/efficacy, hope, optimism and resiliency. They further provide guidance as to how the four PsyCap components can be developed and managed in organizations to foster enhanced performance and competitive advantage.
- Jim Quick and Marilyn Macik-Frey investigate the current state-of-the-science-and-practice concerning healthy, productive work by examining the attributes of healthy individuals and organizations, and by analyzing the current dominant models. They expand the POB arena by introducing individual traits and interpersonal processes into the dialogue. Specifically, they propose interpersonal interdependence and communication competence as critically important factors in studying healthy, productive work.
- Bret Simmons and Debra Nelson present the Holistic Model of Stress, which accentuates the positive form of stress (eustress) and provides a more comprehensive view of the stress experience, including both positive and negative stress responses and consequences. They introduce the concept of savoring eustress as a contrast to coping with distress, and call for research on eustress generation; that is, ways to enhance the pleasurable and motivating aspects of stress at work. Their chapter illustrates the way that the positive movement can bring about a more balanced perspective (positive and negative) to the study of stress, which has consistently focused on the negative.

The second section of the book, which focuses on positive states, traits and processes, highlights the inclusive perspective we advocate by encompassing a wide range of variables reflecting the diversity within positive organizational research.

- Neal Ashkanasy and Claire Ashton-James outline how organizations can engender positive emotion, a necessary precondition for positive organizational behavior. Their multi-level model of emotion includes neuropsychological and cognitive correlates of positive emotion, individual differences, communication of positive emotion, promulgation of positive emotion within groups and creation of positive emotional climates in organizations.

- Gretchen Spreitzer and Kathleen Sutcliffe note that there is more research on slow death at work than exists about thriving, a process characterized by a sense of vitality and a sense of learning at work. The authors examine key antecedents of thriving, and present the features of the work context that produce thriving. They also discuss the positive outcomes of thriving, including self-development, health and performance, and propose that groups, units and organizations can experience collective thriving, which can lead to group and organization-level salutary outcomes.

- Arie Shirom points out that vigor has long been studied as a reflection of physical strength, but it has hardly been studied at work. His focus is on vigor as an affective experience at work reflecting three types of energetic resources: physical strength, emotional energy and cognitive liveliness. Shirom's model of vigor includes antecedents, probable moderators and positive consequences of vigor, including health, life and job satisfaction, job performance and organizational effectiveness.

- Linda Treviño and Michael Brown take a uniquely positive approach to ethics and leadership. In their chapter, they develop the construct of ethical leadership and differentiate it from the transformational and authentic approaches to leadership, acknowledging some overlaps. Ethical leadership specifically looks at leadership from the followers' perspectives. The authors also present their 10-item instrument for measuring ethical leadership.

- Pam Perrewé, Gerald Ferris, Jason Stoner, and Robyn Brouer argue that political skills comprise a central role in the positivity movement because they encompass a positive skill set that is essential for success in contemporary organizations. Political skills have both a dispositional element and an element that can be shaped and developed. The authors demonstrate that political skills have positive effects on job performance, leader effectiveness, reputation and career success, and also that political skills reduce experienced stress in the workplace.

- Kim Cameron analyzes the complexities of forgiveness at both the individual and organizational levels. Forgiveness is an internal state, an interpersonal act and a process. Dispositional forgiveness is the institutionalized capacity to move past trauma and take on a positive orientation. This chapter emphasizes the positive effects of forgiveness on employee behavior, productivity and quality.

- Thomas Britt, James Dickinson, Tiffany Greene-Shortridge and Eric McKibben provide a balanced look at the construct of engagement at work. In reviewing several conceptualizations of engagement, they note that the common factor is that the engaged individual is dedicated to successful work performance through emotional investment. They review the research on predictors of job engagement, and its effects on health and performance. Although engagement is a positive psychological state, it can have negative consequences under certain conditions. Britt et al. remind researchers to build these conditions into their models to provide a more comprehensive view of adaptive functioning at work.

- Tim Judge and Charlice Hurst also take a balanced approach in reviewing the positive aspects and possible costs of positive core self-evaluations (CSE) at work. CSE is a constellation of four traits – self-esteem, locus of control, neuroticism and generalized self-efficacy – and it underscores the idea that some individuals are born with predispositions toward positive feelings and behaviors. Although CSE is related to a host of valued individual and organizational outcomes, the authors note that future research should explore its limitations and costs more fully.

In the third and final section of the book, we focus on the methodological challenges that researchers face as they advance the positive movement. Although these challenges may not be unique to positive organizational behavior, they are formidable and must be acknowledged and dealt with if the positive movement is to go forward.

- Tom Wright tackles two important methodological challenges faced by researchers in the positive movement. One challenge is the decision of whether the variable of interest is a state (typical of the POB domain) or a trait (typical of the POS domain). He suggests supplementing the typical test–retest analysis with tests for parallel and strictly parallel models in order to achieve conceptual clarity and empirical rigor. Further, he suggests moving away from the disease model to study cardiovascular health, using pulse pressure, the composite cardiovascular health measure.
- Laura Little, Janaki Gooty and Debra Nelson bring us full circle in terms of this book by returning to the four variables comprising psychological capital (PsyCap) and examining their construct validity in two separate studies. Convergent, discriminant and predictive validity is investigated for commonly used measures of hope, optimism, resiliency and self-efficacy. Unfortunately, the news is not positive, and they call for more rigorous theory development and measurement development in order to advance the study of POB.

In sum, this book offers a platform for an impressive blend of scholarly research and discussion in the domain of studying positive phenomena at work. Such research should ultimately guide us towards enhancing the experience and consequences of work itself. Our aim in this book is to ensure that the study of POB continues to be a voyage of discovery, and, therefore, a subject of great interest.

References

Cameron, K., Dutton, J.E. and Quinn, R.E. (eds) (2003) *Positive Organizational Scholarship: Foundations of a New Discipline*. San Francisco: Berrett-Koehler.

Diener, E. (2003) 'What is positive about positive psychology: The curmudgeon and Pollyanna', *Psychological Inquiry*, 14, 115–20.

Lazarus, R. (2003) 'Does the positive psychology movement have legs?', *Psychological Inquiry*, 14, 93–109.

Luthans, F. (2002a) 'The need for and meaning of positive organizational behavior', *Journal of Organizational Behavior*, 23, 695–706.

Luthans, F. (2002b) 'Positive organizational behavior: Developing and managing psychological strengths', *Academy of Management Executive*, 16, 57–72.

Seligman, M.E.P. and Csikszentmihalyi, M. (2000) 'Positive psychology', *American Psychologist*, 55, 5–14.

2

Psychological Capital: Investing and Developing Positive Organizational Behavior

Fred Luthans, Carolyn M. Youssef, and Bruce J. Avolio

Several years ago, a growing number of psychologists became concerned that the field had overemphasized the negative at the sacrifice of the positive. In seeking the illusive solutions of healing mental illness and dysfunctional behavior, both academic and practicing psychologists had almost completely ignored strengths and developing and helping healthy, productive people reach even higher levels of functioning. The field had largely ignored the elements that contribute to flourishing, instead focusing on what made individuals fail. The jump start for a more positive psychology came in 1998 when then president of the American Psychological Association Martin Seligman challenged the field to better understand what was right with people instead of solely concentrating on what was wrong with people (Seligman and Csikszentmihalyi, 2000; Sheldon and King, 2001). Indeed, what Seligman was calling for was a more balanced approach to studying what constituted the essence of human functioning and behavior.

The response to Seligman's call for positivity were back-to-back special issues in the *American Psychologist* (2000 and 2001) and, starting in 1999, annual Positive Psychology Summits. There have also been a number of books (e.g. Carr, 2004; Compton, 2005; Peterson and Seligman, 2004; Seligman, 2002), edited handbooks (e.g. Aspinwall and Staudinger, 2003; Keyes and Haidt, 2003; Linley and Joseph, 2004; Lopez and Snyder, 2003; Snyder and Lopez, 2002), journal articles, and a comprehensive website (www.positivepsychology.org) on positive psychology.

Although this rapidly growing body of knowledge on positive psychology has many indirect (and even a few direct, e.g. the *Handbook of Positive Psychology* has one out of 55 chapters on the work domain and Giacalone et al. (2005) have edited a book on positive psychology in business ethics) implications for the workplace, the more direct application has emerged in what we have called positive organizational behavior or simply POB (Luthans, 2002a, 2002b, 2003; also see Wright, 2003) and what a group of scholars mainly from the University of Michigan call positive organizational scholarship or simply POS (Cameron et al., 2003). Whereas POB tends to focus more on micro-level issues related to employee development and performance, POS is aimed more at macro organizational issues, although there is recognized overlap between the two approaches.

Using positive psychology and POB as the foundation and point of departure, we have proposed psychological capital or simply PsyCap as a core construct that can be developed and managed for performance impact (see Luthans et al., 2004, 2007; Luthans and Youssef, 2004). As part of our work on authentic leadership development (see Avolio and Luthans, 2006; Luthans and Avolio, 2003) at the University of Nebraska, Gallup Leadership Institute (see our website: www.gli.unl.edu), we are building the theory, conducting the research and doing developmental interventions on PsyCap (e.g. see Luthans et al., 2005, 2006a, 2006b, 2007). The purpose of this chapter is to briefly summarize this work so far and specifically outline what is meant by PsyCap and provide guidelines for how its major components of confidence/efficacy, hope, optimism and resiliency can be developed and managed/leveraged for performance impact and competitive advantage in today's organizations.

The background and meaning of PsyCap

We first introduced positive organizational behavior or POB as 'the study and application of positively-oriented human resource strengths and psychological capacities that can be measured, developed, and effectively managed for performance improvement in today's workplace' (Luthans, 2002b: 59). Then, to more directly recognize that this positivity can be developed and invested in for performance impact, we proposed the higher-order construct of psychological capital (Luthans and Youssef, 2004; Luthans et al., 2004, 2007). This PsyCap can simply be portrayed as 'going beyond human (what you know) and social (who you know) capital to "who you are" (the actual self) and "what you intend to become" (your possible self)' (Avolio and Luthans, 2006: 147). The comprehensive definition of *PsyCap* is:

> an individual's positive psychological state of development that is characterized by: (1) having confidence (self-efficacy) to take on and put in the necessary effort to succeed at challenging tasks; (2) making a positive attribution (optimism) about succeeding now and in the future; (3) persevering toward goals and, when necessary, redirecting paths to goals (hope) in order to succeed; and (4) when beset by problems and adversity, sustaining and bouncing back and even beyond (resiliency) to attain success. (Luthans et al., 2007: 3)

In total, positive psychological capital, or PsyCap, brings a newly emerging perspective and approach to our understanding and management of human resources in several ways:

- *PsyCap goes beyond human capital.* PsyCap is not just explicit knowledge, skills and abilities that simply can be built through education and training programs, or even through on-the-job experience. Neither is PsyCap equivalent to the organization-specific tacit knowledge that managers and employees build over time through putting in their time and immersing themselves in socialization processes (e.g. Hitt and Ireland, 2002; Hitt et al., 2001). In other words, PsyCap is more than simply important things to know or one's expertise.

- *PsyCap goes beyond social capital.* PsyCap also presents new and exciting opportunities over and above those afforded by social relationships and networking across individuals, departments and organizations (Adler and Kwon, 2002; Coleman, 1988). In other words, PsyCap is more than an influential group of contacts or people with whom you have useful and functional relationships.

- *PsyCap is positive.* Positive psychology has ignited a paradigm shift away from just a negative emphasis on pathology that filled the handbooks, dictionaries and classification systems of clinical psychologists. Similarly, PsyCap offers organizational behavior and human resource management researchers and practitioners a new positive perspective, away from the 'gloom and doom' of focusing on dysfunctional employees, aggression in the workplace, incompetent leaders, stress and conflict, unethical behavior, ineffective strategies and counterproductive organizational structures and cultures. Although these are certainly important avenues for research and practice, trying to fix these problems and weaknesses does not begin to explain human potential.

- *PsyCap is unique.* PsyCap expands the horizons of organizational behavior beyond the traditionally studied constructs such as motivation, goal-setting, empowerment, participation, team-building and organizational culture (e.g. see Locke, 2000). These constructs may be implicitly positive, but most of them have already been extensively studied, and some critics claim these classic constructs remain static (e.g. see Steers, 2001). PsyCap is not intended to be the flipside of the established negative theories and constructs. In other words, it cannot be assumed that seemingly opposite positive and negative constructs are necessarily at the two ends of the same continuum (Peterson and Chang, 2002). PsyCap is a new perspective that can only be captured and utilized through unique and innovative theoretical frameworks, constructs, measures and interventions. Obviously, as PsyCap gains a body of knowledge over time, this uniqueness will no longer hold.

- *PsyCap is theory and research-based.* Considering the avalanche of management fads that continues to be promoted through the unsubstantiated claims of health, wealth and happiness that the popular self-help literature and management 'gurus' offer, it is important to promote and actualize PsyCap as a scientific endeavor. PsyCap is founded on widely recognized theoretical frameworks such as social cognitive theory (Bandura, 1986) and hope theory (Snyder, 2000). It utilizes scientific research methodologies and deductive reasoning to enhance the prediction and causal implications that PsyCap may have on human resource development and performance outcomes in organizations. Each of the constructs comprising overall PsyCap has a history of research to back up its inclusion, but none of them have yet been extensively applied to the workplace, nor have they been combined into a higher-order core construct such as PsyCap.

- *PsyCap is measurable.* For a couple of decades now, there has been an increasing emphasis in management research and practice on quantifying the return on human resource investments (Cascio, 1991; Cascio and Ramos, 1986; Hunter and Schmidt, 1983; Huselid, 1995; Kravetz, 2004). On the other hand, the 'soft' qualities and untested self-assessments that many popular best-sellers offer the general public are lacking any research back-up or meaningful quantitative analysis. In contrast, there is a number of valid and reliable measures that make up PsyCap (e.g. see Lopez and Snyder (2003) for a comprehensive review of positive psychological assessments and in particular the Parker (1998) measure of efficacy; the Snyder et al. (1996) state hope scale; the Wagnild and Young (1993) resiliency scale; and the Scheier and Carver (1985) optimism questionnaire). Drawn from these established measures, we have recently developed and psychometrically supported a PsyCap Questionnaire (PCQ), with sample items shown in Appendix A. Thus, we not only have theoretically based constructs comprising PsyCap, we also have the first survey measure to assess these positive constructs as overall PsyCap that has demonstrated reliability and evidence of construct validity (Luthans et al., 2006b).

- *PsyCap is state-like and therefore open to development.* Many personality traits have been found to relate to performance in the workplace. These include Big Five personality traits (Barrick and Mount, 1991), self-evaluations (Judge and Bono, 2001), Gallup's talents and strengths (Buckingham and Clifton, 2001; Buckingham and Coffman, 1999), cognitive mental abilities (Schmidt and Hunter, 2000) and emotional intelligence (Goleman, 1998). The positive psychology literature is also rich with positive traits that are largely dispositional (e.g. see Peterson and Seligman, 2004). On the other hand, PsyCap is a set of malleable and developmental states that have been demonstrated to significantly increase through relatively brief (1–3 hour), highly focused micro-interventions (see Luthans et al., 2006a). Along with taking a more positive approach to understanding human potential in the workplace, we have proposed to include only those constructs in PsyCap that are state-like. This psychological capital intervention (PCI) is given attention toward the last part of the chapter and the model is found in Appendix B.

- *PsyCap is impactful on work-related performance.* Research to date supports that PsyCap is significantly related to performance in the workplace, both the individual components (efficacy/confidence, hope, optimism and resiliency) and in combination as overall PsyCap (e.g. Luthans et al., 2005, 2006b; Youssef, 2004). This relationship has been shown through utility analysis to make a dramatic contribution to the organization (Luthans et al., 2006a, 2007). Thus, PsyCap becomes a meaningful and justifiable investment and means toward veritable organizational performance and possibly sustained competitive advantage. This performance impact separates PsyCap from many positive psychological capacities that are often viewed as ends in and of themselves (e.g. see Peterson and Seligman, 2004; Snyder and Lopez, 2002) and is given further attention toward the end of the chapter.

The PsyCap states

Four positive psychological capacities have been identified as best meeting the above PsyCap inclusion criteria of being positive, unique, theory and research-based, measurable, developmental and manageable for performance impact in the workplace. These capacities are: self-efficacy/confidence, hope, optimism and resiliency (Luthans, 2002a; Luthans et al., 2007). The following discusses each of these PsyCap components in terms of their theoretical framework and how they can be developed and managed for performance impact in organizations.

Managing PsyCap self-efficacy/confidence

Self-efficacy, or simply confidence, is largely based on Bandura's (1986, 1997) social cognitive theory, and when applied to the workplace can be defined as 'an individual's conviction (or confidence) about his or her abilities to mobilize the motivation, cognitive resources, and courses of action necessary to successfully execute a specific task within a given context' (Stajkovic and Luthans, 1998b: 66). Confident individuals trust their abilities. This enables them to choose challenging tasks, invest the necessary time and energy to achieve their goals and persevere when faced with obstacles and discouraging signals (Stajkovic and Luthans, 1998b). The capacities of symbolizing, forethought, observation, self-regulation and self-reflection allow confident people to purposefully, agentically and proactively set challenging goals, regulate their motivation and actions, and manage and control their learning processes in anticipation of future success (Bandura and Locke, 2003).

Self-efficacy has been found to be strongly correlated with work-related performance (Stajkovic and Luthans, 1998a) and to be readily developable in workplace settings (Bandura, 1997, 2000). Several approaches have been successful in developing self-efficacy. The most effective efficacy-building technique is to allow the developing manager or employee to actually experience success and mastery of the task at hand. Earning success and gradually increasing the level of task complexity in hands-on types of training, either on-the-job or in relevant simulated settings, can provide participants with mastery experiences, which have been clearly shown to enhance their self-efficacy (Bandura, 2000).

Vicarious learning, or simply modeling, is another widely recognized approach for developing self-efficacy. This approach is particularly relevant in settings when actual mastery experiences are difficult, risky or too expensive to provide. Vicarious learning capitalizes on the individual's observational capacities, allowing learning to occur as relevant role models are being observed experiencing success in tasks that are similar to those that the developing manager or employee is expected to perform. Interestingly, even when relevant role models cannot be found, people also seem to be able to draw their confidence from imaginal experiences. They visualize themselves succeeding in the task and use their imagined selves as the role-models (Maddux, 2002).

Other approaches for developing self-efficacy include social persuasion and physiological/psychological arousal (Bandura, 1997). In order for efficacy development to be robust, even when individuals directly experience success, their perceptions and attributions need to internalize this success. The social, psychological and physical context in which mastery experiences are introduced can be managed for further efficacy enhancement. This can be accomplished through positive feedback, social recognition, empowerment and work–life balance. Finally, confidence can be built on the belief in integrated team capacities (i.e. collective efficacy), rather than just one's individual abilities and actions.

Managing PsyCap hope

Drawing from the extensive theory and research of recently deceased positive psychologist C. Rick Snyder, PsyCap hope can be defined as 'a positive motivational state that is based on an interactively derived sense of successful (1) agency (goal-directed energy) and (2) pathways (planning to meet goals)' (Snyder et al., 1991: 287). Thus, hope is developed in two important ways: first, through people's sense of agency or willpower, by increasing their determination to achieve their goals, and second, through the development of pathways, the waypower that enables individuals to proactively design alternative pathways and contingency plans to achieve their goals when they face obstacles and blockages.

An integral part of developing and managing hope is through effective goal-setting. Setting goals that are specific, measurable and challenging, yet realistic and achievable, can help develop a sense of agency for accomplishing those goals. 'Stretch goals' are challenging goals that can expand one's skills and horizons without driving the person to despair. 'Stepping' is another technique in which goals are broken down into smaller and simpler sub-goals. These sub-goals can be accomplished and monitored as milestones toward the eventual attainment of the greater goal. It is also important for goals to be negotiated, shared and communicated in order for managers and employees to be motivated to accomplish them. Most importantly, agency thinking requires the ability to make judgments when unrealistic goals have been pursued, or when over-planning has taken place, to adapt and 're-goal' toward more effective goals (Luthans and Jensen, 2002; Luthans et al., 2001; Snyder, 1995a, 1995b; Snyder et al., 2000a, 2000b).

Besides the agency expressed through goal framing and process, pathways thinking is also vital to hope development. Pathways can be proactively developed through 'mental rehearsals', in which individuals visualize the integral and most challenging components in their goal accomplishment processes, and prepare themselves to overcome important obstacles. Contingency planning and what-if analyses are pragmatic techniques that can be used at both the individual and organizational levels for building the pathways component of hope (Luthans and Jensen, 2002; Luthans and Youssef, 2004; Snyder et al., 2000a; Youssef and Luthans, 2003, 2006).

Managing PsyCap optimism

An optimistic explanatory style attributes positive events to personal, permanent and pervasive causes, and negative events to external, temporary and situation-specific ones (Seligman, 1998). On the other hand, a pessimistic explanatory style externalizes positive events, explaining them in terms of external, temporary and situation-specific reasons, while internalizing negative events and explaining them in terms of personal, permanent and pervasive reasons (Seligman, 1998). In PsyCap, realistic (Schneider, 2001), flexible (Peterson, 2000) optimism is emphasized (Luthans et al., 2007).

PsyCap optimism is a responsible and adaptive form of optimism. It carefully considers and learns from both positive and negative events, as well as their causes and consequences, before taking credit for successes or distancing and externalizing failures. The utility of this type of PsyCap optimism is very relevant in the workplace. In today's organizational environment, responsibility and accountability have become necessary, while at the same time external factors may render many aspects of one's decisions and actions out of one's full control.

Effective developmental approaches for PsyCap optimism include Schneider's (2001) three-step process: leniency for the past, appreciation for the present and opportunity-seeking for the future. As managers and employees toil with the realities of their situations, they need to be sensitive in distinguishing facts from perceptions, giving themselves the benefit of the doubt for misfortunes that were possibly beyond their control. They should carefully assess the utility of holding onto feelings of guilt or shame, because these negative feelings can have a devastating impact on their optimism. They can paralyze their appreciation of and learning from the positives of a situation. They can also hinder future risk-taking and result in stagnation and complacency. Once these negative thoughts and feelings are realistically discounted, they can be replaced with optimistic, positive ones that should lead to a better future. As taken from our definition of PsyCap at the beginning of the chapter, this is the individual's state of development that is characterized by '... making a positive attribution (optimism) about succeeding now and in the future' (Luthans et al., 2007).

Managing PsyCap resiliency

Again drawing from clinical and positive psychology, we define PsyCap resiliency as 'the positive psychological capacity to rebound, to "bounce back" from adversity, uncertainty, conflict, failure or even positive change, progress and increased responsibility' (Luthans, 2002a: 702; also see Luthans et al., 2006c; Youssef and Luthans, 2005). Resilient individuals possess 'a staunch acceptance of reality; a deep belief, often buttressed by strongly held values, that life is meaningful; and an uncanny ability to improvise' (Coutu, 2002: 48). Resilient organizations also have been defined along the dimensions of effective power structures, relationships, sense of reality, attitude to change, differentiation and communication (Hind et al., 1996).

These definitions indicate resiliency does not imply a fortunate, risk-free life, but rather the effective management of scarce resources toward a more fortunate life despite risks and adversities. Along these lines, Masten and Reed (2002: 75) define resiliency at the individual level as 'a class of phenomena characterized by patterns of positive adaptation in the context of significant adversity or risk'. Worline and colleagues (2002) and Klarreich (1998) view resiliency at the organizational level as the structural and processual dynamics that equip an organization with the capacities necessary to absorb strain, retain coherence and bounce back, thus enabling the ongoing engagement of risk.

Various strategies for developing PsyCap resiliency can be classified into three sets: asset-focused strategies, risk-focused strategies and process-focused strategies (Masten, 2001; Masten and Reed, 2002). In times characterized by stability or incremental change, leaders and their associates, as well as their overall organizations, can be encouraged and supported in accumulating various types of assets. These assets include at the organizational level structural, financial and technological, and at the individual level human, social and psychological capital (Luthans and Youssef, 2004; Luthans et al., 2006c; Youssef and Luthans, 2005). Such asset-focused developmental strategies can help mitigate various risk factors and times of adversity. For example, those employees who build their employability assets are more resilient in this era of downsizing and rapid change. By the same token, it is also wise of organizations and their members to avoid unnecessary or exaggerated forms of risk that can jeopardize their well-being. Risk-focused strategies of resiliency are primarily about proactively reducing exposure to risk through various protective mechanisms.

Like hope and optimism, resiliency development is not limited to simply accentuating the positive and eliminating or reducing the negative. It goes beyond that, into proactively engaging in calculated risks and capitalizing on various assets that can transform those risk factors into opportunities for future growth and development. Process-focused strategies emphasize this dynamic interaction between assets and risks, in which the effective handling of adversities and setbacks can result in bouncing back even beyond one's original level of performance, into unexpected realms of learning and growth (Luthans et al., 2006c; Reivich and Shatte, 2002; Ryff and Singer, 2003; Sutcliffe and Vogus, 2003; Youssef and Luthans, 2005). In other words, despite the inevitability of facing difficulties, effectively dealing with hardships may be necessary for resiliency development.

Managing overall PsyCap

Although efficacy/confidence, hope, optimism and resiliency best meet our criteria for PsyCap inclusion, and each has been shown to positively relate to performance outcomes in organizations, our research indicates that PsyCap may be a higher-order, core construct (Luthans et al., 2006b). Specifically, preliminary research indicates that overall PsyCap is a better predictor of performance and satisfaction than each of the four states (Luthans et al., 2006b).

Although considerable attention has been given to the conceptual independence (e.g. see Luthans and Jensen, 2002; Snyder, 2002) and empirically demonstrated discriminant validity (e.g. see Bryant and Cvengros, 2004; Luthans et al., 2006b; Magaletta and Oliver, 1999) of the four positive states, there is also an underlying convergence of positivity and 'moving ahead' among them (Luthans et al., 2006b, 2007). PsyCap as a core construct adds value to the individual states discussed above and has implications for developmental interventions and return on development or what we call ROD (Avolio and Luthans, 2006).

Measurement and development of PsyCap

Besides being based on the theory and research briefly summarized so far, in order to meet our criteria for inclusion, the individual components and overall PsyCap must also be measurable and open to development and change. We have recently developed and provide reliability and validity support for the psychological capital questionnaire or PCQ, with sample items found in Appendix A (see Luthans et al., 2006b, 2007). The preliminary research indicates that this measure of PsyCap significantly relates to performance and satisfaction across diverse samples (emerging adults, as well as service and high-tech manufacturing employees) (Luthans et al., 2006b).

To meet the developmental criterion of PsyCap, we have also recently developed and begun to test the micro-intervention model shown in Appendix B (Luthans et al., 2006a). This psychological capital intervention (PCI) model was drawn from the developmental suggestions and clinical practice guidelines from each of the four components of PsyCap. Like the PsyCap measure, this PCI has been tested with diverse samples. For example, under highly controlled conditions (e.g. random assignment to experimental and control groups), management students/emerging adults (Arnett, 2000) underwent one-hour PCI sessions which increased their measured pre to post PsyCap by a significant 3 percent. The control groups, on the other hand, who went through a one-hour group exercise, non-related to PsyCap, but relevant, showed no increase in their pre to post PsyCap. Similar results were obtained using a cross-sectional sample of managers from all types of organizations and with a sample of engineering managers in a high-tech firm. Through utility analysis, the results from the PCI intervention with the engineering managers yielded 270 percent return on investment in the 2.5 hour PsyCap development session (Luthans et al., 2006a, 2007).

In other words, we were able to demonstrate through very short (1–3 hour sessions depending on the size of the group and number of exercises and video clips used), highly focused micro-interventions following the PCI model shown in Appendix B, that PsyCap can indeed be developed relatively easily. Although we fully realize that more research is needed on both the measure and the micro-interventions, results so far seem quite promising and do seem to indicate that PsyCap can be both measured and developed.

Implications and conclusions

This chapter first summarized the positive psychology and positive organizational behavior background and defined our newly emerging concept of psychological capital. Our recently developed measure and micro-intervention model shown in Appendix A and Appendix B show promise that PsyCap can be directly applicable to both research and practice. Importantly, through utility analysis using the significant positive correlation between PsyCap and performance outcomes from our research so far, and the percentage increase in PsyCap from our micro-interventions, we are able to demonstrate not only developmental and performance impact, but also an impressive return on investment (see Luthans et al., 2006a, 2006b, 2007).

This chapter on positive organizational behavior can serve as a foundation and point of departure for the remaining chapters. Besides background and definition of what we mean by positive organizational behavior, we also give most attention to our newly emerging concept of psychological capital. This PsyCap is made up of criteria meeting strengths and psychological capacities that can be measured, developed and managed for performance impact and competitive advantage. The chapters that follow take different perspectives, but when taken as a whole provide much added value to needed positivity in today's workplace.

References

Adler, P.S. and Kwon, S. (2002) 'Social capital: Prospects for a new concept', *Academy of Management Review*, 27, 17–40.

Arnett, J.J. (2000) 'Emerging adulthood: A theory of development for the late teens through the twenties', *American Psychologist*, 55, 469–80.

Aspinwall, L. and Staudinger, U. (eds) (2003) *A Psychology of Human Strengths: Fundamental Questions and Future Directions for a Positive Psychology.* Washington, DC: American Psychological Association.

Avolio, B.J. and Luthans, F. (2006) *The High Impact Leader: Moments Matter in Accelerating Authentic Leadership Development.* New York: McGraw-Hill.

Bandura, A. (1986) *Social Foundations of Thought and Action.* Englewood Cliffs, NJ: Prentice-Hall.

Bandura, A. (1997) *Self-efficacy: The Exercise of Control.* New York: Freeman.

Bandura, A. (2000) 'Cultivate self-efficacy for personal and organizational effectiveness', in E. Locke (ed.) *Handbook of Principles of Organizational Behavior* (pp. 120–36). Oxford: Blackwell.

Bandura, A. and Locke, E. (2003) 'Negative self-efficacy and goal effects revisited', *Journal of Applied Psychology*, 88, 87–99.

Barrick, M.R. and Mount, M.K. (1991) 'The big five personality dimensions and job performance: A meta-analysis', *Personnel Psychology*, 44, 1–26.

Bryant, F.B. and Cvengros, J.A. (2004) 'Distinguishing hope and optimism', *Journal of Social and Clinical Psychology*, 23, 273–302.

Buckingham, M. and Clifton, D. (2001) *Now, Discover Your Strengths.* New York: Simon & Schuster.

Buckingham, M. and Coffman, C. (1999) *First Break All the Rules: What the World's Greatest Managers Do Differently.* New York: Simon & Schuster.

Cameron, K., Dutton, J. and Quinn, R. (eds) (2003) *Positive Organizational Scholarship.* San Francisco: Berrett-Koehler.

Carr, A. (2004) *Positive Psychology.* New York: Brunner-Routledge.

Cascio, W.F (1991) *Costing Human Resources: The Financial Impact of Behavior in Organizations* (3rd edn). Boston: PWS-Kent.

Cascio, W.F. and Ramos, R.A. (1986) 'Development and application of a new method for assessing job performance and behavioral/economic terms', *Journal of Applied Psychology*, 71, 20–28.

Coleman, J.S. (1988) 'Social capital in the creation of human capital', *American Journal of Sociology*, 94, S95–S120.

Compton, W.C. (2005) *Introduction to Positive Psychology.* Belmont, CA: Thompson Wadsworth.

Coutu, D.L. (2002) 'How resilience works', *Harvard Business Review*, 80, (May), 46–55.

Giacalone, R.A., Jurkiewicz, C. and Dunn, C. (eds) (2005) *Positive Psychology in Business Ethics and Corporate Social Responsibility*. Greenwich, CT: Information Age.

Goleman, D. (1998) *Working with Emotional Intelligence*. New York: Bantam Books.

Hind, P., Frost, M. and Rowley, S. (1996) 'The resilience audit and the psychological contract', *Journal of Managerial Psychology*, 11 (7), 18–29.

Hitt, M.A. and Ireland, D. (2002) 'The essence of strategic management: Managing human and social capital', *Journal of Leadership and Organizational Studies*, 9, 3–14.

Hitt, M.A., Bierman, L., Shimizu, K. and Kochhar, R. (2001) 'Direct and moderating effects of human capital on strategy and performance in professional service firms: A resource-based perspective', *Academy of Management Journal*, 44, 13–28.

Hunter, J.E. and Schmidt, F.L. (1983) 'Quantifying the effects of psychological interventions on employee job performance and work-force productivity', *American Psychologist*, 38, 473–8.

Huselid, M.A. (1995) 'The impact of human resource management practices on turnover, productivity, and corporate financial performance', *Academy of Management Journal*, 38, 635–72.

Judge, T.A. and Bono, J.E. (2001) 'Relationship of core self-evaluations traits – self-esteem, generalized self-efficacy, locus of control, and emotional stability – with job satisfaction and job performance: A meta-analysis', *Journal of Applied Psychology*, 86, 80–92.

Keyes, C. and Haidt, J. (eds) (2003) *Flourishing: Positive Psychology and the Life Well-lived*. Washington, DC: American Psychological Association.

Klarreich, S. (1998) 'Resiliency: The skills needed to move forward in a changing environment', in S. Klarreich (ed.) *Handbook of Organizational Health Psychology: Programs to Make the Workplace Healthier* (pp. 219–38). Madison, CT: Psychosocial Press.

Kravetz, D. (2004) *Measuring Human Capital: Converting Workplace Behavior into Dollars*. Mesa, AZ: KAP.

Linley, P.A. and Joseph, S. (eds) (2004) *Positive Psychology in Practice*. New York: Wiley.

Locke, E. (ed.) (2000) *The Handbook of Principles of Organizational Behavior*. Oxford: Blackwell.

Lopez, S. and Snyder, C.R. (eds) (2003) *Positive Psychological Assessment: A Handbook of Models and Measures*. Washington, DC: American Psychological Association.

Luthans, F. (2002a) 'The need for and meaning of positive organizational behavior', *Journal of Organizational Behavior*, 23, 695–706.

Luthans, F. (2002b) 'Positive organizational behavior: Developing and managing psychological strengths', *Academy of Management Executive*, 16 (1), 57–72.

Luthans, F. (2003) 'Positive organizational behavior (POB): Implications for leadership and HR development and motivation', in R.M. Steers, L.W. Porter and C.A. Begley (eds) *Motivation and Leadership at Work* (pp. 187–95). New York: McGraw-Hill.

Luthans, F. and Avolio, B.J. (2003) 'Authentic leadership: A positive development approach', in K.S. Cameron, J.E. Dutton and R.E. Quinn (eds) *Positive Organizational Scholarship* (pp. 241–58). San Francisco: Berrett-Koehler.

Luthans, F. and Jensen, S.M. (2002) 'Hope: A new positive strength for human resource development', *Human Resource Development Review*, 1, 304–22.

Luthans, F. and Youssef, C.M. (2004) 'Human, social and now positive psychological capital management: Investing in people for competitive advantage', *Organizational Dynamics*, 33, 143–60.

Luthans, F., Avey, J.B., Avolio, B.J., Norman, S.M. and Combs, G.J. (2006a) 'Psychological capital development: Toward a micro-intervention', *Journal of Organizational Behavior*, 27, 387–93.

Luthans, F., Avolio, B.J., Avey, J. and Norman, S. (2006b) 'Psychological capital: Measurement and relationship with performance and satisfaction', *Gallup Leadership Institute, Working Paper*. Lincoln, NE: University of Nebraska.

Luthans, F., Avolio, B.J., Walumbwa, F.O. and Li, W. (2005) 'The psychological capital of Chinese workers: Exploring the relationship with performance', *Management and Organization Review*, 1, 247–69.

Luthans, F., Luthans, K., Hodgetts, R. and Luthans, B. (2001) 'Positive approach to leadership (PAL): Implications for today's organizations', *The Journal of Leadership Studies*, 8 (2), 3–20.

Luthans, F., Luthans, K. and Luthans, B. (2004) 'Positive psychological capital: Going beyond human and social capital', *Business Horizons*, 47 (1), 45–50.

Luthans, F., Vogelgesang, G.R. and Lester, P.B. (2006c) 'Developing the psychological capital of resiliency', *'Human Resource Development Review*, 5 (1), 1–20.

Luthans, F., Youssef, C.M. and Avolio, B.J. (2007) *Psychological Capital*. Oxford: Oxford University Press, 25–44.

Maddux, J.E. (2002) 'Self-efficacy: The power of believing you can', in C.R. Snyder and S. Lopez (eds) *Handbook of Positive Psychology* (pp. 257–76). Oxford: Oxford University Press.

Magaletta, P.R. and Oliver, J.M. (1999) 'The hope construct, will and ways: Their relations with self-efficacy, optimism, and well-being', *Journal of Clinical Psychology*, 55, 539–51.

Masten, A.S. (2001) 'Ordinary magic: Resilience process in development', *American Psychologist*, 56, 227–39.

Masten, A.S. and Reed, M.J. (2002) 'Resilience in development', in C.R. Snyder and S. Lopez (eds) *Handbook of Positive Psychology* (pp. 74–88). Oxford: Oxford University Press.

Parker, S. (1998) 'Enhancing role breadth self-efficacy: The roles of job enrichment and other organizational interventions', *Journal of Applied Psychology*, 6, 835–52.

Peterson, C. (2000) 'The future of optimism', *American Psychologist*, 55, 44–55.

Peterson, C. and Chang, E. (2002) 'Optimism and flourishing', in C. Keyes and J. Haidt (eds) *Flourishing: Positive Psychology and the Life Well-lived* (pp. 55–79). Washington, DC: American Psychological Association.

Peterson, C. and Seligman, M. (2004) *Character Strengths and Virtues: A Handbook and Classification*. Oxford: Oxford University Press.

Reivich, K. and Shatte, A. (2002) *The Resilience Factor: 7 Essential Skills for Overcoming Life's Inevitable Obstacles*. New York: Random House.

Ryff, C. and Singer, B. (2003) 'Flourishing under fire: Resilience as a prototype of challenged thriving', in C. Keyes and J. Haidt (eds) *Flourishing: Positive Psychology and the Life Well-lived* (pp. 15–36). Washington, DC: American Psychological Association.

Scheier, M. and Carver, C. (1985) 'Optimism, coping, and health: Assessment and implications of generalized outcome expectancies', *Health Psychology*, 4, 219–47.

Schmidt, F. and Hunter, J. (2000) 'Select on intelligence', in E. Locke (ed.) *The Handbook of Principles of Organizational Behavior* (pp. 3–14). Oxford: Blackwell.

Schneider, S.I. (2001) 'In search of realistic optimism: Meaning, knowledge and warm fuzziness', *American Psychologist*, 56, 250–63.

Seligman, M. (1998) *Learned Optimism*. New York: Pocket Books.

Seligman, M. (2002) *Authentic Happiness*. New York: Free Press.

Seligman, M. and Csikszentmihalyi, M. (2000) 'Positive psychology', *American Psychologist*, 55, 5–14.

Sheldon, K.M. and King, L. (2001) 'Why positive psychology is necessary', *American Psychologist*, 56, 216–17.

Snyder, C.R. (1995a) 'Conceptualizing, measuring, and nurturing hope', *Journal of Counseling and Development*, 73, 355–60.

Snyder, C.R. (1995b) 'Managing for high hope', *R and D Innovator*, 4 (6), 6–7.

Snyder, C.R. (2000) *Handbook of Hope*. San Diego, CA: Academic Press.

Snyder, C.R. (2002) 'Hope theory: Rainbows in the mind', *Psychological Inquiry*, 13, 249–76.

Snyder, C.R. and Lopez, S. (eds) (2002) *Handbook of Positive Psychology*. Oxford: Oxford University Press.

Snyder, C.R., Ilardi, S., Michael, S.T. and Cheavens, J. (2000a) 'Hope theory: Updating a common process for psychological change', in C.R. Snyder and R.E. Ingram (eds) *Handbook of Psychological Change: Psychotherapy Processes and Practices for the 21st Century* (pp. 128–53). New York: Wiley.

Snyder, C.R., Irving, L. and Anderson, J. (1991) 'Hope and health: Measuring the will and the ways', in C.R. Snyder and D.R. Forsyth (eds) *Handbook of Social and Clinical Psychology* (pp. 285–305). Elmsford, NY: Pergamon.

Snyder, C.R., Sympson, S.C., Ybasco, F.C., Borders, T.F., Babyak, M.A. and Higgins, R.L. (1996) 'Development and validation of the state hope scale', *Journal of Personality and Social Psychology*, 70, 321–35.

Snyder, C.R., Tran, T., Schroeder, L.L., Pulvers, K.M., Adam III, V. and Laub, L. (2000b) 'Teaching the hope recipe: Setting goals, finding pathways to those goals, and getting motivated', *National Educational Service*, Summer, 46–50.

Stajkovic, A.D. and Luthans, F. (1998a) 'Self-efficacy and work-related performance: A meta-analysis', *Psychological Bulletin*, 124, 240–61.

Stajkovic, A.D. and Luthans, F. (1998b) 'Social cognitive theory and self-efficacy: Going beyond traditional motivational and behavioral approaches', *Organizational Dynamics*, 26, 62–74.

Steers, R.M. (2001) 'Call for papers: The future of work motivation theory', *Academy of Management Review*, 26, 331–2.

Sutcliffe, K.M. and Vogus, T. (2003) 'Organizing for resilience', in K.S. Cameron, J.E. Dutton and R.E. Quinn (eds) *Positive Organizational Scholarship* (pp. 94–110). San Francisco: Berrett-Koehler.

Wagnild, G. and Young, H. (1993) 'Development and psychometric evaluation of the resiliency scale', *Journal of Nursing Measurement*, 1 (2), 165–78.

Worline, M.C., Dutton, J.E., Frost, P.J., Kanov, J. and Maitlis, S. (2002) 'Creating fertile soil: The organizing dynamics of resilience', *Paper presented at the National Academy of Management Meeting, Organizational Behavior Division*, Denver, CO.

Wright, T.A. (2003) 'Positive organizational behavior: An idea whose time has truly come', *Journal of Organizational Behavior*, 24, 437–42.

Youssef, C.M. (2004) 'Resiliency development of organizations, leaders and employees: Multi-level theory building and individual-level, path-analytical empirical testing. *PhD Dissertation*, University of Nebraska-Lincoln.

Youssef, C.M. and Luthans, F. (2003) 'Immigrant psychological capital: Contribution to the war for talent and competitive advantage', *Singapore Nanyang Business Review*, 2(2), 1–14.

Youssef, C.M. and Luthans, F. (2005) 'Resiliency development of organizations, leaders and employees: Multi-level theory building for sustained performance', in W. Gardner, B. Avolio and F. Walumbwa (eds), *Authentic Leadership Theory and Practice: Origins, Effects and Development (Monographs in leadership and management, Vol. 3)* (pp. 303–43) Oxford: Elsevier.

Youssef, C.M. and Luthans, F. (2006) 'Time for positivity in the Middle East: Developing hopeful Egyptian organizational leaders', in W. Mobley and E. Weldon (eds) *Advances in Global Leadership (Vol. 4)*. Oxford: Elsevier.

Appendix A

Sample items from the PsyCap Questionnaire (PCQ)

Below are statements that describe how you may think above yourself right now. Use the following scales to indicate your level of agreement or disagreement with each statement.

1 = strongly disagree, 2 = disagree, 3 = somewhat disagree, 4 = somewhat agree, 5 = agree, 6 = strongly agree

1. I feel confident helping to set targets/goals in my work area.
2. I feel confident presenting information to a group of colleagues.
3. There are lots of ways around any problem.
4. I can think of many ways to reach my current work goals.
5. When I have a setback at work, I have trouble recovering from it and moving on. (Reverse scored)
6. I usually take stressful things at work in stride.
7. When things are uncertain for me at work I usually expect the best.
8. I'm optimistic about what will happen to me in the future as it pertains to work.

Source: Drawn from Luthans et al. (2006b). Items adapted from Parker (1998); Snyder et al. (1996); Wagnild and Young (1993); Scheier and Carver (1985).

Note

All 24 items were used conducting reliability and validity analyses of the PCQ. These sample items are not to intended be used for research purposes. For permission to use the PCQ instrument write to the authors at the Gallup Leadership Institute, Dept. of Management, University of Nebraska, Lincoln, NE 68588, USA.

Appendix B

Psychological Capital Intervention (PCI)

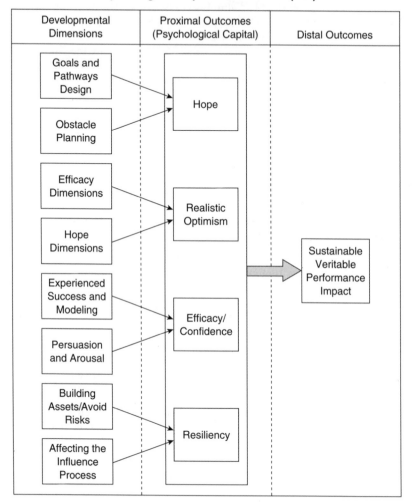

Note: The PCI is intended to affect each state as well as the overall level of PsyCap for performance impact.

Source: Drawn from Luthans et al. (2006a, 2007)

3

Healthy, Productive Work:
Positive Strength through Communication Competence
and Interpersonal Interdependence

James Campbell Quick and Marilyn Macik-Frey

Health and productivity at work are sometimes considered trade-offs that are in conflict rather than attributes which are complementary. We, however, see health and productivity as complementary and healthy, productive work as the basis for both achievement *and* well-being. We arrive at this position by taking a long-term perspective that advances the idea that health is an essential underpinning for sustained productivity and the long-term well-being of the organization. While marshalling resources to maximize productivity in the short-term without consideration for health and individual well-being may maximize outputs and profits, such action ignores the necessity that all systems have for maintenance, resilience and revitalization. Strategic disengagement for energy recovery can be powerfully important to long-term achievement and productivity (Loehr and Schwartz, 2003). By managing energy, we are able to improve health while achieving sustained levels of high performance. At the core of our thinking is the notion that people are human assets to be developed for maximum results rather than personnel costs to be expended for economic gain.

The chapter is organized into four major sections. The first explores the attributes of healthy individuals and healthy organizations. Healthy, productive work must consider the individual and the organizational; both are important. The second section touches on four models of the current state-of-the-science-and-practice in healthy, productive work, then explores the prevention model's implications for positive organizational behavior. The third section is the positive, strength-based contribution of the chapter. This section broadens the POB arena by introducing individual traits and interpersonal processes into the dialogue. More specifically, we consider communication competence and interpersonal interdependence. The concluding section explores the implications for POB.

Attributes of healthy, productive work

What are the attributes of healthy individuals and healthy organizations? Positive organizational behavior has its intellectual roots in positive psychology, which is an outgrowth of one of psychology's three missions. These missions of psychology, first activated by Martin E.P. Seligman during his APA presidency are: (1) to repair damage through psychotherapy and other healing techniques; (2) to prevent mental health and behavior problems; and (3) to build on strength and competency. These broad psychological missions may be translated and applied to a wide range of health and medical contexts. In a medical context, health is often considered the absence of disease or disorders. In line with the aim of accentuating the positive, we want to consider health and the attributes of healthy individuals and healthy organizations in a more positive and proactive way. To do this, we turn to the work of Ryff and Singer (1998). However, first we briefly note the research of three positive pioneering concepts that have paved the way for this more positive approach to people in organizations: personality hardiness, optimism and vigor.

Maddi and Kobasa (1984) brought attention to personality hardiness through their study of 200 executives at Illinois Bell Telephone. Their conceptualization focused on three attributes of the hardy personality: commitment, control and challenge. Commitment concerns curiosity and engagement. Control concerns the ability to exercise influence and take responsibility. Challenge views change as an opportunity for personal development. These clearly emphasize strength and the positive.

Seligman (1990) subsequently brought attention to learned optimism as a non-negative psychological approach to interpreting the good and the bad events that occur in life. The central attribute of optimism is hope. Thus, optimistic thinking leads one to interpret bad events as temporary, limited in their effects, and not ones for which the individual is personally responsible. On the other hand, good events are interpreted as more permanent, more pervasive in their effects, and ones for which the individual takes personal responsibility.

Shirom (2003) has recently drawn attention to the positive attribute of vigor. Vigor is also a three-dimensional construct. The three dimensions are physical strength, emotional energy and cognitive aliveness. Physical strength concerns one's feelings about his or her physical ability. Emotional energy is the interpersonal dimension of vigor and concerns one's feelings regarding expressing sympathy, empathy and other emotions to significant others. Cognitive aliveness relates to one's feelings concerning his or her flow of thoughts, mental agility and cognitive alertness. These three concepts of personality hardiness, optimism and vigor pave the way for our broader discussion of attributes of healthy individuals and healthy organizations.

In addition to these attributes, Ryff and Singer (1998) are on the leading edge of building a more positive approach to the definition of health. The three principles concerning what constitutes 'health' are (Ryff and Singer, 1998):

1. It is a philosophical position pertaining to the meaning of the good life rather than strictly a medical question.
2. Health includes both the mind (mental) and the body (physical) and more importantly how they interact or influence each other.
3. Health is a 'multidimensional dynamic process rather than a discrete end state'.

Whereas, according to these authors, 'health' from a medical perspective has primarily been associated with the body, biology and physiology, this has left the mind and interaction components of life outside the health field and often positioned in the separate science of psychology. Health should overarch medicine and psychology, breaking down the dualism of the mind–body distinction which they, and we, consider to be a false dichotomy. Increasingly, the concept of health is being broadened to encompass emotional, spiritual and even ethical dimensions (Quick et al., 2002).

Therefore, it is important to go beyond both medicine and psychology in understanding a more positive approach to human health. The inclusion of philosophy, and even theology, in the definitional process allows for a more comprehensive insight into 'health' and captures human thriving as well as flourishing ... physically, mentally and socially. Positive affect is important and yet the dynamics of human flourishing are complex (Fredrickson and Losada, 2005). Ryff and Singer's (1998) core features of positive human health suggest that there are two super-ordinate categories which span cultural barriers. That is, cultures may differ in some dimensions of wellness, but these two appear to be common among all.

*   Leading a life of purpose
*   Quality connections to others

A third possible super-ordinate category is positive self-regard and mastery. Finally, Ryff and Singer identify emotion as the critical link between mind and body; life purpose and quality connection to others 'engage the body because they are emotionally laden' (1998: 10). Within this more positive, three-dimensional context of health, we aim to articulate a number of more specific attributes of healthy individuals and healthy organizations.

Healthy individuals

What are the attributes of healthy individuals? Within the overarching, three-dimensional framework noted above, an initial and more complete set of 'attributes' might look like this. These attributes consider the physical, the psychological, the spiritual and even the ethical characteristics of a broader concept of health.

- Leading a life of purpose
  - o Clear mission and goals
  - o Balanced – living within one's value system
  - o Integrity
  - o Productive
  - o Purposeful work
  - o Spiritual or higher purpose basis
  - o Passion or motivation to achieve for the better good
- Quality connections to others
  - o Interdependent: strong, positive social support system
  - o Emotional competence
  - o Mature, intimate connection to family and significant others
  - o Communication competence
- Positive self-regard and mastery
  - o Humor
  - o Optimism
  - o Hope
  - o Self-efficacy or confidence
  - o Self-awareness – strength focus – a component of emotional competence
  - o Subjective well-being/happiness
  - o Hardiness, or adaptability
  - o Vigor, physical and mental energy
  - o Personal challenge and growth goals

We might point out that a number of the attributes under positive self-regard are linked to key CHOSE behaviors advanced by Luthans (2002) and Luthans et al. (2006). Thus, these attributes link directly to the origins of POB. In addition, we earlier noted the pioneering concepts of personality hardiness, optimism and vigor in the domain of positive psychology. These too are reflected in the characteristics of healthy individuals.

Healthy organizations

By employing the same three-dimensional schema used in addressing individual health but at the organizational level, we find that healthy organizations would emphasize, facilitate and support the various categories of health for its members. The organization being made up of individuals that must function together through effective communication to accomplish a shared goal mirrors the same 'health' attributes but in a more macro sense.

- Leading a life of purpose
  - o Clear mission and goals
  - o Give back to the community

- o   Integrity
- o   Quality focus
- o   Principled
- o   Provides opportunities for growth
- o   Rewards or recognizes achievement

- Quality connections to others

  - o   Open, honest communication norms
  - o   Fairness or justice in practices
  - o   Opportunity
  - o   Trust and safety norms
  - o   Mutual purpose and sense of belonging to the bigger whole
  - o   Embrace and encourage diversity of people, skills and ideas
  - o   Cohesiveness and positive affiliation
  - o   Pride in group accomplishments
  - o   Facilitates interdependent workers (high autonomy with strong social supports)

- Positive self-regard and mastery

  - o   Encourage balance
  - o   Growth opportunities
  - o   Support systems for problems
  - o   Fitness support systems
  - o   Positive physical work environment
  - o   High safety focus

This three-dimensional framework offers an approach to broaden the concept of health while tying it to the origins of POB and then extending the positive framework.

Models of occupational health

There are a range of models for occupational health that have grown out of public health, medical sociology, occupational medicine and/or psychology. These models have different key variables, focus on different aspects of the workplace and aim primarily to understand health outcomes for individuals. We touch on three models in this section that have made a clear impact in occupational health. These are the Effort–Reward Model of Siegrist (1996), the Demands–Control Model as advanced by Karasek (1979) and Theorell and Karasek (1996), and the Risk Management Model formulated and revised by Cooper and his colleagues (e.g. Cooper and Marshall, 1978). We then discuss the Preventive Health Management Model of J.C. and J.D. Quick and their colleagues (e.g. Quick et al., 1997) which has implications for POB. For additional information, the reader is directed to Section III on Environmental Health in Wallace et al. (1998) for more specific topics such as ergonomics, occupational health special working groups, occupational health and safety standards, aerospace medicine and toxicology.

The effort–reward model

From a medical sociological perspective, Siegrist (1996) argues that the exchanges in work life between the individual and the organization should be balanced and reciprocal in nature. Hence, he proposes a model that balances effort and reward. Specifically, he suggests that occupational groups who experience lower status control are more likely to have high incidence of high effort–low reward (or, high-cost/low-gain) imbalance, leading to higher stress and strain. Other research suggests that worker compensation stress claims are the result of an imbalance between the employee needs and organizational demands (Woodburn and Simpson, 1994). Finally, this model is consistent with well-established research on the effects of socioeconomic status. Adler et al. (1993) found that those at the bottom of the socioeconomic status ladder have the highest incidence of morbidity and mortality. Hence, strong links exist between occupational effort–reward and health status.

The demands–control model

A second major theory of job stress that developed during this same time period came to be known most commonly as the Demands–Control Model. High strain jobs in the model are characterized by high job demands combined with low job decision latitude (low control). These high strain jobs pose the greatest health risk for job incumbents. The original health risks identified were exhaustion, depression, job and life dissatisfaction, illness days and elevated consumption of tranquilizers and sleeping pills (Karasek, 1979). Subsequent research has considered other health risks associated with high strain jobs, such as cardiovascular problems (Karasek et al., 1988; Theorell and Karasek, 1996). Social support is a third dimension sometimes added to this model. House (1981) was the first to extensively explore social support and work stress. More recently, Lynch (2000) examines the medical and psychological evidence concerning the health risks associated with social isolation.

The risk management model

Cooper and Marshall (1978) extend the organizational stress problems of role conflict and ambiguity originally identified by Robert Kahn and his associates (1964). They do this by bringing attention to additional sources of stress for managers in complex industrial organizations. Their expanded model of sources of managerial stress includes factors intrinsic to the job, career development, organizational structure and climate, interpersonal relations at work, and factors outside the organization, such as family demands, which have spillover effects into the workplace. This approach goes beyond the occupational health risks of physical work

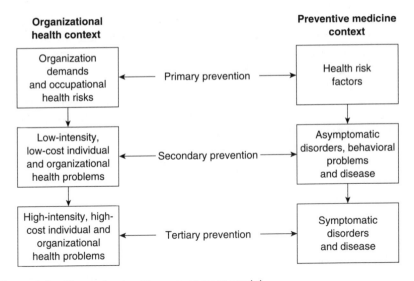

Organizational health context		Preventive medicine context

Figure 3.1   *Preventive health management model*

Source: Quick (1999: 84). Reprinted with permission.

demands and environmental hazards to the wide range of psychosocial demands of the workplace. These psychosocial health risks are more problematic for leaders, managers and white-collar employees. This Risk Management Model considers both the psychosocial risks and the managerial actions that may be taken (Wallace et al., 1998; Wharton, 1992).

Preventive health management model

Prevention is always the best public health strategy for any disease epidemic that threatens the health of a population. The American Institute of Stress has advanced the concern that job stress is in fact a health epidemic which is adversely affecting millions of Americans, as well as having adverse health effects on workers throughout other industrialized nations. If job stress is epidemic, then prevention holds the best hope for addressing this health problem (Elkin and Rosch, 1990; Quick et al., 1997; Wallace et al., 1998). The theory of preventive stress management is based on translating the public health notions of prevention into an organizational context and overlaying them on a stress process model as shown in Figure 3.1 (Quick et al., 1998).

   The prevention strategies in the organizational health context can be classified as primary, secondary and tertiary. Primary prevention aims to modify and manage organizational demands. Secondary prevention aims to modify and manage low-intensity, low-cost health problems in the organizational context. Tertiary prevention aims to help and provide aid to those experiencing high-intensity, high-cost health problems. From a public health perspective, primary prevention is always the preferred point of intervention. This implies for workplace stress and health that job redesign efforts and other interventions that alter, modify or eliminate stressful work conditions are the preferred category of stress management program (Quick and Quick, 1997; Quick et al., 2000).

Originally formulated to address the chronic organizational health risk of stress, this preventive health management model has also been applied to other organizational health risks such as sexual harassment (Bell et al., 2002a, 2002b), workplace violence (Mack et al., 1998), and suicide, organizational restructuring and downsizing (Quick and Tetrick, 2003; Quick et al., 2003).

This prevention model has important implications for POB because a number of the individual and organizational attributes discussed in the first section of the chapter aim to strengthen the host; that is, they aim to make the individual or the organization stronger and heartier. A strong, hearty host is good prevention practice because it is much less susceptible to disease, disorders and a wide range of threats to health. Therefore, the practice of preventive health management goes hand-in-glove with the practice of positive organizational behavior because the two are very complementary. This complementary view of these two approaches (i.e. the preventive approach and POB) leads to the heart of our chapter which focuses on two positive strength factors: communication competence and interpersonal interdependence.

Positive strength through communication competence and interpersonal interdependence

The occupational health models largely grow out of the broader medical model of health, which is predominantly disease based. The allopathic medical model in particular is symptom and disease focused, which the osteopathic model does move more toward a prevention platform. We first connect with the topic of communication within this medical disease model for it is James Lynch (2000) who first brings our attention to the problem of *communicative disease*. From this first understanding of the importance of communication for health, we move to the much more positive model of communication in high performance teams. This then links us to the last subsection of the chapter that addresses interdependence and autonomy at work.

Communicative disease

James Lynch's (1977) original focus was on the medical consequences of loneliness and social isolation while his more recent update in 2000 explores more deeply the salutary effects of heartfelt communication. To understand these health benefits of communication, Lynch first had to understand what he came to call *communicative disease*. Our failure to effectively communicate in deep and meaningful ways he likened to a disease, using the medical model paradigm within which he primarily worked. Communicative disease results in a range of physical, mental and overall health declines. Within the disease-state model, the solution to this dysfunction is to overcome the 'disease' and teach individuals how to overcome communication deficiencies.

We, however, want to shift the paradigm from the disease-state model to a positive psychology, positive organizational behavior model. When we make this shift, we move our thinking from how to overcome the negative to how, and why, we can develop communication competence in interpersonal relationships. Thus, we rethink healthy interactions and attachments with significant others through effective communication. This shift sets the stage for efficient, effective and healthy research and practice in communication and interpersonal relationships. This shift does not totally negate the groundbreaking and seminal work which Lynch (2000) has done. When communication competence falls below a threshold, then treatment, remediation and therapeutic intervention are appropriate. As with all three missions of psychology noted at the outset of the chapter, they work in concert. Placing emphasis on the positive does not negate the appropriate necessity of prevention and/or treatment.

However, in understanding 'healthy' workplaces, the place to begin is not with understanding 'unhealthy' individuals and organizations, which carries with it the assumption that if you eradicate the 'disease' you have health. Rather, understanding 'healthy' individuals and organizations is more than simply the absence of health problems, such as communicative disease. We view communication and interdependence as positive strength factors for building healthy, vibrant and productive work organizations of committed and healthy individuals. This positive competence based approach serves as the foundation for highly effective functional outcomes for all concerned. In other words, you cannot simply train individuals to correct poor communication patterns and expect the same results as seen in these highly effective, communicatively competent counterparts. It is more than the absence of communication disorders; it is the presence of communication competence.

Healthy communication leads to healthy organizations in the interdependence, synergy and cooperation that it inspires. The ability of individuals to safely and effectively express opinions, challenge existing ideas, request support and suggest innovative solution within a climate that minimizes conflict and fear promotes individual growth, a sense of control and a sense of contributing to a greater or mutual purpose. These outcomes are foundational elements of healthy individuals and organizations. Healthy communication is both task-oriented and relationship-oriented; it is personal, subtle and responsive, and is not primarily hinged on authority.

Communication competence in high-performance teams

Communication competence is the key to building positive interpersonal relationships and social support in a wide range of teams, groups and work settings (Macik-Frey et al., 2005). The key role of communication competence to positive, healthy organizational functioning was originally developed in research among high-performance cockpit flight crews (Kanki and Foushee, 1989; Wiener et al., 1993) and surgical teams (Quick et al., 2006). The communication and communication-related characteristics of these high-performance teams are:

- psychological and physical safety
- interpersonal trust and trustworthiness
- willingness to respectfully challenge authority or the prevailing thought
- openness to challenges and to your own ideas
- ability to listen and appreciate others' points of view
- group or team-based orientation versus individual orientation
- open dialogue is the norm and is highly valued
- mistakes are objectively analyzed to find solutions – blame is not the game
- versatile, adaptable communication methods – emergencies may require top down
- more balanced communication patterns between leaders and followers
- team adopts similar communication patterns
- proactive, contingency plans communicated early and problems are anticipated
- leaders are highly motivated, goal-oriented *and* highly interpersonally-oriented
- polite, appropriate assertiveness of followers – give and get feedback
- high group metacognitive skills – shared mental models, shared problem models
- knowledge and information are readily shared to minimize uncertainty

In addition, these high-performance teams display a high incidence rate of problem solving communication in both high work load periods as well as low work load periods (Orasanu, 1990). The problem solving communication frequently centers on one or more of six issues, which are:

- recognize a problem
- state goals or objectives
- plan and strategize
- gather information
- alert and predict
- explain

The development of communication competence and secure, interdependent relationships is influenced by emotional intelligence, cognitive complexity, gender and personality of the team members (Macik-Frey et al.,

2005). Communication competence is more than cerebral, verbal and nonverbal skill in sending and receiving messages. In addition, communication competence concerns a deeper understanding of emotions, of persons, and a deep appreciation of individual differences and personal integrity. Communication competence as we use the term gets to the heartfelt appreciation of the other, when that is appropriate, while attending to the task and performance issues at hand in the workplace.

Interpersonal interdependence and autonomy at work

The understanding of communication competence we just described is one key to building and maintaining a secure set of interpersonal relationships at work. Another key is found in the paradoxical concept of self-reliance, a term first used by Bowlby in the development of his ethnographic approach to personality with Ainsworth (Ainsworth and Bowlby, 1991). The paradox in self-reliance is that is sounds much like 'independence' when in fact the term describes an interpersonal pattern of behavior which is both interdependent and autonomous. Specifically, the self-reliant person is able to easily and comfortably ask for support and help from other people when that is appropriate while having a complementary capacity for solitary and autonomous activity when that is appropriate. Self-reliance thus describes the flexible pattern of interpersonal interdependence coupled with the capacity for autonomous action; hence, the description of this flexible pattern of interpersonal behavior as 'paradoxical'.

Joplin et al. (1999) found that interdependence is reliably measured in the adulthood years among managers and employees. In addition, Nelson et al. (1991) found that interdependence was an important factor for the successful socialization of newcomers in organizations. While attachment theory was evolved by Bowlby and Ainsworth through their studies of childhood and the youthful developmental years, these studies suggest its enduring importance throughout the adulthood years. Further, Nelson and Quick (2006) report that interdependence is important for the health of both female and male senior executives, military trainees and officer candidates, and senior military officers. As a construct, interdependence behaves much more like an enduring trait than like a state attribute because it is relatively stable over time. However, it is amenable to change and development in the longer term. For example, interdependence has been found to increase with both chronological age and with educational level. Interpersonal interdependence is very complementary to communication competence because it focuses on the strengthening of interpersonal bonds and relationships.

Interpersonal interdependence has positive benefits for both health and performance, thus qualifying it as a construct worthy of serious consideration within the POB domain. From a health perspective, interdependence enables individuals to appropriately draw upon the positive resources within a social support system that lead to vitality and well-being. In addition, because of its paradoxical nature, the twin concepts of interdependence and autonomy allow for individuals to establish appropriate balance in their interpersonal relationships for positive and healthy exchange. From a performance perspective, interdependence facilitates the information exchange and coordinated action that leads to effective collaboration and cooperative effort. This is coupled with the individual's capacity to work and perform autonomously when that is the appropriate approach in the work context.

Conclusion and implications

We have considered the emergence of positive organizational behavior (POB) from the new science of positive psychology, which aims to be strength-based in its approach and its emphasis. We have also considered the parallel and complementary tradition of occupational health, focusing in particular on the preventive health model which has direct implications for the emerging domain of POB. However, the core contribution of the chapter rests on the new, positive, strength-based constructs introduced, which are communication competence and interpersonal interdependence. In addition to strengthening individual health, both these positive strength constructs lead to a strengthening of organizational health. Quick et al. (1997) have previously made the case for the interdependence of individual and organizational health; the two cannot be severed. Our primary concern and emphasis in the domain of healthy, productive work is on the important outcome variables of individual and organizational health *and* individual and organizational productivity. While Quick et al. (1997) argue that individual and organizational health cannot be severed, we advance the case that health and productivity cannot be severed; rather, they go hand-in-glove.

A number of the constructs that we captured in our review of individual and organizational health, most specifically those with a POB origin, appear as state-like variables rather easily amenable to modification and change. The two new constructs at the heart of this chapter do not fit this mold. Rather, communication competence may be cast as having either individual trait-like qualities or interpersonal process qualities. Similarly, interpersonal interdependence may be cast as an individual trait-like variable. We say this due to their enduring and more stable quality over time. At the same time, we suggest that these are not 'fixed' variables or characteristics.

Our aim is to build on the traditions of POB, positive psychology and occupational health in approaching the issue of healthy, productive work. We have done this by introducing two new positive strength variables into the domain. POB can broaden its reach and enhance its impact through the consideration of individual traits and interpersonal processes without forsaking its strong and positive roots in state-like variables. We need to renew our focus on healthy people and healthy organizations, which has long roots in the US Surgeon General's Report on Health Promotion and Disease Prevention (Levi, 1979). We need to review this focus because it is in our collective best interests and because it has important implications for the well-being of the nation. However, the refocusing needs to consider the more contemporary and positive approaches to individual and organizational health as discussed in the first section of the chapter.

Purpose, connection to others, positive self-regard, and mastery offer a stronger and more positive framework for understanding and defining health. In a content analysis of 28 senior executives and leaders conducted by the Goolsby Leadership Academy, 'purpose' was the only common attribute of exceptional leaders (Macik-Frey et al., 2006). While there was significant variance on the definitions of leadership and on the common attributes, there was no variance on that one construct: purpose. Hence, the spiritual and the emotional come into play as we take a new and more positive approach to the understanding of individual and organizational health along with its important implications for performance and productivity.

References

Adler, N.E., Boyce, W.T., Chesney, M.A., Folkman, S. and Syme, S.L. (1993) 'Socio economic inequalities in health: No easy solution', *Journal of the American Medical Association*, 269, 3140–45.

Ainsworth, M.D.S. and Bowlby, J. (1991) 'An ethdogical approach to personality,' *American Psychologist*, 46, 333–41.

Bell, M.P., Cycota, C. and Quick, J.C. (2002a) 'Affirmative defense: The prevention of sexual harassment', in D.L. Nelson and R. Burke (eds) *Gender, Work Stress and Health: Current Research Issue* (pp. 191–210). Washington, DC: American Psychological Association.

Bell, M.P., Quick, J.C. and Cycota, C. (2002b) 'Assessment and prevention of sexual harassment: An applied guide to creating healthy organizations', *International Journal of Selection and Assessment*, 10 (1/2), 160–7.

Cooper, C.L. and Marshall, J. (1978). 'Sources of managerial and white collar stress', in C.L. Cooper and R. Payne (eds) *Stress at Work* (pp. 81–105). Chichester: John Wiley & Sons.

Elkin, A.J. and Rosch, P.J. (1990) 'Promoting mental health at the workplace: The prevention side of stress management', *Occupational Medicine: State of the Art Review*, 5 (4), 739–54.

Fredrickson, B.L. and Losada, M.F. (2005) 'Positive affect and complex dynamics of human flourishing', *American Psychologist*, 60 (7), 678–86.

House, J.S. (1981) *Work Stress and Social Support*. Reading, MA: Addison-Wesley.

Joplin, J.R.W., Nelson, D.L. and Quick, J.C. (1999) 'Attachment behavior and health: Relationships at work and home', *Journal of Organizational Behavior*, 20, 783–96.

Kahn, R.L., Wolfe, R.P., Quinn, R.P., Snoek, J.D. and Rosenthal, R.A. (1964) *Organizational Stress: Studies in Role Conflict and Ambiguity*. New York: John Wiley & Sons.

Kanki, B.G. and Foushee, H.C. (1989) 'Communication as group process mediator of aircrew performance', *Aviation, Space and Environmental Medicine*, 60, 402–10.

Karasek, R.A. (1979) 'Job demands, job decision latitude, and mental strain: Implications for job redesign', *Administrative Science Quarterly*, 24 (June), 285–308.

Karasek, R.A., Theorell, T., Schwartz, J.E., Schnall, P.L., Pieper, C.F. and Michela, J.L. (1988) 'Job characteristics in relation to the prevalence of myocardial infarction in the US health examination survey (HES) and the health and nutrition examination survey (HANES)', *American Journal of Public Health*, 78, 910–18.

Levi, L. (1979) 'Psychosocial factors in preventive medicine', in *Healthy People: The Surgeon General's Report on Health Promotion and Disease Prevention Background Papers* (pp. 207–52). Washington, DC: US Department of Health, Education, and Welfare.

Loehr, J. and Schwartz, T. (2003) *The Power of Full Engagement: Managing Energy, not Time, Is the Key to High Performance and Personal Renewal*. New York: Free Press.

Luthans, F. (2002) 'Positive organizational behavior: Developing and managing psychological strengths', *Academy of Management Executive*, 16, 57–75.

Luthans, F., Youssef, C. and Avolio, B.J. (2006) 'Leveraging positive psychological capital for organizational performance', in D.L. Nelson and C.L. Cooper (eds) *Positive Organizational Behavior: Accentuating the Positive at Work* (in press). Thousand Oaks, CA: Sage Publications.

Lynch, J.J. (1977) *The Broken Heart: The Medical Consequences of Loneliness*. New York: Basic Books.

Lynch, J.J. (2000) *A Cry Unheard: New Insights into the Medical Consequences of Loneliness*. Baltimore, MD: Bancroft.

Macik-Frey, M., Quick, J.C. and Quick, J.D. (2005) 'Interpersonal communication: The key to social support for preventive stress management', in C.L. Cooper (ed.) *Handbook of Stress, Medicine, and Health, 2nd edn* (pp. 265–92). Boca Raton, FL: CRC Press.

Macik-Frey, M., Shinoda, P., Gray, D.A., Mack, D.A., Quick, J.C. and Keller, N. (2006) Strength of Purpose: Positive Direction for Leadership Action. Paper presented at the British academy of Management Annual Meeting, 13 August.

Mack, D.A., Shannon, C., Quick, J.D., and Quick, J.C. (1998) 'Chapter IV – Stress and the preventive management of workplace violence', in R.W. Griffin, A. O'Leary-Kelly and J. Collins (eds) *Dysfunctional Behavior in Organizations – Volume 1: Violent Behavior in Organizations* (pp. 119–41). Greenwich, CT: JAI Press.

Maddi, S.R. and Kobasa, S.C.O. (1984) *The Hardy Exeuctive: Health Under Stress*. Homewood, IL: Dow Jones-Irwin.

Nelson, D.L. and Quick, J.C. (2006) *Organizational Behavior: Foundations, Realities and Challenges, 5th edn*. Mason, OH: South-Western/Thompson.

Nelson, D.L., Quick, J.C. and Joplin, J. (1991) 'Psychological contracting and new-comer socialization: An attachment theory foundation', *Journal of Social Behavior and Personality*, 6, 55–72.

Nelson, D.L., Quick, J.C. and Simmons, B.L. (2001) 'Preventive management of work stress: Current themes and future challenges', in A. Baum, T. Revenson and J. Singer (eds) *Handbook of Health Psychology* (pp. 349–64). Mahwah, NJ: Lawrence Erlbaum Associates.

Orasanu, J.M. (1990) *Shared Mental Models and Crew Decision Making* (Cognitive Science Laboratory Report #46). Princeton, NJ: Princeton University.

Quick, J.C. (1999) 'Occupational Health Psychology: Historial Roots and Future Directions', *Health Psychology*, 18(1) January, 82–88.

Quick, J.C., Cooper, C.L., Quick, J.D. and Gavin, J.H. (2002) *The Financial Times Guide to Executive Health*. London and New York: FT/Prentice Hall.

Quick, J.C., Murphy, L.R. and Hurrell, J.J. Jr (1992) *Stress and Well-being at Work: Assessments and Interventions for Occupational Mental Health*. Washington, DC: American Psychological Association.

Quick, J.C., Nelson, D.L. and Simmons, B. (2000) 'Work conditions', in N. Schmitt (ed.) Industrial/Organizational Section *Encyclopedia of Psychology* (pp. 269–74). Washington, DC: American Psychological Association and Oxford University Press.

Quick, J.C. and Quick, J.D. (1997) 'Stress Management Programs', in C. Argrlis and C.L. Cooper (eds) *The Blackwell Encyclopedia of Management* (pp. 338–39). Oxford, England: Basil Blackwell Ltd.

Quick, J.C., Quick, J.D., Nelson, D.L. and Hurrell, J.J. Jr (1997) *Preventive Stress Management in Organizations*, Washington, DC: American Psychological Association. (Original work published in 1984 by J.C. Quick and J.D. Quick.)

Quick, J.C., Saleh, K.J., Sime, W.E., Martin, W., Cooper, C.L., Quick, J.D. and Mont, M.A. (2006) 'Stress management skills for strong leadership: Is it worth dying for', *Journal of Bone & Joint Surgery*, 88 (1), 217–25.

Quick, J.C. and Tetrick, L. (2003) *Handbook of Occupational Health Psychology*. Washington, DC: American Psychological Association.

Quick, J.C., Tetrick, L., Adkins, J.A. and Klunder, C. (2003) 'Occupational health psychology', in I. Weiner (ed.) *Comprehensive Handbook of Psychology* (pp. 569–89). New York: John Wiley & Sons, Inc.

Quick, J.D., Quick, J.C. and Nelson, D.L. (1998) 'Chapter 12 – The theory of preventive stress management in organizations', in C.L. Cooper (ed.) *Theories of Organizational Stress* (pp. 246–68). Oxford and New York: Oxford University Press.

Ryff, C.D. and Singer, B. (1998) 'The contours of positive human health', *Psychological Inquiry*, 9 (1), 1–28.

Seligman, M.E.P. (1990) *Learned Optimism*. New York: Knopf.

Shirom A. (2003) 'Feeling vigorous at work? The construct of vigor and the study of positive affect in organizations', in D. Ganster and P.L. Perrewé (eds) *Research in Organizational Stress and Well-being* (Vol. 3, pp. 135–65). Greenwich, CT: JAI Press.

Siegrist, J. (1996) 'Adverse health effects of high-effort/low-strain reward conditions', *Journal of Occupational Health Psychology*, 1, 30.

Theorell, T. and Karasek, R.A. (1996) 'Current issues relating to psychosocial job strain and cardiovascular disease research', *Journal of Occupational Health Psychology*, 1, 9–26.

Wallace, R.B., Doebbeling, B.N. and Last, J.M. (1998) *Maxcy-Rosenau-Last Public Health and Preventive Medicine, 14th edn*. Stamford, CT: Appleton & Lange.

Wiener, E.L., Kanki, B.G. and Helmreich, R.L. (1993) *Cockpit Resource Management*. San Diego, CA: Academic Press.

Wharton, F. (1992) 'Risk management: Basic concepts and general principles', in J. Ansell and F. Wharton (eds) *Risk: Analysis, Perception, & Management*. Chichester: Wiley.

Woodburn, L.T. and Simpson, S. (1994) 'Employer types: Who will be the next stress claimant?', *Risk Management*, 41, 38–44.

4

Eustress at Work:
Extending the Holistic Stress Model

Bret L. Simmons and Debra L. Nelson

The positive movement in behavioral research emphasizes the emotions, attitudes and actions that lead to well-being, positive individuals, and thriving workplaces, in contrast to a familiar focus on pathology that results in a model of the human being lacking the positive features that make life worth living. Researchers have come to understand quite a bit about how people survive and cope when confronted with adversity, but we know comparatively little about how normal people thrive under challenging circumstances. Positive psychology advocates a preoccupation with building positive qualities in individuals and workplaces in addition to repairing the negative aspects of work and careers (Seligman and Csikszentmihalyi, 2000). The study and application of these positive qualities of individuals for performance improvement at work is termed positive organizational behavior (POB) (Luthans, 2002).

We believe that a model of work stress provides an excellent way to illustrate how demands at work manifest themselves in both positive and negative responses, and how these responses ultimately affect valued outcomes at work. This chapter will discuss some of the new directions in the study of work and stress that are consistent with POB. Our organizing framework is The Holistic Stress Model (Figure 4.1), which incorporates positive as well as negative responses. In this model, responses can take the form of psychological states, emotions, attitudes, and behaviors. This chapter focuses on the positive responses and their effects on performance and health. We further extend our Holistic Stress Model by elaborating on our concept of savoring the positive, and we introduce the concept of expectation alignment, which moderates the relationship between responses and outcomes.

The central tenets of our model, which we will briefly elaborate on throughout this chapter, are as follows:

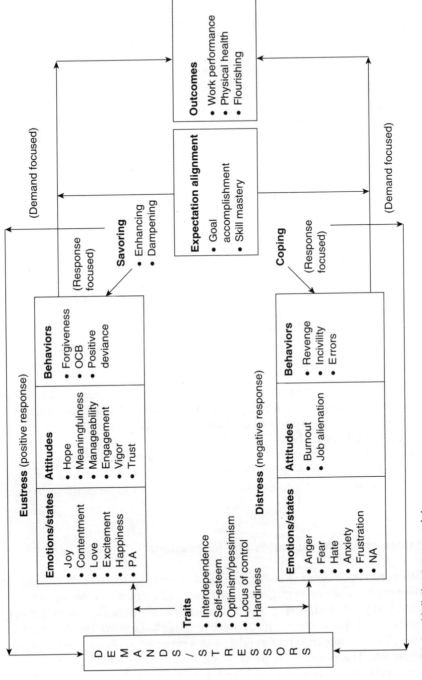

Figure 4.1 *Holistic stress model*

- Demands or stressors are inherently neutral.
- The cognitive appraisal of any given demand or stressor produces a simultaneous positive and negative response. It is the *response* to demands that has positive and/or negative valence based on the degree of attraction and/or aversion the individual experiences toward the event or object.
- Individual differences/traits affect the way in which demands are appraised; therefore, they moderate the relationship between demands and responses.
- Positive and negative responses are complex and mixed; therefore, they manifest themselves in a variety of distinct physiological, psychological and behavioral indicators. Degrees of *both* positive and negative indicators of response will be present for any given demand. (Our model does not focus on physiological indicators because they are less observable by managers interacting with employees, and therefore are less subject to managerial intervention.)
- Individuals select strategies to either eliminate or alleviate their negative responses to demands, or to accentuate or potentially dampen their positive responses. These strategies can be focused either on the perceived demand or on the perceived response.
- Positive and negative responses differentially affect valued outcomes at work.
- The relationship between responses and outcomes is moderated by both explicit and implicit contracts that govern what is expected of and accepted from employees at work.

While OB has considered a number of positive constructs (e.g. satisfaction, citizenship behavior, positive affect), too often these constructs have been embedded in models of dysfunction and disease. With hindsight as a guide, POB then should avoid the criticisms that it makes of existing models of work. By incorporating both positive and negative, we believe that the Holistic Stress Model answers the call for the more balanced view of human behavior that POB must supply in order to be credible (Wright, 2003).

Stress and distress: basics and foundations

Stress has been defined as the naturally occurring mind–body *response* to demanding and/or emergency *situations*, either of a chronic or episodic nature (Quick et al., 1987). The advantage of this definition is that it suggests a familiar stimulus–response framework. Leaving out the descriptive clauses, stress can be thought of as a process involving responses to a situation. The physical or psychological stimuli to which the individual responds are commonly referred to as either *stressors* or *demands*. Demands at work take the form of role demands, interpersonal demands, physical demands, workplace policies, and job conditions (Barnett, 1998; Quick et al., 2000).

When a person encounters a stressor, she or he *evaluates* the encounter with respect to its significance for well-being. This evaluative process is the essence of cognitive appraisal. The negative *response* to stressors that results from appraisals where stressors are perceived by the individual to be either threatening or harmful is commonly termed *distress*. It is distress that is commonly studied for its relationship to adverse health outcomes, absenteeism, and turnover (Quick et al., 2000). Distress, as such, is negative and dysfunctional (i.e. bad stress).

Eustress: the positive response to stress

Some have also suggested that there is also good stress, which Selye (1976a, 1976b) termed *eustress*. Quick et al. (2000) associate eustress with healthy, positive outcomes. Positive appraisals of stressors 'occur if the outcome of an encounter is construed as positive, that is, if it preserves or enhances well-being or promises to do so' (Lazarus and Folkman, 1984: 32). As indicators of the positive response to stressors resulting from positive appraisals, they suggest looking for the presence of positive or pleasurable psychological states and attitudes. A major issue in the study of eustress is to simultaneously establish the presence of both positive and negative psychological states, rather than merely inferring eustress by the absence of negative states. Instead of representing opposite ends of a single continuum, positive (eustress) and negative (distress) states may represent two distinct constructs, which would require separate multi-variate indices for their measurement (Edwards and Cooper, 1988).

Consider the analogy of a bathtub to illustrate the point of thinking of eustress and distress as two distinct constructs. As a minimum, we are concerned about two things when we settle in for a bath – the level of water in the tub and the temperature of water in the tub. Essentially two things determine the level of water in the bathtub – the flow of water into the bathtub and the flow of water out of the bathtub over time. Likewise, the *simultaneous* flow of *both* hot and cold water into the bathtub determines the temperature of the water in the tub. If we liken the study of stress to the study of water in the bathtub, our current approach is like studying a bathtub with a single water faucet – cold water, representing distress. We know a lot about the sources of cold water, and we can tell individuals how to either decrease the flow of cold water into or increase the flow of cold water out of their bathtub. We also know quite a bit about the physiological, behavioral, and psychological consequences of sitting in a tub of cold water for a prolonged period of time. Our knowledge of cold water (distress) is important, but does not present a complete understanding of the water (stress) in the bathtub. A more complete model of stress would acknowledge that the bathtub does indeed have two faucets – hot and cold – and both are necessary to get the level and temperature of the water just right for a comfortable bath.

Positive Organizational Behavior encompasses valued subjective experiences. The approach to stress that incorporates subjective experiences is the cognitive appraisal approach most commonly associated with the work of Richard Lazarus (1966). The essence of this approach to understanding stress is that people can have different responses to stressors they encounter depending on whether they appraise a relevant stressor as positive or negative. Although Lazarus acknowledged the existence of positive responses, he, like the majority of stress researchers, focused almost exclusively on negative responses.

When a person encounters a stressor, she or he *evaluates* the encounter with respect to its significance for well-being. If a stressor is not appraised as irrelevant, Lazarus and Folkman (1984) asserted that appraisals can be complex and mixed, depending on person factors and the situational context. They essentially describe two types of appraisals and associated response patterns: positive and stressful.

Positive appraisals 'occur if the outcome of an encounter is construed as positive, that is, if it preserves or enhances well-being or promises to do so' (Lazarus and Folkman, 1984: 32). As indicators of positive appraisals, they suggest looking for the presence of positive or pleasurable psychological states (e.g. exhilaration).

Stressful appraisals can also be thought of as negative appraisals. Negative appraisals include harm/loss, threat, and challenge. In *harm/loss*, some damage to the person has already occurred (e.g. injury, illness, loss of a loved one, damage to self-esteem). *Threat* involves harms or losses that have not yet occurred but are anticipated. *Challenge* appraisals occur if the outcome of an encounter holds the potential for gain or growth. As indicators of challenge appraisals, they suggest looking for some of the same positive or pleasurable psychological states they identify as indicators of the positive response (e.g. exhilaration).

Lazarus and Folkman (1984) did not view challenge and threat as poles of a single continuum. They believe that challenge and threat responses can occur simultaneously, as the result of the same stressor, and should be considered as separate but related constructs. While threat is clearly a negative appraisal, challenge is better thought of as a positive appraisal (they share the same indicators).

As such, the reasoning they apply to the distinction between challenge and threat to the higher levels of positive and negative response can be extended. Accordingly, positive and negative responses can occur simultaneously, as a result of the same demand or stressor, and should be considered separate but related constructs. Thus, for any given demand, an individual can have *both* a degree of positive and a degree of negative response. This is consistent with Lazarus and Folkman's (1984) view that any psychophysiological theory of stress or emotion that positions the response as unidimensional disequilibrium or arousal is untenable or at least grossly incomplete. They support this assertion with research on emotions and autonomic nervous system activity (Elkman et al., 1983) as well as research on hormonal response to arousing conditions (Frankenhauser et al., 1978; Mason, 1974). Evidence is mounting that indicates that our brains may indeed be wired to simultaneously experience positive and negative emotions separately (Davidson, 2000; Tomarken et al., 1992; Wheeler et al., 1993).

At this point, we wish to reiterate that in order to remain consistent with our interpretation of cognitive appraisal, our model does not attempt to label demands or stressors as challenging (positive) or threatening (negative). Others have taken the approach of labeling *stressors* believed to hold potential gains for individuals as challenge stress, and *stressors* believed to constrain or interfere with work achievement as hindrance stress (Boswell et al., 2004; LePine et al., 2004). The Holistic Stress Model contends that any given demand could hold the potential for both challenge and constraint, the appraisal of which would be manifest in an array of both positive and negative emotions, attitudes, and behaviors. We believe that the leverage lies in understanding how individual differences affect the relationships between stressors and responses. So, for example, demands encountered by pessimists and those with low self-esteem may manifest themselves more strongly in negative responses, but the same demands may manifest with more positive and less negative responses for optimists or those with high self-esteem.

Eustress reflects the extent to which cognitive appraisal of a situation or event is seen to either benefit an individual or enhance his/her well-being. We expect that most work situations elicit a mixed bag of both positive and negative responses in individuals. For example, a recently promoted individual should be expected to experience joy and satisfaction associated with the recognition of achievement and excitement about the opportunity to pursue new goals and challenges at work. At the same time, and as a result of the same situation, the individual may also experience a degree of disappointment if the additional compensation associated with the promotion is perceived as inadequate, or may experience the beginnings of the anxiety they anticipate about having to tell friends, family, and colleagues that the new promotion involves relocation to another city. On the other hand, an individual recently downsized out of a job can be expected to experience hostility associated with the loss and anxiety due to the uncertainty of having to find a new job. Yet at the same time they may feel relief to be leaving an overworked job in a sinking ship, or may see it as an opportunity to spend more coveted time with family.

We posit that positive and negative responses are separate, distinct, multivariate, and potentially interactive in nature. To assume the presence of the positive by simply observing the absence of the negative, or vice versa, is an unacceptably simplistic approach to understanding the sources, responses, and consequences of stress. The full range of the stress response cannot be appreciated without a strategy to assess eustress and distress concurrently.

Support for the Holistic Stress Model

We have examined our model in studies of hospital nurses, home health-care nurses, university professors, pastors, and assisted living center employees (Gooty et al., 2005; Little et al., 2006; Nelson and Simmons, 2003, 2004; Simmons and Nelson, 2001, 2005; Simmons et al., 2001, 2003). Of the demands and stressors we have studied – role ambiguity, work–family conflict, family–work conflict, death of a patient, workload – we have consistently found no direct relationship between stressors and outcomes like perception of health and supervisor-rated performance.

Using the positive psychological states hope, positive affect, meaningfulness, and manageability as indicators of eustress, and the negative psychological states job alienation, negative affect, anxiety and anger as indictors of distress, we found some evidence of a second order factor of eustress, but we were unable to confirm the entire model. In our studies, hope, the belief that one has the will and the way to accomplish valued goals at work (Snyder et al., 1996), has been our most effective indicator of eustress. Satisfaction with work and satisfaction with supervision emerged in our studies as significant predictors of hope at work. We have consistently found a significant, positive relationship between hope and self-reported perceptions of health; however, our preliminary studies have found an equivocal relationship between hope and supervisor-rated performance.

The individual difference variable that we believe holds significant promise in our model is interdependence (Nelson et al., 1991; Quick and Macik-Frey Chapter 3 of this volume; Quick et al., 1990). Interdependence is a trait based on attachment theory (Ainsworth and Bowlby, 1991; Bowlby, 1982, 1988). Interdependence is a healthy, secure attachment style that enables individuals to work comfortably autonomously as well as to seek help from others when appropriate. We found that hope fully mediated the significant, positive relationship between interdependence and perception of health in home healthcare nurses (Simmons et al., 2003). We concluded that it is not that hope has a greater effect on health in those that are interdependent, but that those who are interdependent are more likely to be hopeful, and therefore healthy. Our most recent findings in a study of 161 assisted living center employees suggests that interdependent individuals reap the work-related benefits of trust in the supervisor, perceptions of health, effective performance in the eyes of their supervisors, and affective commitment to the organization (Gooty et al., 2005).

We have recently attempted to extend our model beyond sole reliance on psychological states to including behavioral indicators of eustress and distress. In a study of pastors, we used forgiveness behaviors, along with positive affect and engagement, as indicators of eustress, and revenge behaviors, along with negative affect and burnout, as indictors of distress (Little et al., 2006). As part of the study, pastors were asked to think about a recent time in their current position when another person had offended them. Examples of items used to measure forgiveness behaviors were: 'I gave them a new start, a renewed relationship' and 'I made an effort to be more friendly and concerned'. Examples of items used to measure revenge behaviors were: 'I got even with them', and 'I told them something was wrong with them'. Contrary to our expectations, we did not find a significant relationship between forgiveness behaviors and the pastor's perception of his health. Only positive affect and revenge emerged as significant predictors of perceptions of health in this study.

In a post-hoc analysis, the variable with the strongest significance to revenge behavior was engagement (Britt et al., 2001). We concluded that although engagement did not have a direct effect on health, it may have an indirect influence on health through its negative relationship with revenge behavior. Having a strong felt responsibility and commitment to one's job may buffer one from committing revenge behaviors. The pleasurable state of engagement in work is absorbing, and may act as an antidote to committing vengeful acts against others in the face of stressors.

Although we have not yet been able to test our full model, we are finding that the relationships between a variety of stressors and outcomes like health and performance are mediated by both positive and negative psychological states, attitudes, and behaviors. The role of individual differences in our model, antecedent to responses, has also been partially verified. The Holistic Stress Model can be extended by including emotions as indicators of eustress and distress, identifying additional behaviors indicators, expanding the concept of savoring eustress, and suggesting some variables that might moderate the relationship between positive/negative responses and outcomes.

Positive emotions and behaviors as indicators of eustress

Although the research we have done on our model to date has included a number of psychological states, we have yet to incorporate emotions. We believe emotions merit a place in our model as legitimate indicators of responses resulting from the cognitive appraisals of demands.

Emotions can be conceptualized by multi-component response tendencies that unfold over a relatively short time span. They occupy the foreground of consciousness, and they always have an object or focus. As such, emotions require cognitive appraisals, and they are associated with action readiness, or the readiness for changes in behavior toward the environment (Fredrickson, 2002; Frijda, 1999; Lucas et al., 2003). The valence for emotions (categorized as either positive or negative) is dependent upon whether they motivate either approach or avoidance behavior when activated. Emotions can be thought of as positive if they lead to approach behavior (Lucas et al., 2003). Research on positive emotions suggests that joy, contentment, love, excitement, and happiness may be good indicators to add to our Holistic Stress Model.

Generating and savoring eustress

We have previously called for research that moved from emphasizing models of preventive distress management to models that focus on *generative* eustress management (Simmons and Nelson, 2001). We suggested that managers attempt to identify aspects of the work environment that employees find most engaging, and more importantly to find out *why* individuals find the work pleasurable so that managers could enhance the aspects of the workplace that employees were appraising as enjoyable. Similar to the notion of primary preventive stress (distress) management (Quick et al., 2000), generative eustress management is the most proactive approach managers can take when partnering with employees to accentuate the positive at work.

Several recent studies of the happy-productive worker hypothesis provide additional support for the need to develop a model of eustress generation. One study found that a pleasantness-based measure of dispositional affect predicted rated job performance, although the same was not true of state positive affect in this study (Wright and Staw, 1999). A second set of studies indicated that psychological well-being was predictive of job performance for 47 human service workers (Wright and Cropanzano, 2000). Unfortunately, psychological well-being was operationalized as the absence of the negative (e.g. how often have you felt depressed or very unhappy), again supporting the prevailing primacy of the distress model.

We have also suggested the concept of savoring eustress. Savoring the positive would literally mean enjoying it with anticipation or dwelling on it with satisfaction or delight (Nelson and Simmons, 2004). We see savoring eustress as a contrast to coping with distress, and see it as a related but separate and distinct mechanism. Coping, as reactions to feelings of distress, consists of voluntary activities involving cognition, emotion, and behavior in a process of self-regulation (Ashkanasy et al., 2004). The strategies an individual formulates to reduce or eliminate distress can be problem-focused, intended to address the perceived source of distress, or emotion-focused, intended to deal with the perceived experience and ramifications of distress (Lazarus and Folkman, 1984).

Some employ the concept of positive coping in an attempt to focus on the positive (Folkman and Moskowitz, 2000). Consistent with our model, positive coping accepts the fact that both positive and negative response (e.g. affect) can co-occur during a stressful period of time. In contrast to the approach presented here, positive coping suggests that positive and negative responses are produced by different events (stressors); furthermore, the effects of the positive response are viewed as a coping strategy, a way to adapt to distress and its negative effects. As such, we believe that positive coping is still embedded in the disease model of stress.

Fredrickson's *broaden-and-build* theory of positive emotions posits that positive emotions *broaden* people's habitual models of thinking and acting and *build* enduring personal resources (Fredrickson, 1998, 2002). The experience of positive emotions can help individuals transform themselves to become more creative, connected, resilient, and ultimately healthy individuals. The concept of *broad-minded coping* is part of the broaden-and-build approach, and while it is very appealing, we believe that it is still ultimately conceptualized and operationalized is a distress/ disease model, as a method to help individuals cope with adversity.

While research on coping with distress is plentiful, research involving positive affect regulation is relatively rare. There is, however, research to suggest that processes of positive affect regulation are separate and distinct from processes of negative affect regulation (Bryant, 1989; Larsen, 2000). People who are experiencing positive emotions typically strive to maintain the emotions by approaching things they believe caused the experience and avoid things that threaten to cut short their good feelings. Yet there may be times when people attempt to *dampen* positive feelings by calming down and refocusing themselves. They may do this, for example, when they anticipate engaging in a demanding task or interacting with someone of importance (Wood et al., 2003).

We would like to see new research that examines how individuals identify both positive and negative emotions, psychological states, and behaviors in themselves. Because the extant research has already addressed how individuals avoid or cope with the negative, we would like to see studies that focus on how individuals generate or savor the positive.

Expectation alignment

We believe that there may be very important moderating variables between positive/negative responses and valued outcomes at work. As we previously stated in this chapter, our preliminary research on the relationship between hope and supervisor-rated performance was equivocal. How can we explain that? We suspect that it is possible that, at least in our studies, employees and supervisors were 'hoping' for different things. Our supervisor ratings of performance captured aspects of work related to accomplishing goals established by the supervisors. Yet employees engaged in their work may be 'absorbed' in the work itself, and therefore more focused on mastering skills associated with the work they are attempting to savor.

Individuals with high performance goals may become concerned with failure and therefore may reduce effort because they obtain few intrinsic rewards from sustaining the effort required to achieve high performance.

And individuals focused on mastering skills are less concerned about the implications of failure for challenging tasks, because negative as well as positive outcomes may provide useful feedback about their current task strategies and effort (Kristof-Brown and Stevens, 2001). We believe that the relationship between positive emotional, attitudinal, and behavioral responses and valued outcomes at work will be strongest when both employees and their supervisors develop relationships where they can engage each other in meaningful dialogue about important, challenging, yet shared understandings about what is expected at work.

Flourishing

Flourishing is a promising new outcome variable for POB researchers. Flourishing is based on the broaden-and-build theory of positive emotions, and means to live within an optimal range of human functioning (Fredrickson and Losada, 2005). As a measure of positive mental health, it could offer a much needed complement to the important outcome variable of employee physical health. Healthy employees are productive employees, and health should be broadly conceptualized as the presence of the positive – physically, mentally, spiritually – and not just the absence of the negative (e.g. disease). The challenge for researchers interested in exploring flourishing at work will be conceptualizing and measuring it in ways distinct from other constructs presented in our holistic stress model. We simply must find ways to keep the causes and indicators of flourishing separate and distinct; otherwise, we risk confounding an important concept in POB. In our models, because positive emotions, attitudes, and behaviors *cause* an individual to flourish, they cannot also be used as indicators of flourishing.

Conclusion

The study of work stress and well-being is best thought of as a constellation of theories and models that each addresses a meaningful process or phenomenon, and as such the stress serves as a general rubric for workplace experiences, individuals' reactions to those experiences, and various manifestations of employee well-being (Perrewé and Ganster, 2005). We believe the Positive Organizational Behavior perspective adds considerable value to the study of stress and health by informing a comprehensive model with a wide range of constructs of interest to both managers and scholars. We also believe that one of the most important contributions POB can make is to bring balance back to the field. We offer the Holistic Stress Model in order to provide the requisite balance between the multifaceted positive and negative aspects of work. Future studies in POB should include *both* positive and negative constructs as we attempt to challenge and advance our specific areas of research interest.

References

Ainsworth, M.D.S. and Bowlby, J. (1991) 'An ethological approach to personality', *American Psychologist*, 46, 333–41.

Ashkanasy, N.M., Ashton-James, C.E. and Jordan, P.J. (2004) 'Performance impacts of appraisal and coping with stress in workplace settings', in P.L. Perrewé and D.C. Ganster (eds) *Research in Occupational Stress and Well Being (Volume 3): Emotional and Physiological Processes and Positive Intervention Strategies* (pp. 1–43). Oxford: Elsevier.

Barnett, R.C. (1998) 'Toward a review and reconceptualization of the work/family literature', *Genetic, Social, and General Psychology Monographs*, 124, 125–82.

Bowlby, J. (1982) *Attachment*, 2nd edn. New York: Basic Books.

Bowlby, J. (1988) *A Secure Base*. New York: Basic Books.

Boswell, W.R., Olson-Buchanan, J.B. and LePine, M.A. (2004) 'Relations between stress and work outcome: The role of felt challenge, job control, and psychological strain,' *Journal of Vocational Behavior*, 64, 165–81.

Britt, T.W., Adler, A.B. and Bartone, P.T. (2001) 'Deriving benefits from stressful events: The role of engagement in meaningful work and hardiness', *Journal of Occupational Health Psychology*, 6, 53–63.

Bryant, F.B. (1989) 'A four-factor model of perceived control: Avoiding, coping, obtaining, and savoring', *Journal of Personality*, 57, 773–97.

Davidson, R.J. (2000) 'Affective style, psychopathology, and resilience: Brain mechanisms and plasticity', *American Psychologist*, 55, 1196–1214.

Edwards, J.R. and Cooper, C.L. (1988) 'The impacts of positive psychological states on physical health: A review and theoretical framework', *Social Science Medicine*, 27, 1147–1459.

Elkman, P., Levenson, R.W. and Friesen, W.V. (1983) 'Autonomic nervous system activity distinguishes among emotions', *Science*, 221, 1208–10.

Folkman, S. and Moskowitz, J.T. (2000) 'Positive affect and the other side of coping', *American Psychologist*, 55, 647–54.

Frankenhauser, M., Von Wright, M.R., Collins, A., Von Wright, J., Sedvall, G. and Swahn, C.G. (1978) 'Sex differences in psychoendocrine reactions to examination stress', *Psychosomatic Medicine*, 40, 334–43.

Fredrickson, B.L. (1998) 'What good are positive emotions?', *Review of General Psychology*, 2, 300–19.

Fredrickson, B.L. (2002) 'Positive emotions', in C.R. Snyder and S.J. Lopez (eds) *Handbook of Positive Psychology* (pp. 120–34). Oxford: Oxford University Press.

Fredrickson, B.L. and Losada, M.F. (2005) 'Positive affect and the complex dynamics of human flourishing', *American Psychologist*, 60, 678–86.

Frijda, N.H. (1999) 'Emotions and hedonic experience', in D. Kahneman, E. Diener and N. Schwarz (eds) *Well-being: The Foundations of Hedonic Psychology* (pp. 190–210). New York: Russell Sage Foundation.

Gooty, J., Nelson, D.L. and Simmons, B.L. (2005) 'Interdependence and trust in the supervisor'. Unpublished manuscript, Oklahoma State University.

Kristof-Brown, A.L. and Stevens, C.K. (2001) 'Goal congruence in project teams: Does the fit between members' personal mastery and performance goals matter?', *Journal of Applied Psychology*, 86, 1083–95.

Larsen, R.J. (2000) 'Toward a science of mood regulation', *Psychological Inquiry*, 11, 129–41.

Lazarus, R.S. (1966) *Psychological Stress and the Coping Process*. New York: McGraw-Hill.

Lazarus, R.S. and Folkman, S. (1984) *Stress, Appraisal, and Coping*. New York: Springer Publishing Company.

LePine, J.A., LePine, M.A. and Jackson, C.L. (2004) 'Challenge and hindrance stress: Relations with exhaustion, motivation to learn, and learning performance', *Journal of Applied Psychology*, 89, 883.

Little, L.M., Simmons, B.L. and Nelson, D.L. (2006) 'Health among leaders: Positive and negative affect, engagement and burnout, forgiveness and revenge', *Journal of Management Studies*, forthcoming.

Lucas, R.E., Diener, E. and Larsen, R.J. (2003) 'Measuring positive emotions', in S.J. Lopez and C.R. Snyder (eds) *Positive Psychological Assessment* (pp. 201–18). Washington, DC: American Psychological Association.

Luthans, F. (2002) 'The need for and meaning of positive organizational behavior', *Journal of Organizational Behavior*, 23, 695–706.

Mason, J.W. (1974) 'Specificity in the organization response profiles', in P. Seeman and G. Brown (eds) *Frontiers in Neurology and Neuroscience Research*. Toronto: University of Toronto Press.

Nelson, D.L. and Simmons, B.L. (2003) 'Health psychology and work stress: A more positive approach', in J.C. Quick and L.E. Tetrick (eds) *Handbook of Occupational Health Psychology* (pp. 97–119). Washington, DC: American Psychological Association.

Nelson, D.L. and Simmons, B.L. (2004) 'Eustress: An elusive construct, an engaging pursuit', in P.L. Perrewé and D.C. Ganster (eds) *Research in Occupational Stress and Well Being (Volume 3): Emotional and Physiological Processes and Positive Intervention Strategies* (pp. 265–322). Oxford: Elsevier.

Nelson, D.L., Quick, J.C. and Joplin, J.R. (1991) 'Psychological contracting and newcomer socialization: An attachment theory foundation', *Journal of Social Behavior and Personality*, 6, 55–72.

Perrewé, P.L. and Ganster, D.C. (2005) 'Overview', in P.L. Perrewé and D.C. Ganster (eds) *Research in Occupational Stress and Well Being (Volume 3): Emotional and Physiological Processes and Positive Intervention Strategies* (p. vii). Oxford: Elsevier.

Quick, J.C., Nelson, D.L. and Quick, J.D. (1990) *Stress and Challenge at the Top: The Paradox of the Successful Executive*. Chichester: John Wiley and Sons.

Quick, J.C., Quick, J.D., Nelson, D.L. and Hurrell, J.J. (2000) *Preventive Stress Management in Organizations*. Washington, DC: American Psychological Association.

Quick, J.D., Horn, R.S. and Quick, J.C. (1987). 'Health consequences of stress', *Journal of Organizational Behavior Management*, 8, 19–36.

Selye, H. (1976a) *Stress in Health and Disease*. Boston: Butterworths.

Selye, H. (1976b) *The Stress of Life: rev edn*. New York: McGraw-Hill.

Seligman, M.E.P. and Csikszentmihalyi, M. (2000) 'Positive psychology', *American Psychologist*, 55, 514.

Simmons, B.L. and Nelson, D.L. (2001) 'Eustress at work: The relationship between hope and health in hospital nurses,' *Health Care Management Review*, 26: 718.

Simmons, B.L. and Nelson, D.L. (2005) 'Extending the case for hope at work as the most unique organizational capacity.' Working paper presented at the 2005 Meeting of the National Academy of Management.

Simmons, B.L., Nelson, D.L. and Neal, L.J. (2001) 'A comparison of positive and negative work attitudes of home healthcare and hospital nurses', *Health Care Management Review*, 26, 64–75.

Simmons, B.L., Nelson, D.L. and Quick, J.C. (2003) 'Health for the hopeful: A study of attachment behavior in home health care nurses', *International Journal of Stress Management*, 10, 361–71.

Snyder, C.R., Sympson, S.C., Ybasco, F.C., Borders, T.F., Babyak, M.A. and Higgins, R.L. (1996) 'Development and validation of the state hope scale', *Journal of Personality and Social Psychology*, 70, 321–35.

Tomarken, A.J., Davidson, R.J., Wheeler, R.E. and Doss, R.C. (1992) 'Individual differences in anterior brain asymmetry and fundamental dimensions of emotion', *Journal of Personality and Social Psychology*, 62, 676–87.

Wheeler, R.E., Davidson, R.J. and Tomarken, A.J. (1993) 'Frontal brain asymmetry and emotional reactivity: A biological substrate of affective style', *Psychophysiology*, 30, 82–9.

Wood, J.V., Heimpel, S.A. and Michela, J.L. (2000) 'Savoring versus dampening: Self-esteem differences in regulating positive affect', *Journal of Personality and Social Psychology*, 85, 566–80.

Wright, T.A. (2003) 'Positive organizational behavior: An idea whose time has truly come', *Journal of Organizational Behavior*, 24, 437.

Wright, T.A. and Cropanzano, R. (2000) 'Psychological well-being and job satisfaction as predictors of job performance', *Journal of Occupational Psychology*, 5, 84–94.

Wright, T.A. and Staw, B.M. (1999) 'Affect and favorable work outcomes: two longitudinal tests of the happy-productive worker thesis', *Journal of Organizational Behavior*, 20, 1–2.

PART TWO

POSITIVE STATES, TRAITS AND PROCESSES

5

Positive Emotion in Organizations:
A Multi-level Framework

Neal M. Ashkanasy and Claire E. Ashton-James

The fundamental tenet of 'Positive Organization Scholarship' (Cameron et al., 2003) is that organizational management and decision settings need to be reframed in a positive light. It follows therefore that managers need to shift their focus to the positive aspects of organizational functioning and achievement, rather than dwell on the defensive measures needed to deal with real and imagined negative contingencies. A corollary of this view, first advanced by Staw et al. (1994), and more recently confirmed by Lyubomirsky et al. (2005), is that such organizations need also to be characterized by positive, rather than negative emotion. More recently, Ashkanasy and Daus (2002) have described these organizations in terms of a 'healthy emotional climate'. Consistent with this proposition and based on a multi-level model of emotions in organizations (Ashkanasy, 2003a; Ashkanasy and Ashton-James, 2005), we outline in this chapter how organizations can engender positive emotion, and conclude that positive emotion is a necessary precondition of positive organizational behavior.

Although Isen and Baron (1991) identified the importance of mild positive affect in organizational behavior 15 years ago, since then much of the literature that has dealt with emotions in the workplace has focused on negative emotions. For example, Fitness (2000) studied 'anger in the workplace', Ashkanasy and Nicholson (2003) studied the 'climate of fear', while Frost (2003) focused on 'toxic emotions', including their antecedents and consequences, and prescriptions for dealing with toxic emotions. In this chapter, we return to the spirit of Isen and Baron's seminal article and emphasize the link between positive emotion and exceptional performance in organizational contexts. Also, and consistent with Isen (2003), we argue that positive emotions are associated with individual and group creativity. More recently, Lyubomirsky et al. (2005) found, in an extensive meta-analysis, that positive affect leads to more successful outcomes than negative affect across a range of contextual domains, including in the workplace. The theory of positive affect in organizations that we set out here thus provides a basis upon which to understand how and when organizations can foster positive emotion, and why positive emotions should be associated with positive behavior. The multi-level perspective we present in this chapter to address these issues is based on the 5-level model of emotion in organizations described by Ashkanasy (2003a):

Level 1. neuropsychological and cognitive correlates of positive emotion at the within-person level of analysis;

Level 2. individual differences in positive emotion at the between-persons level of analysis;

Level 3. communication of positive emotion at the dyadic (relationships) level of analysis;

Level 4. promulgation of positive emotion at the group level of analysis; and

Level 5. creation of a positive emotional climate at the organizational level of analysis.

Antecedents of positive emotions in organizations

The majority of research on the antecedents of positive emotions focuses on the cognitive appraisal process that initiates emotional reactions to positive events (e.g. Lazarus, 1991). The nature of the specific events that trigger positive emotions in the organizational environment has only recently been considered, however (see Fredrickson and Brannigan, 2001). To address this in the specific context of the workplace, we base our discussion on Weiss and Cropanzano's (1996) Affective Events Theory (AET), and use this as a basic framework to describe the situational determinants of positive emotion in workplace settings.

Weiss and Cropanzano (1996) argue that events and conditions in the workplace that facilitate the attainment of workplace goals constitute positive 'affective events', and it is these events that ultimately determine the occurrence of moods and emotions. Such emotions and moods can lead to the formation of more long-term attitudes, reflected in job satisfaction and affective commitment, or even organizational loyalty (see Wright et al., 1993; Wright and Cropanzano, 1998). The seminal contribution of AET is that it represents an attempt to understand why employees' moment to moment moods fluctuate in the workplace environment. A further outcome of AET is the importance of *accumulation* of hassles and uplifts. Thus, rather than the *intensity* of major events being the source of attitudes and behavior at work, according to AET, emotions are determined more by the *frequency* with which hassles or uplifts occur (see Fisher, 2000;

Fisher and Noble, 2004; Weiss and Beal, 2005). This conclusion implies in respect of negative emotions that people are more capable of handling once-off incidents than they are of dealing with ongoing hassles. A further corollary of this is that the accumulation of negative events can be offset by positive support from colleagues, friends, and family (see Grzywacz and Marks, 2000). Finally, this idea is consistent with Isen and Baron's (1991) contention that 'positive affect states induced by seemingly minor, everyday events can have significant effects on social behavior and cognitive processes that can be important for the functioning of organizations' (p. 2).

It is clear from AET that contextual factors play a pivotal role as determinants of employees' fluctuating moods and emotions in the workplace. It is also important, however, first to understand the internal neurological and cognitive mechanisms that determine the impact of positive affective events on organizational behavior.

Level 1: Positive emotion at the within-person level of analysis

Neuropsychological correlates of positive emotion

At the most basic level of understanding, neurobiological processes underlie the experience of emotion, including perception, and understanding and display of positive emotional expression. Mirroring the emphasis on negative emotions in organizational research, however, much of the literature in emotions research in general has been oriented towards the negative emotions. LeDoux, for example, based his pioneering work on a study of fear (see LeDoux, 1998). More recently, it has become clear that positive emotion is perceived, integrated and expressed by discrete neurobiological mechanisms that are quite distinct from the mechanisms associated with negative emotion (see LeDoux, 2000). In particular, recent research has revealed that positive environmental stimuli are recognized by the *basal ganglia* region of the brain, while negative or aversive environmental stimuli are processed primarily by the *amygdala*.

The basal ganglia are programmed to encode sequences of behavior that, over time, have been repeated and rewarded – or at least not punished (Lieberman, 2000). The affective representations that are encoded by the basal ganglia support not only the execution of habitual behaviors but the prediction of what comes next in a sequence of thoughts or actions (LeDoux et al., 1989). These implicit skills are essential because they allow us to make automatic the sequences of thought and action that lead to adaptive success.

Further, basal ganglia activation has been found to be associated with the experience of positive emotions in response to positive environmental stimuli (McPherson and Cummings, 1996). As such, and as Brieter and Rosen (1999) have shown, degeneration of the basal ganglia is associated with depression and a lack of motivation to adaptive environmental demands. The ability to perceive and integrate positive emotional stimuli thus has important implications for adaptive social functioning, and is mediated by the basal ganglia.

Isen (2003) argues further that positive affect is a key facilitator of creativity. Consistent with the neuropsychological view noted earlier in this chapter, Isen and her colleagues (Ashby et al., 1999) posit that this process is mediated by the neurotransmitter dopamine. In their theory, dopamine levels in the blood are increased as a result of positive emotions, and the presence of this neurotransmitter in the anterior cingulate cortex is responsible for more creative and flexible cognitions.

In effect, there is strong evidence that positive and negative affect are driven by distinct neural circuits. Moreover, in support of Ashkanasy's (2003a) multi-level model, Isen (2003) argues that the impact of positive affect on creativity at the group and organizational level derives from fundamental differences in mechanisms underlying the production of positive and negative affect, and differences in the impact of positive and negative affect on cognitive functioning. In the following, we describe theoretical frameworks for understanding the differential impact of positive and negative mood on cognitive processing.

Cognitive correlates of positive emotion

Several cognitive mechanisms have been proposed to underlie the differential impact of positive and negative affect on cognitive functioning. Affect influences both the content of cognition, and the strategies that people use to process information. As such, positive and negative mood have different effects on the content and processes of cognition.

Content effects

The content effects of mood have received considerable attention in affect and cognition research (Forgas and Bower, 1987). The primary finding here relates to the notion of 'mood congruence', which holds that individuals in a positive mood are likely to evaluate situational cues as correspondingly optimistic or positive, so that their associated judgments and decisions are also more likely to be positive. For example, people in a positive mood tend to form more positive impressions of others (Forgas et al., 1984), and to make more optimistic risk assessments (Lerner and Keltner, 2000). People in a negative mood, on the other hand, are more likely to make more pessimistic risk assessments (Mittal and Ross, 1998), and to evaluate other people and situations more negatively (Forgas and Bower, 1987). A number of cognitive theories of affect congruence have been proposed. For example Bower's

(1981) 'Affect Priming Theory' and Schwarz and Clore's (1983) 'Affect-as-Information Model'.

Affect priming is based on an associative network model of mental representation (Bower, 1981; Isen et al., 1978). Fundamental to this model is the assumption that affective and cognitive representations are linked in an associative semantic network. Affect can infuse judgments by facilitating or priming access to related cognitive categories (Bower, 1981). As such, judgment and decision processes that rely on recall processes may be affected by positive affect. Consequently, when in a positive mood, managers are likely to be more optimistic, entrepreneurial, and to take more risks as their perception and assessment of situations is positively biased.

The affect-priming account suggests an indirect influence of affect on judgments, via the priming of affect-congruent semantic categories. The *affect-as-information* model suggests on the other hand that mood may also have direct informational effects, serving as a heuristic cue from which to infer judgments. When presented with a judgmental target, instead of deriving a response from a constructive, elaborate information search, people may simply ask themselves, 'How do I feel about it?' and base their judgments on this affective response (Schwarz, 1990).

Moderators of affect-congruence

While there is much empirical support for both content and processing effects of moods, there are many instances where affect infusion may not occur, and neither the affect priming nor the affect-as-information accounts can explain all such instances. Furthermore, there are cases in which the mood congruence literature and the mood and information processing literature make opposite predictions for the outcome of mood on cognition and behavior (Forgas, 1995). In response to this discrepancy, Forgas (1995) proposed the *Affect Infusion Model* (AIM) to explain the individual, situational and task differences that moderate the impact of moods and emotions on cognition and behavior, via their impact on processing strategy (see also Forgas, 2002, for a comprehensive review).

The primary assumption of the AIM is *process mediation*: the nature and extent of mood effects depends on the information processing strategy used for a particular task. The second assumption of the AIM is *effort minimization*: people should adopt the least effortful processing strategy capable of producing a response, all other things being equal (see Figure 5.1). Mood congruence effects are most likely when some degree of open, constructive processing is used (heuristic and substantive strategies), and less likely when closed strategies are used (direct access and motivated processing).

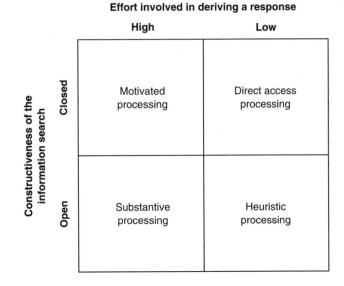

Effort involved in deriving a response

Figure 5.1   *The affective infusion model (Forgas, 1995)*
Source: Based on Forgas, 2002

Level 2: Positive emotion at the between-person (individual difference) level of analysis

Level 2 of the Ashkanasy (2003a) model encompasses the between-person effects. In this section, we look at individual difference factors that moderate the frequency, intensity, and duration of the experience of positive affect. We address in particular trait affect and emotional intelligence.

Trait affect

Trait affect represents a personal disposition to be in a long-term positive or negative affective state. Fox and Spector (2000) and Staw and Barsade (1993) examined the effect of trait affect, and found that it plays a small but significant role as a determinant of personal outcomes in organizational settings. Of course, when negative trait affect becomes chronic, the result is burnout, with more severe consequences for the individual concerned. More recently, Judge and Larsen (2001) proposed a theory of job satisfaction based on trait affect, where they found that positive affect is an important precursor of job satisfaction.

Emotional intelligence

A second dimension of individual difference that we discuss is the relatively recent concept of emotional intelligence. This variable relates to individual differences in an individual's ability to perceive, to use (assimilate), to understand, and to manage or regulate their own and others' moods and emotions (Mayer and Salovey, 1997). Differences in emotional intelligence account for between-person variation in an individual's affective responses to affective events in the workplace, and the way that positive and negative emotions affect their cognitions and behaviors in the workplace.

Fisher and Ashkanasy (2000) note that much had been expected of the emotional intelligence concept in terms of its relationship with positive organizational outcomes, but the impact of emotional intelligence on positive organizational outcomes continues to be unclear. While emotional intelligence is consistently correlated with trait positive affect and well-being, scholars continue to determine its relationship with work attitudes and outcomes (e.g. see Ashkanasy and Daus, 2005; Jordan et al., 2002).

Ashkanasy et al. (2002) present a list of some key findings that appear to be providing a clearer picture of emotional intelligence, however. These are that emotional intelligence:

- appears to be distinct from, but positively related to, other intelligences;
- is an individual difference, where some people are more endowed, and others are less so;
- develops over a person's life span and can be enhanced through training;
- involves, at least in part, a person's abilities to identify and to perceive emotion (in self and others); and
- includes skills to understand and to manage emotions successfully.

Emotional intelligence thus addresses an individual's ability to perceive emotion accurately, and to deal with it appropriately. Thus, while emotional intelligence does not ostensibly address positive emotion, Boyatzis and McKee (2005) make the case that emotional intelligence is a form of adaptive resilience, where high emotional intelligence employees are able to deal effectively with employment challenges such as job insecurity through adopting a positive view, while low emotional intelligence employees resort to maladaptive coping mechanisms (see also Jordan et al., 2002). This parallels recent findings by Tugade and Fredrickson (2004) that positive emotional states contribute to emotional resilience.

Level 3: Positive emotion at the interpersonal (dyadic) level of analysis

In discussing within-person differences in positive emotion (Level 1), we addressed the influence of positive emotions on the content of cognitive appraisals, and on information processing strategies. These effects of mood on cognition also have important consequences for interpersonal relationships. As proposed in AET and the AIM, positive affective events affect the content of situation appraisals and the way in which information is processed, which in turn influences people's behavior in the workplace. That is, positive mood has a significant impact upon the way in which people interpret one another's behavior, which has implications for subsequent interactions.

For example, Forgas et al. (1984) demonstrated that happy people perceive significantly more positive and skilled behaviors and fewer negative, unskilled behaviors both in themselves and in their partners than did sad people. In terms of the AIM, these effects occur because affect priming influences the kinds of interpretations, constructs, and associations that become available as people evaluate intrinsically complex and indeterminate social behaviors in the course of substantive, inferential processing. In the workplace, therefore, the same performance review between a manager and employee that is judged to be positive and constructive by a happy person may be perceived to be negative and critical by someone in a bad mood.

A behavior that is of particular relevance to workplace functioning is requesting. There are several workplace situations in which the ability to formulate a request confidently, in a manner which maximizes the likelihood of compliance, is of strategic importance to the achievement of workplace or personal goals. For example, requesting help from colleagues may be critical to one's ability to complete a task, and the achievement of compliance in the request for a pay rise may significantly affect one's future job satisfaction and personal well-being. In terms of the AIM, happy people should adopt a more confident, direct processing style, as a result of the greater availability and use of positively valenced thoughts and associations in their minds as they assess the felicity conditions for their requests (Forgas, 1998a). Consequently, people in a positive mood are more likely to be granted their request, as their requests are less equivocal and demonstrate less hedging, leaving the person receiving the request little opportunity to avoid meeting the object of the request (Forgas, 1999). Moreover, Forgas (1998a) has also demonstrated that people respond to people's requests more positively when in a positive mood than when in a negative mood.

Negotiation is another interpersonal task that is critical to organizational outcomes. Particularly with regards to top management, the ability to negotiate or bargain for optimal organizational outcomes is of great importance. Again, Forgas (1998b) has shown that happy people are more confident during the negotiation process, are more assertive and persistent in reaching their desired goals, behave more cooperatively, and are more willing to use integrative strategies and make reciprocal deals than were those in a negative mood. As such, positive mood produces better outcomes for happy people than for sad individuals.

Level 4: Positive emotion at the group level of analysis

Schermerhorn et al. (2001) define a group as 'a collection of two or more people who work with one another regularly to achieve common goals'

(p. 174). As such, group members interact on a dyadic and collective basis, and naturally encounter all of the perceptions and experiences that we have outlined earlier in reference to individuals and their interactions. Nonetheless, groups introduce additional dimensions of cohesiveness, collective values, and leadership that render an added level of complexity to the discussion of emotions in workplace settings. In this respect, De Dreu, et al. (2001) see group settings as a sort of 'emotional incubator', where the emotional states of the group members combine to produce an overall group-level emotional tenor that, in turn, affects all group members.

Kelly and Barsade (2001) argue more specifically that teams possess an 'affective composition' or a group mood, which begins either with the emotional characteristics of team members, and then develops through a process of emotional contagion (see also Barsade, 2002; Hatfield et al., 1992), or the emotional expression of the group leader, which evokes emotion in group members.

Emotional contagion

Emotion contagion is 'a process in which a person or group influences the emotions or behavior of another person or group through the conscious or unconscious induction of emotion states and behavioral attitudes' (Schoenewolf, 1990: 50). Emotions are 'caught' by group members when they are exposed to the emotional expressions of other group members. Hatfield et al. (1992, 1994) posited that the degree to which emotional contagion occurs is mediated by attentional processes, with greater emotional contagion occurring when more attention is allocated.

When the emotional expression is observed, an affective state of the same valence (positive or negative) is then experienced by the observer group members. The actual mechanisms by which emotions are transferred are subconscious, automatic and 'primitive' (Hatfield et al., 1994). Psychological researchers have found that this process involves automatic non-conscious mimicry, in which people spontaneously imitate each others' facial expressions and body language (Chartrand and Bargh, 1999), speech patterns (Ekman et al., 1976) and vocal tones (Neumann and Strack, 2000). The second step of this primitive contagion process comes from the affective feedback people receive from mimicking others' nonverbal behaviors and expressions. This is also an automatic process. Several studies (e.g. Duclos et al., 1989) have demonstrated that the mimicking of nonverbal expressions of emotion results in the experience of the emotion itself through physiological, visceral, and glandular feedback responses (see Hatfield et al., 1994 for a review). While group members ultimately become aware of this feeling, the initial process of emotion contagion is subconscious and automatic.

Zurcher (1982) argues that displays of positive emotion in group situations constitute an essential ingredient necessary for establishment of group cohesion. Furthermore, Lawler (1992) posits that emotion is the essential social process in group formation and maintenance. This is because positive emotions strengthen feelings of control. As such, positive emotion is a necessary precursor of group cohesiveness. In the context of organizational work groups, George (1990) has shown also that positive affect is a key ingredient for group effectiveness and satisfaction (see also George and Brief, 1992). Barsade (2002) found that positive emotion contagion amongst group members affects individual-level attitudes and group processes. Group members who experienced positive emotional contagion demonstrated improved cooperation, decreased conflict, and increased perceived task performance (Barsade, 2002).

Group leadership and emotion

The role of leadership in communicating, expressing, and managing emotions in groups is axiomatic (see Graen and Uhl-Bien, 1995). According to Pfeffer (1981) leadership is seen as a process of symbolic management, and involves creating and maintaining shared meanings among followers. Ashforth and Humphrey (1995) argue that this process depends intrinsically on evocation of emotion. Based on Ortner's (1973) model, they note that symbols generate interacting cognitive and emotional responses, and they conclude, 'symbolic management involves orchestrating summarizing and elaborating symbols to evoke emotion which can be generalized to organizational ends' (p. 111). Thus, leaders engage in communication of symbols designed to make followers feel better about themselves, and to strengthen followers' commitment to the organization (see also Fineman, 2001; Van Maanen and Kunda, 1989).

It follows therefore that leadership entails perception, recognition, and management of emotional cues by both the leader and the led, which we described earlier as emotional sensitivity. A leader's displayed emotion is a critical determinant of the quality of relationships with group members, and consequently of the leader's ability to communicate emotionally evocative symbols (Avolio, et al., 1999). Thus, facilitated by processes of emotional contagion, positive group affect energized by emotionally aware leaders, can enhance organizational creativity performance by facilitating group cohesion and positive affect.

Level 5: Positive emotion at the organizational level of analysis

Finally, at Level 5, the conditions necessary for positive emotion at the other levels of the model must be built and sustained across the whole organization through a healthy emotional climate (Ashkanasy and Daus, 2002). Level 5 of Ashkanasy's (2003a) multi-level model is qualitatively different from the other levels. At the lower levels, organizational policies and values are interpreted in the context of face-to-face interactions, where all the basic biological and neurophysiological and physiological mechanisms we have discussed up to this point are salient. Thus, at this level of organization, a manager can recognize cues of real or felt emotion, and identify the positive emotional indicators of employees who are genuinely motivated toward goal achievement and confident of achieving their goals. When dealing with the organization-wide or macro view, on the other hand, the situation is much less clear. Although some members of a large organization will have meetings with senior managers, these meetings are likely to be brief and infrequent (Mintzberg, 1973), and are also likely to be constrained by power differences (Gibson and Schroeder, 2002). Instead, it is necessary to deal with the more nebulous concept of *emotional climate*, defined by De Rivera (1992) as 'an objective group phenomenon that can be palpably sensed – as when one enters a party or a city and feels an attitude of gaiety or depression, openness or fear' (p. 197).

In the context of work organizations, *organizational climate* has been studied for some time now (see Ashkanasy et al., 2000; Reichers and Schneider, 1990), and constitutes the collective mood of organizational members toward their jobs, the organization, and management. The concept is distinct from *organizational culture*, in that climate is essentially an emotional phenomenon, while culture is more stable, and rooted in beliefs, values, and embedded assumptions (Ashkanasy et al., 2000; Ott, 1989; Schein, 1985). Nonetheless, Schein makes it clear that assumptions underlying organizational culture are associated with deeply felt feelings. More recently, Beyer and Niño (2001) demonstrated how culture and organizational members' emotional views and states are intimately and reciprocally related. As such, both organizational climate and organizational culture arguably have emotional underpinnings.

A number of writers in the organizational literature have noted the emotional basis of organizational culture (e.g. Beyer and Niño, 2001; Fineman, 2001; Hochschild, 1983; Rafaeli and Sutton, 1987, 1989; Van Maanen and Kunda, 1989), but primarily in the context of displayed emotional states, rather than felt emotion. This begs the question as to how to ascertain real emotional climate (or culture) in organizations. Although Härtel et al. (in press) measured emotional climate and reported a correlation with job satisfaction, most advocates of an ethnographic approach (e.g. Schein, 1985; Trice and Bayer, 1993) argue that only through active day-to-day involvement in organizations is it possible to sense real as opposed to displayed emotion. De Rivera (1992) notes, however, that emotional climate is an objective phenomenon and is therefore amenable to objective perception and interpretation, provided the observer knows what to look for. In effect, his point is that observers need to be sensitive to markers of felt rather than displayed emotion. In this case, however, the markers are not so much in the individual expressions of organizational members, but in the social structures and patterns of behavior that are manifest in the organization. De Rivera argues further that people are sensitive to such cues, and shape their beliefs and behaviors accordingly. It follows that the arguments developed earlier in the present paper in respect of interpersonal relationships and small groups may be extendable to the organization as a whole, especially since organizational policies ultimately come down to the perceptions, understanding, and behavior of individuals, interacting dyads, and groups.

Conclusions

In this chapter, we have outlined the 5-level model of emotions set out in Ashkanasy (2003a), with an emphasis on positive emotion. We argue, consistent with Isen and Baron (1991) and Lyubomirsky et al. (2005), that mild, positive affect, experienced as a result of everyday events, is a catalyst for creativity and effectiveness in organizational settings. The logical sequence was presented from the bottom-up, in that we began with the neurobiological bases of within-person emotion, and then moved progressively to the individual, dyadic, group, and organizational levels of analysis. We also argued, consistent with Ashkanasy (2003b), that the neurobiological processes represent the integrating medium across these levels of analysis. The important point here is that the view we present is internally consistent across all five levels of organizations. From a strategic perspective, this means that a manager who engenders a positive emotional climate can expect that this will lead to positive emotions at all of the other levels. Members in an organization characterized by a positive climate can therefore expect to work in cohesive groups where positive emotion is transferred from leaders to member, and between members, and where the resulting positive affect is likely to create the conditions that facilitate positive organizational behavior, and where genuine creativity can flourish.

Finally, we note that research in this field is still at an early stage of development. Although research on the role played by emotion in organizational settings has progressed enormously over the 15 years since Isen and Baron (1991) published their seminal article on positive affect, there still remains considerable scope for research to understand in more detail the role of affect and emotions in organizational life in general, and positive emotions in particular. We hope the multi-level perspective outlined in this chapter will provide a framework to advance this research further into the future.

Acknowledgment

This research was funded by a grant of the Australian Research Council. We acknowledge with thanks the assistance of Kaylene W. Ascough and Marie T. Dasborough in preparing this manuscript. An earlier version of this chapter was presented in an All-Academy Symposium at the 64th Annual Meeting of the Academy of Management, New Orleans, Louisiana, USA (August 2004), chaired by A. Caza and L.E. Sekerka.

References

Ashby, F.G., Isen, A.M. and Turken, A.U. (1999) 'A neuropsychological theory of positive affect and its influence on cognition', *Psychological Review*, 106, 529–50.

Ashforth, B.E. and Humphrey, R.H. (1995) 'Emotion in the workplace: A reappraisal', *Human Relations*, 48, 97–125.

Ashkanasy, N.M. (2003a) 'Emotions in organizations: A multilevel perspective', in F. Dansereau and F.J. Yammarino (eds) *Research in Multi-level Issues, Vol. 2: Multi-level Issues in Organizational Behavior and Strategy* (pp. 9–54). Oxford: Elsevier Science.

Ashkanasy, N.M. (2003b) 'Emotions at multiple levels: An integration', in F. Dansereau and F.J. Yammarino (eds) *Research in Multi-level Issues, Vol. 2: Multi-level Issues in Organizational Behavior and Strategy* (pp. 71–81). Oxford: Elsevier Science.

Ashkanasy, N.M. and Ashton-James, C.E. (2005) 'Emotion in organizations: A neglected topic in I/O Psychology, but with a bright future', in G.P. Hodgkinson and J.K. Ford (eds) *International Review of Industrial and Organizational Psychology, Vol. 20* (pp. 221–68). Chichester: John Wiley and Sons.

Ashkanasy, N.M. and Daus, S.D. (2002) 'Emotion in the workplace: The new challenge for managers', *Academy of Management Executive*, 16 (1), 76–86.

Ashkanasy, N.M. and Daus, C.S. (2005) 'Rumors of the death of emotional intelligence in organizational behavior are vastly exaggerated', *Journal of Organizational Behavior*, 26, 441–52,

Ashkanasy, N.M. and Nicholson, G.J. (2003) 'Climate of fear in organizational settings: Construct definition, measurement, and a test of theory', *Australian Journal of Psychology*, 55, 24–9.

Ashkanasy, N.M., Härtel, C.E.J. and Daus, C.S. (2002) 'Advances in organizational behavior: Diversity and emotions', *Journal of Management*, 28, 307–38.

Ashkanasy, N.M., Wilderom, C.P.M. and Peterson, M.F. (2000) 'Introduction', in N.M. Ashkanasy, C. Wilderom and M. Peterson, *Handbook of Organizational Culture and Climate* (pp. 1–18). Thousand Oaks, CA: Sage Publications.

Avolio, B.J., Howell, J.M. and Sosik, J.J. (1999) 'A funny thing happened on the way to the bottom line: Humor as a moderator of leadership style effects', *Academy of Management Journal*, 42, 219–27.

Barsade, S.G. (2002) 'The ripple effect: Emotional contagion and its influence on group behavior', *Administrative Science Quarterly*, 47, 644–75.

Beyer, J. and Niño, D. (2001) 'Culture as a source, expression, and reinforcer of emotions in organizations', in R.L. Payne and C.L. Cooper (eds) *Emotions at Work: Theory, Research, and Applications for Management* (pp. 173–197). Chichester: John Wiley and Sons.

Bower, G.H. (1981)'Mood and memory', *American Psychologist*, 36, 129–48.

Boyatzis, R.E. and McKee, A. (2005) *Resonant Leadership: Renewing Yourself and Connecting with Others through Mindfulness, Hope, and Compassion.* Cambridge, MA: Harvard University Press.

Brieter, H.C. and Rosen, B.R. (1999) 'Functional magnetic resonance imaging of brain reward circuitry in the human', *Annals of the New York Academy of Sciences*, 877, 523–47.

Cameron, K., Dutton, J.E. and Quinn, R.E. (eds) (2003) *Positive Organizational Scholarship: Foundations of a New Discipline.* San Francisco: Berrett-Koehler Publishers.

Chartrand, T. and Bargh, J. (1999) 'The chameleon effect', *Journal of Personality and Social Psychology*, 76, 893–910.

De Dreu, C.K.W., West, M.A., Fischer, A.H. and MacCurtain, S. (2001) 'Origins and consequences of emotions in organizational teams', in R.L. Payne and C.L. Cooper (eds) *Emotions at Work: Theory, Research, and Applications for Management* (pp. 199–217). Chichester: Wiley.

De Rivera, J. (1992) 'Emotional climate: Social structure and emotional dymamics', *International Review of Studies of Emotion*, 2, 197–218.

Duclos, S.E., Laird, J.D., Scheider, E., Sexter, M., Stern, L. and Van Lighten, O. (1989) 'Emotion-specific effects of facial expressions and postures on emotional experiences', *Journal of Personality and Social Psychology*, 57, 100–8.

Ekman, P., Friesen, W.V. and Scherer, K.R. (1976) 'Body movement and voice pitch in deceptive interaction', *Semiotica*, 16, 23–7.

Fineman, S. (2001) 'Emotions and organizational control', in R.L. Payne and C.L. Cooper (eds), *Emotions at Work: Theory, Research, and Applications for Management* (pp. 219–40). Chichester: Wiley.

Fisher, C.D. (2000) 'Mood and emotions while working: Missing pieces of job satisfaction', *Journal of Organizational Behavior*, 21, 185–202.

Fisher, C.D. and Ashkanasy, N.M. (eds) (2000) Special issue on Emotions in Work Life. *Journal of Organizational Behavior*, 21, (3).

Fisher, C.D. and Noble, C.S. (2004) 'A within-person examination of correlates of performance and emotions while working', *Human Performance*, 17, 145–68.

Fitness, J. (2000) 'Anger in the workplace: An emotion script approach to anger episodes between workers and their superiors, co-workers, and subordinates', *Journal of Organizational Behavior*, 21, 147–62.

Forgas, J.P. (1995) 'Mood and judgment: The Affect Infusion Model (AIM)', *Psychological Bulletin*, 117, 39–66.

Forgas, J.P. (1998a) 'Asking nicely? Mood effects on responding to more or less polite requests', *Personality and Social Psychology Bulletin*, 24, 173–85.

Forgas, J.P. (1998b) 'On feeling good and getting your way: Mood effects on negotiation strategies and outcomes', *Journal of Personality and Social Psychology*, 74, 565–77.

Forgas, J.P. (1999) 'On feeling good and being rude: Affective influences on language use and request formulations', *Journal of Personality and Social Psychology*, 76, 928–39.

Forgas, J.P. (2002) 'Feeling and doing: Influences on interpersonal behavior', *Psychological Inquiry*, 13, 1–28.

Forgas, J.P. and Bower, G.H. (1987) 'Mood effects on person perception judgments', *Journal of Personality and Social Psychology*, 53, 53–60.

Forgas, J.P., Bower, G.H. and Krantz, S. (1984) The influence of mood on perceptions of social interactions', *Journal of Personality and Social Psychology*, 20, 497–513.

Fox, S. and Spector, P. (2000) 'Relations of emotional intelligence, practical intelligence, general intelligence, and trait affectivity with interview outcomes: It's not all just "G"', *Journal of Organizational Behavior*, 21, 203–20.

Fredrickson, B.L. and Brannigan, C. (2001) 'Positive emotions', in. G. Bonnano and T. Mayne (eds) *Emotions: Current Issues and Future Directions* (pp. 123–52). New York: Guilford Press.

Frost, P.J. (2003) *Toxic Emotions at Work: How Compassionate Managers Handle Pain and Conflict*. Boston, MA: Harvard Business School Press.

George, J.M. (1990) 'Personality, affect, and behavior in groups', *Journal of Applied Psychology*, 76, 299–307.

George, J.M. and Brief, A.P. (1992) 'Feeling good – doing good: A conceptual analysis of the mood at work-organizational spontaneity relationship', *Psychological Bulletin*, 112, 310–29.

Gibson, D.E. and Schroeder, S.J. (2002) 'Grinning, frowning, and emotionless: Agent perceptions of power and their effect on felt and displayed emotions in influence attempts', in N.M. Ashkanasy, W.J. Zerbe and C.E.J. Härtel (eds), *Managing Emotions in the Workplace* (pp. 184–211). Armonk, NY: ME Sharpe.

Graen, G.B. and Uhl-Bien, M. (1995) 'Development of leader–member exchange (LMX) theory of leadership over 25 years: Applying a multi-level multi-domain perspective', *Leadership Quarterly*, 6, 219–47.

Grzywacz, J.G. and Marks, N.F. (2000) 'Reconceptualizing the work–family interface: An ecological perspective on the correlates of positive and negative spillover between work and family', *Journal of Occupational Health Psychology*, 5, 111–26.

Härtel, C.E.J., Gough, H. and Härtel, G.F. (in press) 'Work group emotional climate, emotion management skills and service attitudes and performance', *Asia Pacific Journal of Human Resources*.

Hatfield, E., Cacioppo, J. and Rapson, R.L. (1992) 'Primitive emotional contagion', *Review of Personality and Social Psychology*, 14, 151–77.

Hatfield, E., Cacioppo, J. and Rapson, R.L. (1994) *Emotional Contagion*. New York: Cambridge University Press.

Hochschild, A.R. (1983) *The Managed Heart: Commercialization of Human Feeling*. Berkeley, CA: University of California Press.

Isen, A.M. (2003) 'Positive affect, systematic cognitive processing, and behavior: Toward integration of affect, cognition, and motivation', in F. Dansereau and F.J. Yammarino (eds) *Research in Multi-level Issues, Vol. 2: Multi-level Issues in Organizational Behavior and Strategy* (pp. 55–72). Oxford: Elsevier Science

Isen, A.M. and Baron, R.A. (1991) 'Positive affect as a factor in organizational behavior', *Research in Organizational Behavior*, 13, 1–53.

Isen, A.M., Shalker, T.E., Clark, M. and Karp, L. (1978) 'Affect, accessibility of material in memory, and behavior: A cognitive loop?', *Journal of Personality and Social Psychology*, 36, 1–12.

Jordan, P.J., Ashkanasy, N.M. and Härtel, C.E.J. (2002) 'Emotional intelligence as a moderator of emotional and behavioral reactions to job insecurity', *Academy of Management Review*, 27, 361–72.

Judge, T.A. and Larsen, R.J. (2001) 'Dispositional affect and job satisfaction: A review and theoretical extension', *Organizational Behavior and Human Decision Processes*, 86, 67–98.

Kelly, J.R. and Barsade, S.G. (2001) 'Mood and emotions in small groups and work teams', *Organizational Behavior and Human Decision Processes*, 86, 99–130.

Lawler, E.J. (1992) 'Affective attachment to nested groups: A choice-process theory', *American Sociological Review*, 57, 327–39.

Lazarus, R.S. (1991) *Emotion and Adaptation*. New York: Oxford University Press.

Lerner, J.S. and Keltner, D. (2000) Beyond valence: Toward a model of emotion-specific influences on judgments and choice', *Cognition and Emotion*, 14, 473–95.

LeDoux, J. (1998) 'Fear and the brain: Where have we been, and where are we going', *Biological Psychiatry*, 44, 1229–38.

LeDoux, J. (2000) 'Emotion circuits in the brain', *Annual Review of Neuroscience*, 23, 155–84.

LeDoux, J.E., Romanski, L. and Xagoraris, A. (1989) 'Indelibility of sub-cortical emotional memories', *Journal of Cognitive Neuroscience*, 1, 238–43.

Lieberman, M.D. (2000) 'Intuition: A social cognitive neuroscience approach', *Psychological Bulletin*, 126, 109–37.

Lyubomirsky, S., King, L. and Deiner, E. (2005) 'The benefits of frequent positive affect: Does happiness lead to success?', *Physchological Bulletin*, 131, 803–55.

Mayer, J.D. and Salovey, P. (1997) 'What is emotional intelligence?', in P. Salovey and D.J. Sluyter (eds) *Emotional Development and Emotional Intelligence: Educational Implications* (pp. 3–31). New York: Basic Books.

McPherson, S. and Cummings, J.L. (1996) 'Neuropsychological aspects of Parkinson's disease and Parkinsonism', in I. Grant and K.M. Adams (eds) *Neurological Assessment of Neuropsychiatric Disorders* (pp. 288–311). New York: Oxford University Press.

Mintzberg, H. (1973) *The Nature of Managerial Work*. New York: Harper and Row.

Mittal, V. and Ross, W.T. (1998) 'The impact of positive and negative affect and issue framing on issue interpretation and risk taking', *Organizational Behavior and Human Decision Processes*, 76, 298–324.

Neumann, R. and Strack, F. (2000) ' "Mood contagion": The automatic transfer of mood between persons', *Journal of Personality and Social Psychology*, 79, 211–23.

Ortner, S.B. (1973) 'On key symbols', *American Anthropologist*, 75, 1338–46.

Ott, J.S. (1989) *The Organizational Culture Perspective*. Pacific Grove, CA: Brooks/Cole.

Pfeffer, J. (1981) 'Management as symbolic action: The creation and maintenance of organizational paradigms', *Research in Organizational Behavior*, 3, 1–52.

Rafaeli, A. and Sutton, R.I. (1987) 'Expression of emotion as part of the work role', *Academy of Management Review*, 12, 23–37.

Rafaeli, A. and Sutton, R.I. (1989) 'The expression of emotion in organizational life', *Research in Organizational Behavior*, 11, 1–42.

Reichers, A.E. and Schneider, B. (1990) 'Climate and culture: An evolution of constructs', in B. Schneider (ed.) *Organizational Climate and Culture* (pp. 5–39). San Francisco: Jossey-Bass.

Schein, E.H. (1985) *Organizational Culture and Leadership*. San Francisco: Jossey-Bass.

Schermerhorn, Jr, R.R., Hunt, J.G. and Osborn, R.N. (2001) *Organizational Behavior*, 7th edn. New York: Wiley.

Schoenewolf, G. (1990) *Turning Points in Analytic Therapy: The Classic Cases*. London: Jason Aronson Press.

Schwarz, N. (1990) 'Feelings as information: Informational and motivational functions of affective states', in E.T. Higgins and R. Sorrentino (eds) *Handbook of Motivation and Cognition, Volume 2: Foundations of Social Behavior* (pp. 527–61). New York: Guilford Press.

Schwarz, N. and Clore, G.L. (1983) 'Mood, misattribution, and judgments of well-being: Informative and directive functions of affective states', *Journal of Personality and Social Psychology*, 45, 513–23.

Staw, B.M. and Barsade, S.G. (1993) 'Affect and managerial performance: A test of the sadder-but-wiser vs. happier-and-smarter hypotheses', *Administrative Science Quarterly*, 38, 304–28.

Staw, B.M. Sutton, R.I. and Pelled, S.H. (1994) 'Employee positive emotions and favorable outcomes at the workplace', *Organization Science*, 5, 51–71.

Trice, H.M. and Bayer, J.M. (1993) *The Cultures of Work Organizations*. Englewood Cliffs, NJ: Prentice Hall.

Tugade, M.M. and Fredrickson, B.L. (2004) 'Resilient individuals use positive emotions to bounce back from negative emotional experiences', *Journal of Personality and Social Psychology*, 86, 320–33.

Van Maanen, J. and Kunda, G. (1989) '"Real feelings": Emotional expression and organizational culture', *Research in Organizational Behavior*, 11, 43–103.

Weiss, H.M. and Beal, D.J. (2005) 'Reflections on affective events theory', in N.M. Ashkanasy, W.J. Zerbe and C.E.J. Härtel (eds) *Research on Emotion in Organizations, Vol. 1: The Effect of Affect in Organizational Settings* (pp. 1–22). Oxford: Elsevier/JAI Press.

Weiss, H.M. and Cropanzano, R. (1996) 'Affective events theory: A theoretical discussion of the structure, causes and consequences of affective experiences at work', *Research in Organizational Behavior*, 18, 1–74.

Wright, T.A., Bonett, D.G. and Sweeney, D.A. (1993) 'Mental-health and work performance: Results of a longitudinal field study', *Journal of Occupational and Organizational Psychology*, 66, 277–84.

Wright, T.A. and Cropanzano, R. (1998) 'Emotional exhaustion as a predictor of job performance and voluntary turnover', *Journal of Applied Psychology*, 83, 486–93.

Zurcher, L.A. (1982) 'The staging of emotion: A dramaturgical analysis', *Symbolic Interaction*, 5, 1–22.

6

Thriving in Organizations

Gretchen M. Spreitzer and Kathleen M. Sutcliffe

Consider these contrasting images of individuals in relation to their work.

Slow death

- 'Here we house the legions of the walking dead.'
  When people join the legions of the walking dead, they begin to live lives of quiet desperation. They tend to experience feelings of meaningless-ness, hopelessness, and impotence in their work roles. (Quinn, 1996: 20)
- 'Seventy-five percent of our middle managers have opted for peace and pay.' Peace and pay means don't rock the boat, maintain the status quo, keep your head in a shell, come in at eight and leave at five, don't take any risks. (Quinn, 1996: 22)

In slow death, employees are stagnant, stale, and lifeless. Now consider a different image of individuals at work.

Thriving at work

- Thriving is about 'being energized, feeling valued, feeling what you do is valuable. For me thriving is a sense of connectedness. Feeling good about what you do … So thriving is being productive, still being able to learn new things … I think thriving is being open to challenges presented and to learn and grow, and having those opportunities to grow.' (A mid-level manager in a large metropolitan non profit; Spreitzer et al., 2005: 38)
- '… I know thriving as I feel it. It is like going forward. It is not staying in place. It is not stagnant. You are moving forward; not necessarily in job titles or positions, but just being able to move forward thinking and in the activities that you are engaged in and in your mindset, all of those things.' (A social worker; Spreitzer et al., 2005: 538)

In these thriving images, individuals are growing, full of life, and engaged. While both slow death and thriving depict actual organizational realities, we know much more about the causes of slow death than of thriving. In the organization studies literature, work contexts are often blamed for their untoward consequences on individuals. And many studies have shown the ways in which work contexts cause stress and contribute to health problems (e.g. French et al., 1982; Wright and Cropanzano, 1998; Danna and Griffin, 1999). However, as the thriving images reflect, work contexts can do more than generate stress and corrode health. They can enable employees to thrive and thereby can contribute positively to their health and well-being (Harter et al., 2003).

This chapter provides an introduction and overview of research on thriving in organizations. We build on a small but growing body of research that suggests that when people have opportunities to thrive at work, positive outcomes follow. And because thriving may offer key insights into how work contexts can positively enable individuals, we seek to understand the process of thriving at work. We define thriving at work, examine key outcomes of thriving, and articulate the mechanisms through which features of work contexts produce their salutary effects. In doing so, we shift the research away from a focus on the negative aspects of work and work contexts (e.g. stress factors) to a focus on the positive, enabling potential of work contexts. We also begin to explore the notion of collective thriving.

What is thriving?

In medicine, there is a diagnosis pertaining to infants and the frail elderly known as failure to thrive. A 'failure to thrive' diagnosis is denoted by an acute lack of growth and is manifest in listlessness, immobility, apathy, and lack of an appetite (Bakwin, 1949). While failure to thrive focuses on not growing, thriving then is about personal growth and development. We draw on the work of Spreitzer et al. (2005: 538) to define thriving as 'the psychological state in which individuals experience both a sense of vitality and a sense of learning at work'. Vitality refers to the positive feeling of having energy available (Nix et al., 1999). Learning refers to the sense that one is acquiring, and can apply, knowledge and skills. To bring these dimensions of thriving alive, consider these narratives from two employees about their experiences of thriving at work (drawn from qualitative work conducted as part of Sonenshein et al., 2006):

- 'Feeling that there's some upper thrust to your life instead of just mediocrity going on.'
- 'When you can look back and you can see how far that you have prospered, when you can see how far that you have advanced, when you can see how far, just see how far you've come.'

These quotes capture thriving as the joint experience of vitality and learning. According to Spreitzer and colleagues (2005), both vitality and learning are essential components of thriving. If one is learning, but feels depleted and burned out, one is not thriving. When thriving, individuals feel alive and vibrant – they have a zest for life (Miller and Stiver, 1998). Conversely, if one is energized, but finds his or her learning to be stagnant, that person is not thriving. Consequently, these two dimensions encompass both the affective (vitality) and cognitive (learning) dimensions of psychological experience. Moreover, the definition of thriving as growing in terms of both learning and vitality captures both the hedonic (vitality) and eudaimonic (learning) aspects of psychological functioning and development (Waterman, 1993).

Thriving as conceived by Spreitzer and colleagues is closely aligned with perspectives on personal growth (e.g. Carver, 1998; Ryff, 1989). Ryff (1989: 1072), for example, suggests that when individuals grow, they consider themselves to be expanding in ways that reflect enhanced self-knowledge and effectiveness. Thriving reflects 'continually developing and becoming, rather than achieving a fixed state wherein one is fully developed' (Ryff, 1989: 1071). Individuals have a sense of realizing their own potential and seeing improvement in the self and their behaviors over time (Ryff, 1989). Likewise, Carver (1998) conceives of thriving as the psychological experience of growth in a positive capacity (i.e. a constructive or forward direction). The learning element of this definition of thriving is also consistent with Ryff and Keyes' (1995) personal development element of psychological well-being. In short, thriving involves active, intentional engagement in the process of personal growth.

But thriving is not a dichotomous state. As Spreitzer et al. (2005) point out; thriving is a continuum where people are more or less thriving at any point in time. And individuals can experience a range of thriving experiences rather than experiencing thriving or not thriving. And thriving is a psychological state and not an individual disposition. Individuals' thriving is malleable and shaped by their work context. Depending on a person's work context, he or she can experience thriving as increasing, decreasing, or constant in comparison to the person's thriving at a previous point in time.

Recent research on peoples' experience of thriving at work (Sonenshein et al., 2006) demonstrates that everyone has had thriving experiences at work. No one was stumped when they were asked to describe an experience of thriving at work. And interestingly, when asked to reflect on an experience of thriving at work, people appear to focus on a past experience rather than a current experience. There are several plausible explanations for why this might be the case. First, people may remember past experiences more positively than present experiences. We may filter out the negative elements of past experiences. As such, we may remember past experiences as being ones in which we were thriving. Second, although it is clear that people can sense their current level of vitality or energy, it may be more difficult for them to gauge the extent to which they are learning in the moment. As a result, people may see more learning in past experiences than current experiences.

Why does thriving matter? Some outcomes of thriving at work

Thriving is associated with important individual and organizational outcomes.

Self-development

First, thriving can be a powerful gauge (Spreitzer et al., 2005) for people about whether what they are doing and how they are doing it is helping them to develop in a positive direction – that is an individual's sense of improvement in short-term individual functioning and long-term adaptability to the work environment (Hall and Fukami, 1979; Kolb, 1984). Individuals can track the magnitude and changes in their sense of thriving to gauge whether and how they should take action in the context of work to sustain or renew their thriving. Thus, thriving serves an adaptive function that helps individuals navigate and change their work contexts in order to promote their own development.

Health

Second, when individuals are thriving, they are more likely to be healthy. Why? When individuals feel a sense of vitality and aliveness, they are less likely to be anxious and depressed, and thus more likely to be mentally healthy (Keyes, 2002). Consistent with this line of thinking, Christianson and colleagues (2005) found that individuals who report higher levels of thriving (measured as energy and increasing complexity) have better mental and physical health, even when controlling for the separate effects of depression, anxiety, panic attacks, body mass index, and chronic conditions. In addition, a sense of learning by itself can contribute to positive physical health. Alfredsson et al. (1985: 378) concluded that 'workers ... with few possibilities to learn new things' had a heightened probability of being hospitalized for heart attacks. Similarly, Ettner and Grzywacz (2001) found that employees who reported more learning at work also were more likely to report that work contributed positively to their mental and physical health.

Performance

Third, thriving may have implications for individual and organizational performance. We know less about performance outcomes of thriving but can speculate on this relationship. The health effects described above may have important implications for organizations because vitality and personal development have been associated with better individual work productivity (in terms of work effort and days lost to illness) and less health care usage (Keyes and Grzywacz, 2005). And when people use less health care, companies can cut health care costs which are skyrocketing out of control for many organizations.

We can also expect that individuals who feel more energized at work (i.e. one dimension of thriving) will expend more effort and be more committed to their work and organizations (Marks, 1977). Conceptually, Quinn and Dutton (2005) articulate the crucial role that energy plays in coordinated activities in organizations. Empirically, Cross et al. (2003) found that those who are energizers in organizations have higher job performance, and are more likely to have their ideas considered and put into action.

And individuals who experience more learning at work (i.e. the other dimension of thriving) are likely to be able to leverage that learning for performance improvements. The learning may capture new skills, abilities, and knowledge about how to function more productively at work. And that learning can be shared vicariously or directly with others to produce more organizational learning.

Contagion to others

We know that positive affect (and energy is considered an element of positive affect) can be spread from one person to another. Emotional contagion is 'a process in which a person or group influences the emotions or behavior of another person or group through the conscious or unconscious induction of affect states and behavioral attitudes' (Schoenewolf, 1990: 50). Through emotional contagion, emotions such as energy among group members become shared (e.g. Barsade, 2002; Bartel and Saavedra, 2000; Totterdell, 2000). So if one person is energized, others are likely to catch their energy, leading to a more energized group, unit or organization.

Spillover to home life

Although we know very little about positive spillover, we know that stress at work spills over into home life. For example, a study of more than 2000 male executives and their spouses over a five-year period showed that the fatigue, tension and worry experienced by some executives at work caused emotional spillover into private life (Evans, 1981). However, the researchers also found evidence that other executives who endured the same long hours and tension-filled jobs went home full of energy and excited by the day. What differentiated these two groups of executives? The findings revealed that when individuals felt competent, had high levels of job satisfaction, and felt challenged by what they were doing (which appears to be consistent with recent conceptualizations of thriving), they were able to experience their work as invigorating, not depleting. Quinn (1996) finds something similar in his research on the fundamental state of leadership. He found that when people engaged their work to move from a state of slow death to deep change, they not only felt more alive at work but also more alive in their home life. Their actions permeated their whole beings as people. So both of these bodies of research suggest the possibility of a positive spillover from thriving at work to thriving at home.

Of course an equally plausible alternative hypothesis is that there is a zero-sum relationship between thriving at work and thriving in other aspects of life. If one is thriving extensively at work, that thriving at work may crowd out the possibility of thriving in home life. Some executives give so much of themselves to their work lives that they ignore their home life. They devote all of their energy to work so that they literally have nothing left to give at home (Loehr and Schwartz, 2003). They sacrifice close connections to family and friends. In an extension of Evan's longitudinal research on the lives of executives, he found that some executives literally lost their will to live after retiring. They succumbed to death within two years of retirement (Evans, 2005). Clearly, the potential for positive spillover of thriving at work into private life is a fertile area for future research.

What contributes to thriving at work? Some antecedents

Spreitzer et al.'s (2005) model of thriving is based on the idea that thriving is socially embedded. By this, we mean that when individuals are situated in particular contexts they are more or less likely to thrive (see Figure 6.1). As the framework shows, three sets of factors which include (1) unit contextual features, (2) agentic work behaviors, and (3) resources produced in the doing of work contribute to thriving at work. Unit contextual features reflect the dominant way that work is accomplished and include such things as how decisions are made, how information is shared, and the extent to which interactions are infused with trust and respect. Agentic working behaviors reflect the ways that individuals experience their work context and how they carry out daily work activities. To be more specific, individuals are more likely to thrive to the extent that they (a) have a task focus to get their work done, (b) explore new ways of working and being to enhance their learning, and (c) heedfully relate with others in their work environment. Resources produced in the doing of work reflect the knowledge, affective, and relational assets that enable people to enact schemas to guide action. The dual arrow between the resource box and the agentic work behaviors box indicates that resources enable thriving but also are produced through the agentic behaviors of thriving employees. In this way, the resources are renewable and produced through thriving at work.

While this framework has not yet been subject to rigorous empirical testing, we do have some initial encouraging empirical findings on several elements. Christianson et al. (2005) have found that in a nationally

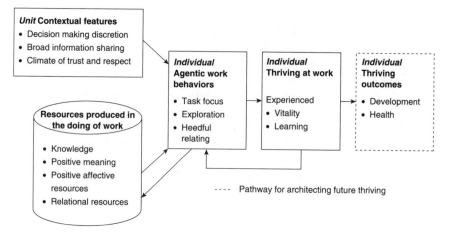

Figure 6.1   *The social embeddedness of thriving at work*

representative sample of mid-life adults, positive affective resources and agentic work behaviors were significant predictors of thriving at work. While no measure of unit contextual features was available, the research did not find significant differences across occupational types. The level of thriving experienced by blue collar workers and their white collar or professional counterparts was similar. This finding is important because it suggests that individuals in all types of jobs have the potential to thrive if they have an opportunity to exercise agency over their work and can create and nurture the necessary resources in doing their work.

Qualitative research also provides some insight about the subjective experience of thriving and growth at work. For example, Sonenshein et al. (2006) studied how people experience thriving at work and analyzed narrative accounts from a broad set of respondents. Respondents' accounts revealed that most experiences of thriving (76 percent) involve learning, recognition and accomplishment; but almost 40 percent of thriving experiences emphasize relationships and helping connections as well. Furthermore, Sonenshein and colleagues found that properties of work (challenge, novelty, variety, etc.), working closely with others (including supervisors, colleagues, and clients), and organizational properties (culture, structure, and physical space) were all described as enabling people to thrive and grow at work.

Thriving organizations

As described above, individual thriving is an important means through which people self-regulate their own growth. But is thriving limited to individuals? Can collectives (i.e. groups, units, or even organizations) thrive as well? And why should we care about thriving collectives? What are the implications and outcomes of thriving at the collective level? At present, to our knowledge, there is no research explicitly focused on thriving at the unit or organizational levels. Yet, these are important questions and ones that we will speculate about in the remainder of this chapter.

What is collective thriving?

Is a thriving group, unit, or organization merely the sum of its parts? That is, is it merely a set of individuals who are thriving? We do not expect a one-to-one correspondence between individual thriving and collective thriving. It may be that while individuals in an organization may be thriving, they may not be thriving in a way that benefits the organization. For example, at United Technologies, employees can enroll in any kind of educational program in which they have an interest – whether it is gourmet cooking, belly dancing, or fly fishing. While these employees are learning and likely to be highly energized, this learning is not necessarily aligned with the needs of the organization and hence may not relate to organizational thriving in the sense that the learning may not add to the organization's capabilities or growth in any substantive way.

On the other hand, an organization may be thriving, but its individual members may not be. The organization may be learning and energized as a whole, but individual members may feel overwhelmed and depleted. For example, in today's business environment, many organizations strive to be lean even though it may mean laying off high performing employees who may not be part of the strategic future of the firm. And people who stay may be stretched too thin. In both cases, although their organization may be thriving, if employees see little future in the organization or if they are overwhelmed, they are not likely to feel that they themselves are thriving.

So what is collective thriving? A group, unit, or organization is thought to thrive when the collective is both learning and energized. Thriving collectives are not afraid to try new things, take risks, and learn from mistakes. They build capabilities (i.e. sets of routines) and new competencies from their learning. This collective capability can be used to respond to the demands of an unpredictable world. A thriving collective is also energized – energy which contributes to the collective capacity to cope with obstacles, challenges, setbacks and failures and to persist in their efforts (Glynn et al., 1994).

What might be some ways to measure or assess the extent to which a group, unit, or organization is thriving? Certainly, we would expect that employees and outsiders would perceive the collective as growing. From an energy standpoint, we would expect a thriving collective to have high levels of employee vitality which may show up through increased activity, persistence, innovation. The energy network methodology of Baker et al. (2003) may be a useful method for identifying the magnitude of positive and negative energy in a collective. From a learning standpoint, we would expect that thriving collectives have more cognitive and behavioral complexity that comes from their learning orientation.

Why does collective thriving matter?

Why should we care whether groups, units or organizations thrive? Organizational scholarship typically has tended to emphasize performance outcomes, at the expense of considering social and public objectives (Walsh et al., 2003). We take seriously the idea that organizations are social entities as well as economic ones. Thus, thriving matters at the collective level because it enhances the vitality of our social and public environments. Most economists agree that knowledge economies differ from goods-producing economies. If we accept that previous industrial economic indicators may provide an inadequate account of the state of nations in a knowledge economy (David, 1999, as cited in Barley and Kunda, 2001), it is quite possible that the collective vitality of the workforce may be an important economic indicator and a way to conceptualize value in a postindustrial world. If so, our ideas about thriving can provide some insight to organizational theorists about how this alternative production value is created and the underlying logic of organizing to achieve it.

It is plausible to think that thriving collectives have a number of outcomes which would enhance the long-term sustainable performance of the collective. First, scholars have noted that the world confronting organizations is increasingly characterized as discontinuous, uncertain, and chaotic. Uncertain conditions favor organizations that are flexible and can adapt quickly to changing conditions. It is possible that organizations with many thriving individuals will be more responsive to these conditions.

Second, we would expect that the learning inherent in thriving may lead to new behavioral routines/repertoires. This could enable increased capability to improvise or recombine competencies to solve new problems. The energy inherent in thriving can contribute to an increased ability to build, repair, sustain, and endure challenges/problems/crises. In short, we expect that thriving collectives are likely to be more resilient in the face of adversity or hardship.

Third, given that prior research has found that individuals who thrive at work are likely to be healthier, perhaps the most obvious implication and important outcome for thriving collectives is reduced health care costs. It may be that thriving organizations can save millions of dollars in health care costs. The non-profit/non-partisan National Coalition on Health Care estimates that the average total cost to organizations for health care benefits rose 14.7 percent in 2002, at a time when general inflation hovered around 2 percent, and it continues to rise. For each automobile it produces, General Motors spends more on health care (approximately $1500/automobile) than it does on steel.

Possible concerns about thriving as a domain of study

Although we think thriving is a useful concept in organization studies, we suggest that future studies should undertake a critical review of some of the assumptions manifest in the perspective proposed here. Some scholars may see these ideas about thriving at work as totalitarian. Willmott (2003: 77) for example, asserts that promoting allegiance to a particular set of norms is 'ethically dubious' not only because it reduces practical autonomy, but also because it systematically suppresses alternative ideas and practices. We are not trying to colonize individuals' affective domains (Willmott, 2003), or constrain variety (in fact we are trying to enhance it), nor are we suggesting that employees adopt particular ways of thinking. Rather, we are simply suggesting that a particular set of socio-contextual conditions are more salutary for individuals, groups, units, and organizations (and possibly societies) than others.

Conclusion

In this chapter we draw attention to the paucity of research on work contexts and their salutary effects for individuals and organizational collectives and make the case for why scholars ought to pay more attention to understanding thriving in organizations. Thriving is the psychological state in which individuals experience both a sense of vitality and a sense of learning at work (Spreitzer et al., 2005). We have proposed that thriving is an important precursor to employee health and well-being and may contribute in positive ways to organizational capabilities for long-term adaptability in a dynamic and changing world. Interest in thriving reflects both growth in social trends recognizing that employee well-being and health include positive aspects that transcend economic productivity and wealth and growth in scholarship that seeks to understand the elements of positive functioning in ordinary circumstances rather than under conditions of adversity.

Acknowledgment

We would like to thank our colleagues in the Thriving Lab (Marlys Christianson, Kathryn Dekas, Jane Dutton, Adam Grant, Brent Rosso, Scott Sonenshein and J. P. Stephens) for their intellectual contributions to the development of the thriving construct.

Figure 6.1 reprinted by permission, Gretchen Spreitzer, Kathleen Sutcliffe, Jane Dutton and Adam M. Grant, 'A socially embedded model of thriving at work', *Organizational Science*, 16(5), 2005, 537–549. Copyright 2005, the Institute for Operations Research and the Management Sciences, 7240 Parkway Drive, Suite 310, Hanover, MD 21076, USA.

References

Alfredsson, L., Spetz, C.L. and Theorell, T. (1985) 'Type of occupation and near-future hospitalization for myocardial infarction and some other diagnoses', *International Journal of Epidemiology*, 14, 378–88.

Baker, W., Cross, R. and Parker, A. (2003) 'What creates energy in organizations?', *Sloan Management Review*, 44 (4), 51–6.

Bakwin, H. (1949) 'Emotional deprivation in infants', *Journal of Pediatrics*, 35, 512–21.

Barley, S.R. and Kunda, G. (2001) 'Bringing work back in', *Organization Science*, 12 (1), 76–95.

Barsade, S.G. (2002) 'The ripple effect: Emotional contagion and its influence on group behavior', *Administrative Science Quarterly*, 47, 644–75.

Bartel, C.A. and Saavedra, R. (2000) 'The collective construction of work group moods', *Administrative Science Quarterly*, 45, 197–231.

Bergland, A. and Kirkevold, M. (2001) 'Thriving – a useful theoretical perspective to capture the experience of well-being among frail elderly in nursing homes', *Journal of Advanced Nursing*, 36, 426–32.

Carver, C.S. (1998) 'Resilience and thriving: Issues, models, and linkages', *Journal of Social Issues*, 54 (2), 245–66.

Christianson, M., Spreitzer, G., Sutcliffe, K. and Grant, A. (2005) 'An empirical examination of thriving at work.' Working paper, Center for Positive Organizational Scholarship, Ross School of Business, University of Michigan.

Cross, R., Baker, W. and Parker, A. (2003) 'What creates energy in organizations?', *Sloan Management Review*, Summer, 51–6.

Danna, K. and Griffin, R.W. (1999) 'Health and well-being in the workplace: A review and synthesis of the literature', *Journal of Management*, 25 (3), 357–84.

Ettner, S.L. and Grzywacz, J. (2001) 'Workers' perceptions of how jobs affect health: A social ecological perspective', *Journal of Occupational Health Psychology*, 6 (2), 101–13.

Evans, P. (1981) *Must Success Cost so Much?* New York: Basic Books.

Evans, P. (2005) Personal communication. INSEAD, May 18.

French, J.R.P., Caplan, R.D. and Van Harrison, R. (1982) *The Mechanisms of Job Stress and Strain*. New York: Wiley.

Glynn, M., Lant, T. and Milliken, F. (1994) 'Mapping learning processes in organizations: A multi-level framework linking learning and organizations', in C. Stubbert, J. Meindel and J. Porac (eds) *Advances in Managerial Cognition and Organizational Information Processing*, Vol. 5 (pp. 48–83). Greenwich, CT: JAI Press.

Hall, D.T. and Fukami, C.V. (1979) 'Organization design and adult learning', in B.M. Staw (ed.) *Research in Organizational Behavior*, Vol. 1. (pp. 126–68). Greenwich, CT: JAI Press.

Harter, J.K., Schmidt, F.L. and Keyes, C.L.M. (2003) 'Well-being in the workplace and its relationship to business outcomes: A review of the Gallup studies', *Flourishing: Positive Psychology and the Life Well-Lived* (pp. 205–24). Washington, DC: American Psychological Association.

Keyes, C.L.M. (2002) 'The mental health continuum: From languishing to flourishing in life', *Journal of Health and Social Behavior*, 43, 207–22.

Keyes, C.L.M. and Grzywacz, J.G. (2005) 'Health as a complete state: The added value in work performance and healthcare costs', *Journal of Occupational and Environmental Medicine*, 47 (5), 523–32.

Kolb, D.A. (1984) *Experiential Learning: Experience as the Source of Learning and Development*. Englewood Cliffs, NJ: Prentice Hall.

Loehr, J. and Schwartz, T. (2003) *The Power of Full Engagement: Managing Energy, not Time, is the Key to High Performance and Personal Renewal*. New York: Free Press.

Marks, S.R. (1977) 'Multiple roles and role strain: Some notes on human energy, time, and commitment', *American Sociological Review*, 42 (6), 921–36.

Miller, J.B. and Stiver, I.P. (1998) *The Healing Connection: How Women Form Relationships in Therapy and in Life*. Boston: Beacon Press.

Nix, G., Ryan, R.M., Manly, J.B. and Deci, E.L. (1999) 'Revitalization through self-regulation: The effects of autonomous and controlled motivation on happiness and vitality', *Journal of Experimental Social Psychology*, 25, 266–84.

Quinn, R.E. (1996) *Deep Change*. San Francisco: Jossey-Bass.

Quinn, R.E. and Dutton, J. (2005) 'Coordination as energy in conversation: A process theory of organizing', *Academy of Management Review*, 30, 36–57.

Ryff, C.D. (1989) 'Happiness is everything, or is it? Explorations on the meaning of psychological well-being', *Journal of Personality and Social Psychology*, 57, 1069–81.

Ryff, C.D. and Keyes, C.L.M. (1995) 'The structure of psychological well-being', *Journal of Personality and Social Psychology*, 69, 719–27.

Schoenewolf, G. (1990) 'Emotional contagion: Behavioral induction in individuals and groups', *Modern Psychoanalysis*, 15, 49–61.

Sonenshein, S., Dutton, J., Grant, A., Spreitzer, G. and Sutcliffe, K. (2006) 'Narrating Growth at Work: Rationalist and Socio-Emotionalist and Logics of Development. Working paper, Center for Positive Organizational Scholarship, Ross School of Business, University of Michigan.

Spreitzer, G.M., Sutcliffe, K., Dutton, J.E., Sonenshein, S. and Grant, A.M. (2005) 'A socially embedded model of thriving at work', *Organizational Science*, 16 (5), 537–50.

Totterdell, P. (2000) 'Catching moods and hitting runs: Mood linkage and subjective performance in professional sport teams', *Journal of Applied Psychology*, 85, 848–59.

Walsh, J.P., Weber, K. and Margolis, J.D. (2003) 'Social issues and management: Our lost cause found', *Journal of Management*, 29 (6), 859–81.

Waterman, A. (1993) 'Two conceptions of happiness: Concepts of personal expressiveness (eudemonia) and hedonic enjoyment', *Journal of Personality and Social Psychology*, 64, 678–91.

Willmott, H. (2003) 'Renewing strength: Corporate culture revisited', *M@n@gement*, 6 (3), 73–87.

Wright, T.A. and Cropanzano, R. (1998) 'Emotional exhaustion as a predictor of job performance and voluntary turnover', *Journal of Applied Psychology*, 83, 486–93.

7

Explaining Vigor: On the Antecedents and Consequences of Vigor as a Positive Affect at Work

Arie Shirom

The focus of this study is on vigor as a positive affect experienced at work, its antecedents and consequences. Vigor refers to individuals' feelings that they possess physical strength, emotional energy and cognitive liveliness, a set of interrelated affective experiences. This focus is congruent with recent calls that researchers study human strengths and positive psychological capacities (Peterson and Seligman, 2004; Seligman et al., 2005). Vigor has very rarely been the topic of any conceptual and integrative analysis. Vigor may be described as the affective dimension of the energy reservoirs that employees possess and therefore is directly related to the construct of work motivation. Work motivation is often viewed as a set of energetic forces that originate within as well as beyond an individual's being, to initiate work-related behavior and to determine its form, direction, intensity, and duration (Latham and Pinder, 2005). Thus motivational processes in organizations represent in part individuals' decisions to allocate energy over time from their energetic resources among different activities. It follows that one could consider a certain threshold of perceived vigor, and individuals' feelings that they possess it as action orientations or motivation predisposition (Ellsworth and Scherer, 2003), as a prerequisite to any motivational processes in organizations.

Following widely accepted views of emotions and moods (Gray and Watson, 2001), vigor combines elements of a specific emotion in that it is contextualized in individuals' work situation, but it is closer to a mood state in that it tends to last days and even weeks. Therefore, I refer to vigor as an affective state that combines elements of an emotion and of a mood state. It represents, like all other specific affective states (e.g. Watson, 2002), a fundamental action tendency. Individuals' appraisals of their energetic resources are discussed below as theoretically distinct from the feeling of vigor, following Lazarus and Folkman's appraisal theory (1984: 273–4, 284–5). In nature, these appraisals and the feeling of vigor probably appear conjoined, mutually affecting each other over time. The focus on vigor as an affective state follows the cognitive-motivational-relational theory developed by Lazarus and his colleagues (Lazarus, 2001; Smith and Lazarus, 1993). This theory implies a discrete-category approach to affective states, each having its own core relational themes and coping implications. Furthermore, it posits that conceptualizing the distinctive characteristics, antecedents and consequences of each enriches and extends our understanding of employees' attempts to survive and flourish in their work environment (Lazarus and Cohen-Charash, 2001).

The chapter is organized in three sections. The first section provides a summary of past conceptual approaches to vigor and of measures constructed to assess it. Elaborating and considerably extending an earlier conceptualization of vigor (Shirom, 2004), I describe in the next section a theoretical model that specifies its antecedents and consequences. This theoretical model is based on the conservation of resources theory. I conclude by pointing out a few open research questions that concern the study of vigor at work.

Vigor as a positive affective state

The construct of vigor represents one of the affective states referred to in the emerging research area of positive affect (Dahlsgaard et al., 2005; Peterson and Seligman, 2004; Snyder and Lopez, 2002). A leading model in this research area is the positive emotions model (PEM), which proposes that positive emotions, like happiness, joy, pride, and love, have health-protecting physiological effects, including low autonomic reactivity relative to the effects of negative emotions (Fredrickson, 2002; Tugade et al., 2004). Fredrickson's (2002) broaden-and-build theory posits that positive emotions tend to enhance activity levels while negative emotions have the opposite effect of narrowing activity levels. The enhancing effects of positive feelings on physical health and longevity are supported by an accumulating body of evidence (Faragher et al., 2005; Lyubomirsky et al., 2005; Rozanski and Kubzansky, 2005; Salovey et al., 2000a). The biological mechanisms underlying these effects of positive emotions are likely to include their enhancing the immune system's capacity to mount an effective response to challenges and the adoption of healthy life-style habits like smoking abstention (Rozanski and Kubzansky, 2005; Ryff et al., 2004).

How does vigor relate to other affective states? Russell (1980, 2003) proposed that each affective state can be identified and differentiated from other affective states by where it lies on the two-dimensional space that consists of the horizontal dimension of pleasure–displeasure and of the vertical dimension of arousal–sleepiness. In this two-dimensional space, vigor represents positive arousal or a combination of moderate amounts of arousal and pleasure. In the same space, vigor's counterpart in the quadrant of displeasure–arousal is anxiety, and its mirror-image in the quadrant of displeasure–sleepiness is burnout, combining displeasure with lack of arousal. In contrast to burnout and anxiety, however, vigor is a component of the approach-oriented behavior facilitation system. This system, according to Watson (2002), directs organisms toward situations and experiences that potentially may yield pleasure and reward and facilitates the procuring of resources like food, shelter and sexual partners – resources that are essential for the survival of both the individual and the species. Carver and Scheier's (1998) model of regulated behavior expresses an analogous theoretical perspective in that it regards positive emotions as resulting from advancement or doing better on goal attainment at a pace faster than expected.

Mood states and vigor

In past research, vigor has been studied predominantly as a mood state, hardly as an emotion, and primarily in clinical samples. However, in actual research practice, virtually identical techniques, such as gift-giving, were used for inducing positive moods as well as positive emotions (Fredrickson, 2002).

The Profile of Mood States (POMS). The Profile of Mood States (POMS: McNair et al., 1971) was one of the earliest measures of any positive mood, and included, among the six subscales of different moods, an eight-item subscale gauging vigor, using items like feeling cheerful, lively, alert, active and vigorous. In the studies using the POMS, results that concern the vigor subscale have often been reported. In the area of sports psychology, a recent meta-analysis of studies that have used the POMS in association with either athletic achievement or athletic performance (Beedie et al., 2000) found a moderate effect size between the POMS vigor subscale and performance outcomes. Studies that have used the POMS and its vigor subscale to predict physiological outcomes abound in the literature. For example, the vigor subscale was found to positively predict sleep quality (Bardwell et al., 1999), as well as shorter duration of recovery from injury (Quinn and Fallon, 1999). As Payne (2001) noted, different aspects of the construct validity of this scale have been extensively studied, but primarily with clinical samples such as cancer patients, drug abusers and brief psychotherapy patients, with hardly any past use in work organizations.

Other measures of vigor as a mood state. Following the above limitations of POMS, the Brunel Mood Scale, largely based on it and including simplified items but the same dimensions as POMS, was developed (Terry et al., 1999). Its vigor scale was found to be positively associated with athletic (Lane and Lane, 2002) and scholastic (Lane et al., 2005) performance. Yet another widely used measure of mood is the Activation-Deactivation Adjective Check List, available in short and long forms (Thayer, 1996). It includes a subscale that gauges energy level. Mood inventories developed by other researchers also include measures of vigor or energy levels. The

UWIST Mood Adjective Checklist (Matthews et al., 1990) includes a subscale of energetic arousal that contained eight items, including the four items of 'active', 'energetic', 'alert', and 'vigorous', and also four tiredness items, like 'sluggish', 'tired', and 'passive' (Payne, 2001). Matthews et al. (1990) reported that the subscale of energetic arousal was negatively correlated with workload and that it was the only mood measure sensitive to drugs.

This review of past attempts to gauge vigor leads to the following conclusions. First, vigor has hardly been studied at work; in most past studies, respondents were mentally ill persons, students, or sportsmen. Second, in all past research, vigor has been conceptualized to reflect one form of energy – physical strength. This differs from the current focus on vigor as an affective experience at work reflecting three interrelated forms of energetic resources. Third, most measures of vigor as a mood state were based on the theoretical position that the pair of vigor and fatigue, burnout or tiredness represents bipolar affective states that cannot be experienced simultaneously. This theoretical position is reflected in the practice of reverse-scoring tiredness or fatigue items in the vigor scales to arrive at a total score representing the positive mood of vigor. This practice has been followed by several researchers who have assessed vigor either as a component of job-related affective well-being (Daniels, 2000; Payne, 2001), or as a stress reaction (Williams and Cooper, 1998). In contrast, I argue for the theoretical position that vigor and burnout are obliquely related and do not represent the extreme poles of the same continuum, perhaps with the exception of situations characterized by very high levels of stress (Reich and Zautra, 2002). This theoretical position rests first on the fact that the biological systems underlying approach and avoidance activations have been shown to be basically independent (Cacioppo et al., 1999). Second, positive and negative affective states are physiologically represented in different systems (Davidson, 2000). Third, positive and negative affective states are known to have different antecedents (Baumeister et al., 2001), may function relatively independently (Davis et al., 2004), and are differentially represented in peoples' behaviors (Gendolla, 2000). Therefore, it could be concluded that the affective state structure is flexible, and that the relationships between positive and negative affective states is not bipolar but bivariate.

The set of studies on engagement by Schaufeli and his colleagues (Schaufeli and Bakker, 2004) is not covered here because these investigators have defined the vigor component in the conceptualization of engagement as comprising high levels of energy, motivation to invest effort at work, and resilience; it follows that they refer to vigor as a cluster of different evaluative or attitudinal facets and not as an affective state. In sharp contrast, vigor, as conceptualized in this chapter, refers to it as an affective state and does not confound it with motivational processes or with individuals' behaviors following encounters with adverse events – namely resilience (Davidson, 2000). Vigor at work can be experienced with or without encounters with adverse events. While I have proposed above that vigor and motivation to invest effort at work are closely related, they belong to different conceptual domains, those of affect and action orientations, respectively.

A theoretical model of vigor

Vigor represents a positive affective response to one's ongoing interactions with significant elements in one's job and work environment that comprises the interconnected feelings of physical strength, emotional energy, and cognitive liveliness. Theoretically, this view of vigor is derived from Hobfoll's (1989, 1998) Conservation of Resources (COR) theory. The COR theory's central tenets are that people have a basic motivation to obtain, retain and protect that which they value. The things that people value are called resources, of which there are several types, including material, social and energetic resources. Hobfoll maintained that resources are those personal energies and characteristics, objects and conditions that are valued by individuals or that serve as the means for the attainment of other objects, personal characteristics, conditions or energies (Hobfoll, 2002). Examples of internal personality factors that are considered resources are optimism, self-esteem and self-efficacy. Examples of external resources are employment, social support and economic status. The concept of vigor relates to proximal energetic resources only, namely to physical, emotional and cognitive energies. These three types of energetic resources are individually owned, closely interrelated, and socially embedded in that emotional energy always concerns significant others in one's social milieu. Vigor represents an affective state that individuals attribute to their job and workplace when asked about it and do so spontaneously, in contrast to affective traits like positive affectivity that refers to the tendency to experience positive affect across situations and times (cf. Fox and Spector, 2002).

The theoretical rationale for focusing on the combination of physical strength, emotional energy and cognitive liveliness in the conceptualization of vigor is as follows. First, these forms of energy are individually possessed. The COR theory predicts that the three factors constituting vigor are closely interrelated (cf. Hobfoll and Shirom, 2000). The COR theory argues that personal resources affect each other and exist as a resource pool, and that an expansion of one is often associated with the other being augmented (Hobfoll, 2002). Second, this focus on proximal energetic resources is theoretically justified in that they are a major precondition to any goal-directed behavior and thus are essential for one's survival (Hobfoll, 2002). Third, they represent a coherent set that does not overlap any other established behavioral science concept, like resilience or potency, or any aspect of the self-concept, such as self-esteem and self-efficacy. Furthermore, this

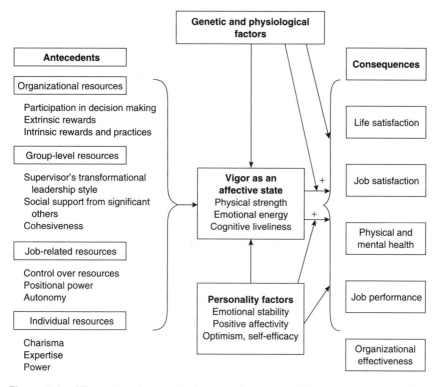

Figure 7.1   *Vigor at work: expected antecedents, possible consequences and probable moderators*

conceptualization of vigor clearly differentiates it from its likely consequences like engagement or job involvement.

For the sake of simplicity, vigor is depicted in the following theoretical model as a unidimensional variable, although it is possible for each of its components to be differentially associated with the antecedents and consequences of vigor. Vigor is associated with the approach biobehavioral tendency, and therefore it is expected to be more closely associated with mental health outcomes rather than with performance outcomes; however, I do not discuss the relative proximity of vigor's consequences or predictors (see Figure 7.1).

Predictors of vigor: personality factors

Personality and physiological factors are likely to impact directly vigor and moderate its relationships with its consequences. I expect that men would experience higher levels of physical vigor than women because the accepted norms associated with the masculine gender role emphasize strength, independence, and invulnerability (Stanton et al., 2002). The literature on dispositional influences on affective states may lead to the expectation that those high on the personality trait of extraversion (or positive affectivity) are more likely to experience vigor relative to those high on the trait of neuroticism (cf. Brief and Weiss, 2002).

Work-related predictors of vigor

Because employees' work-related affective states reflect their appraisals of their on-the-job experiences, organizations do not have a direct way of eliciting specific affective responses in their employees. Organizations do attempt to regulate employees' emotions, including by means of pre-scribing, neutralizing, buffering, or normalizing them (cf. Ashforth and Humphrey, 1995). In the following, I will discuss work elements and features likely to increase the likelihood of employees feeling invigorated.

Job-related resources. Hackman and Oldham (1980) have developed one of the most influential models explaining, inter alia, employee positive affective states by certain job features. The job characteristic model (Hackman and Oldham, 1980) posits that the higher the levels of five job characteristics, namely task autonomy, significance, feedback, identity and skill variety, the more pronounced the resultant psychological states which lead in turn to higher employee job satisfaction and performance. Empirical research has shown that the most powerful predictors of employee job satisfaction and performance were job autonomy and feedback (Fried and Ferris, 1989). Brousseau (1983) has argued that autonomous jobs, namely jobs that allow employees to formulate more elaborated work plans and pursue self-determined goals, would enhance feelings of personal efficacy and thereby enhance their feelings of cognitive liveliness.

Group-level resources. Work groups tend to share emotions because of common socialization experiences and common organizational features, norms and regulations that govern the expression of emotions, task inter-dependence, and the phenomenon of emotional contagion (Brief and Weiss, 2002). It has been found that work teams characterized by mutual trust and high social support tend to be more cohesive and goal-directed, and that these qualities in turn lead to favorable employee morale and job-related well-being (Karasek and Theorell, 1990). Specifically, work group cohesion was found to predict vigor, measured as a mood state (Terry et al., 2000).

Leadership style. There are indications in the literature that leaders who feel energetic are likely to energize their followers (cf. Brief and Weiss, 2002). Displaying vigor is probably expected from employees in managerial roles (e.g. Church and Waclawsk, 1998). In a similar vein, the leadership literature often makes the claim that transformational leaders often exhibit energizing emotions in order to arouse similar emotional states among their followers (Avolio, 1999). This literature suggests that intellectual stimulation, a component of transformational leadership which consists of encouraging followers to think creatively (Avolio, 1999), is likely to have a direct positive effect on cognitive liveliness, a component of vigor.

Organizational resources. Employee participation in decision making has the potential to increase one's exposure to many sources of information, enhance one's being able to adjust more flexibly to the demands of diverse role partners, and enable one's capability to develop cognitive skill such as finding creative solutions that integrate diverse viewpoints (Spector, 1986).

Consequences of vigor

Job performance and organizational effectiveness

Existing research on positive affect has supported the view that both naturally occurring and induced positive affective states tend to facilitate flexible, effective problem solving and decision making (Baumann and Kuhl, 2005; Isen, 2001). A body of studies suggests that positive affective states are closely associated with more efficient cognitive processing of information and therefore have direct impact on the ability component of task performance (Isen, 2004). In addition, positive affective states have been found to antecede creativity in work organizations (James et al., 2004; Staw and Barsade, 1993). However, there has been relatively little consideration of the impact of vigor as an affective state on various individual- and organizational-relevant outcomes.

The close relationship between vigor and motivation was noted in the introductory section. Recently, it has been shown that when the mental representation of a behavioral goal is associated with positive affects, it automatically signals to the person that the goal is desired and worth pursuing and therefore promotes motivational activity designed to accomplish the goal (Custers and Aarts, 2005). Vigor, like most other positive affects, facilitates goal-directed behavior (Carver and Scheier, 1990) or approach behavior (Fredrickson, 2002; Watson, 2002) and therefore could be expected to prompt individuals to engage with their job and work environment.

Several studies have documented the role of positive emotions in promoting performance (Huy, 1999; Rafaeli and Worline, 2001; Staw et al., 1994). Indeed, performance is interwoven with emotion in organizational life. Positive emotions have been linked to several performance-related behaviors, including enhanced creativity, more effective decision-making, sales-related prosocial behaviors, and the use of more successful negotiation strategies (Baron, 1990; Forgas, 1998; George, 1991; Staw and Barsade, 1993). While vigor is not specifically referred to in the above literature, I assume that the relationship between vigor and job performance will be positive, and that it is likely to be reciprocal rather than recursive.

Physical and mental health

Individuals' level of vigor may be considered as an indicator of their optimal psychological functioning. The reason: many investigators defined the conceptual domain of health-related quality of life as including vigor. To illustrate, the operational definition of well-being by the World Health Organization (WHOQOL Group, 1994), used in their questionnaire, includes items like 'I feel energetic', 'I feel active', 'I feel vigorous', and 'I wake up feeling fresh', items used in part in the measure of vigor described elsewhere (Shirom, 2004).

While vigor's likely effects on mental well-being are straightforward, its effects on physical well-being are more complex (cf. Edwards and Cooper, 1988). One of the limitations regarding the body of knowledge on the effects of positive emotions on physical health is that while we know that these effects tend to be positive in sign, the nature of the physiological pathways linking these two entities are hardly understood (Ryff and Singer, 2002). It has been suggested that positive emotions change the levels of brain dopamine (Ashby et al., 1999), thereby simultaneously expanding cognitive functioning and regulating cardiovascular activity. Another possible physiological pathway is that linking positive emotions with improved immune function (e.g. Salovey et al., 2000a).

Directions for future research

The suggested focus on vigor is in tune with the new development of the field of positive psychology (Seligman et al., 2005) and the emergence of positive organizational behavior (Luthans, 2002). Vigorous feelings at work possibly allow employees to effectively cope with work-related demands, and more importantly are likely to have a positive impact on their well-being. Researchers' future efforts to increase our understanding of the antecedents and etiology of vigor at work may be aided by the conceptual framework of vigor described in this chapter. This conceptual framework integrates past disparate efforts and allows researchers to pose new research questions and offer new theoretical interpretations.

From the review of past attempts to assess vigor, primarily as a mood state, it appears that this core affect tends to promote goal-directed behavior likely to increase individuals' personal resources. Hobfoll (2002) hypothesized that such increases in individuals' pool of personal resources may initiate an upward spiral toward further increases in these individuals' personal resources. Fredrickson and Joiner (2002) found that positive emotions broaden the scopes of attention and cognition and, by consequence, initiate upward spirals toward increasing emotional well-being. The augmented personal resources can be drawn on to cope with any work-related demand that may arise in one's job. In work organizations, employee vigor should promote skill building and learning, prosocial behaviors, and organizational commitment, among other important aspects of organizational effectiveness.

The study of vigor at work may offer new insights into the process of goal-directed behaviors, or the process by which employees initiate, regulate and maintain over time and over changing circumstances their task-related behaviors. DeSchon and Gillespie (2005) proposed that goal-directed behaviors be viewed as specific manifestations of self-regulation efforts. Individuals self-regulate their behaviors to a considerable extent based on their feeling states, as documented above. One way of assessing the validity of the proposition that views vigor as a prerequisite of goal-directed behavior is to examine these relationships over time. Such a longitudinal study may also test the propositions that elevations in vigor lead to a positive spiral of resource augmentation and to more effective coping with work-related demands.

There are several open questions awaiting empirical clarification with regard to using vigor in actual research. Are there individual differences in the ability to 'intelligently' use vigor as a means of guiding and maintaining one's behavior? Feelings provide meaning to work-related employee experiences. In line with recent thinking on emotional intelligence, the ability to identify and regulate feelings and use the information provided by feelings are considered important for adaptive social behavior (Salovey et al., 2000). If such differences are found to exist, do they reflect differences in the above skills, and can these skills be learnt (Salovey et al., 2000)? Emotional intelligence represents just one, albeit important, possible modulator of vigor's relationship with behavioral responses.

Another open question has to do with the effects of vigorous feelings at work on organizations. In this chapter, the emphasis has been on job and work characteristics conducive to employee vigor, and on the influence of employee vigor on job performance. However, how does employee vigor affect the organization as a whole? Are there vigorous organizations and, if so, what are their inherent characteristics? Vigorous organizations could be regarded as organizations whose managerial apex effectively create the conditions that generate, foster and maintain employee vigor throughout the organization and mobilize these energetic resources in the pursuit of organizational effectiveness. Based on emotional and cognitive contagion processes (Barsade, 2002), organizational vigor probably reflects the synergistic accumulation of individual employees' level of vigor. Vigorous organizations could be expected to be highly innovative, proactively adjust to environmental changes, and otherwise distinguish themselves in their product and labor markets (Bruch and Ghoshal, 2003; Cross et al., 2003).

The emphasis throughout this chapter has been on vigor at work. However, vigor may be experienced in and outside of work. That is, it may be experienced as an affective response to events and situations that individuals encounter outside of work. It is possible that vigor felt at work spills over to the family and other life domains and vice versa. These are open questions that need to be addressed in future research. The same is true regarding the possible reciprocal relations between vigor and job performance or proactive behavior in organizations.

Vigor represents an affect experienced at work. While available research on vigor at work is in its infancy, existing research on vigor as a mood state would suggest that it is strongly related to individuals' well-being and health. The link proposed above between vigor and physical health, indirectly supported by the body of studies that have examined positive affect–physical health relationships, indicates that additional research on vigor at work may provide an understanding of possible pathways by which organizations can reduce absenteeism and health care costs. Therefore, there exists a need for future research on vigor at work.

Acknowledgment

I would like to acknowledge the financial support of the Israel Science Foundation (Grant 926/02-1).

Note

1. The full scale is also available for downloading in Word format at: http://www.tau.ac.il./~ashirom/

References

Ashby, F.G., Isen, A.M. and Turken, A.U. (1999) 'A neuropsychological theory of positive affect and its influence on cognition', *Psychological Review*, 106, 529–50.
Ashforth, B.E. and Humphrey, R.H. (1995) 'Emotions in the workplace: A reappraisal', *Human Relations*, 48, 97–125.
Avolio, B.J. (1999) *Full Leadership Development*. London: Sage.
Bardwell, W.A., Berry, C.C., Ancoli-Israel, S. and Dimsdale, J.E. (1999) 'Psychological correlates of sleep apnea', *Journal of Psychosomatic Research*, 47, 583–96.
Baron, R.A. (1990) 'Environmentally induced positive affect: Its impact on self-efficacy, task performance, negotiation, and conflict', *Journal of Applied Social Psychology*, 20, 368–84.
Barsade, S.G. (2002) 'The ripple effect: Emotional contagion and its influence on group behavior', *Administrative Science Quarterly*, 47 (4), 644–77.
Baumann, N. and Kuhl, J. (2005) 'Positive affect and flexibility: Overcoming the precedence of global over local processing of visual information', *Motivation and Emotion*, 29 (2), 123–34.
Baumeister, R.F., Bratslavsky, E., Finkenauer, C. and Vohs, K.D. (2001). 'Bad is stronger than good', *Review of General Psychology*, 5 (4), 323–70.
Beedie, C.J., Terry, P.C. and Lane, A.M. (2000). 'The profile of mood states and athletic performance: Two meta-analyses', *Journal of Applied Sport Psychology* 12, 49–68.
Brief, A.P., and Weiss, H.M. (2002) 'Organizational behavior: Affect in the workplace', *Annual Review of Psychology*, 53, 279–307.
Brousseau, K.R. (1983) 'Toward a dynamic model of job–person relationship: Findings, research, questions, and implications for work system design', *Academy of Management Review*, 8, 33–45.

Bruch, H. and Ghoshal, S. (2003) 'Unleashing organizational energy', *MIT Sloan Management Review*, 44 (1), 45–51.

Cacioppo, J.T., Gardner, W.L. and Brenston, G.G. (1999) 'The affect system has parallel and integrative components: Form follows function', *Journal of Personality and Social Psychology*, 76, 839–54.

Carver, C.S. and Scheier, M.F. (1990) 'Origins and functions of positive and negative affect: A control-process view', *Psychological Review*, 97, 19–35.

Carver, C.S. and Scheier, M.F. (1998) *On the Self-regulation of Behavior*. New York: Cambridge University Press.

Church, A. and Waclawsk, J. (1998) 'The relationship between individual orientation and executive leadership behavior', *Journal of Occupational and Organizational Psychology*, 71, 99–127.

Cross, R., Baker, W. and Parker, A. (2003) 'What creates energy in organizations?', *MIT Sloan Management Review*, 44 (1), 51–6.

Custers, R. and Aarts, H. (2005) 'Positive affect as implicit motivator: On the nonconscious operation of behavioral goals', *Journal of Personality and Social Psychology*, 89 (2), 129–42.

Dahlsgaard, K., Peterson, C. and Seligman, M.E.P. (2005) 'Shared virtue: The convergence of valued human strengths across culture and history', *Review of General Psychology*, 9 (3), 203–13.

Daniels, K. (2000) 'Measures of five aspects of affective well-being at work', *Human Relations*, 53, 275–94.

Davidson, R.J. (2000) 'Affective style, psychopathology, and resilience: Brain mechanisms and plasticity', *American Psychologist*, 55 (11), 1196–1214.

Davis, M.C., Zautra, A.J. and Smith, B.W. (2004) 'Chronic pain, stress, and the dynamics of affective differentiation', *Journal of Personality*, 72 (6), 1133–60.

DeSchon, R.P. and Gillespie, J.Z. (2005) 'A motivated action theory account of goal orientation', *Journal of Applied Psychology*, 90 (6), 1096–1127.

Eaton, L.G. and Funder, D.C. (2000) 'Emotional experience in daily life: Valence, variability, and rate of change', *Emotion*, 1, 413–21.

Edwards, J.R. and Cooper, C.L. (1988) 'The impact of positive psychological states on physical health: A review and theoretical framework', *Social Science and Medicine*, 27, 1447–59.

Ellsworth, P.C. and Scherer, K.R. (2003) 'Appraisal processes in emotion', in R.J. Davidson, H. Goldsmith and K.R. Scherer (eds) *Handbook of Affective Sciences* (pp. 572–95). New York: Oxford University Press.

Faragher, B., Cass, M. and Cooper, C.L. (2005) 'The relationship between job satisfaction and health: A meta-analysis', *Occupational and Environmental Medicine*, 62 (2), 105–12.

Folkman, S. and Moskowitz, J.T. (2000) 'Positive affect and the other side of coping', *American Psychologist*, 55, 647–54.

Forgas, J.P. (1998) 'On feeling good and getting your way: Mood effects on negotiator cognition and bargaining strategies', *Journal of Personality and Social Psychology*, 73, 565–77.

Fox, S. and Spector, P.E. (2002) 'Emotions in the workplace: The neglected side of organizational life introduction', *Human Resource Management Review*, 12, 167–71.

Fredrickson, B.L. (1998) 'What good are positive emotions?', *Review of General Psychology*, 2, 300–19.

Fredrickson, B.L. (2002) 'Positive emotions', in C.R. Snyder and S.J. Lopez (eds) *Handbook of Positive Psychology* (pp. 120–34). New York: Oxford University Press.

Fredrickson, B.L. and Joiner, T. (2002) 'Positive emotions trigger upward spirals toward emotional well-being', *Psychological Science*, 13, 172–5.

Fried, Y. and Ferris, G.R. (1987) 'The validity of the job characteristic model: A review and a meta-analysis', *Personnel Psychology*, 40, 287–322.

Gendolla, G.H.E. (2000) 'On the impact of mood on behavior: An integrative theory and a review', *Review of General Psychology*, 4(4), 378–408.

George, J.M. (1991) 'State or trait: Effects of positive mood on prosocial behaviors at work', *Journal of Applied Psychology*, 76, 299–307.

Gray, E. and Watson, D. (2001) 'Emotion, mood, and temperament: Similarities, differences, and a synthesis', in R.L. Payne and C.L. Cooper (eds) *Emotion at Work* (pp. 21–45). Chichester: Wiley.

Hackman, J.R. and Oldham, G.R. (1980) '*Work Redesign*. Reading, MA: Addison-Wesley.

Hobfoll, S.E. (1989) 'Conservation of resources: A new attempt at conceptualizing stress', *American Psychologist*, 44, 513–24.

Hobfoll, S.E. (1998) *The Psychology and Philosophy of Stress, Culture, and Community*. New York: Plenum.

Hobfoll, S.E. (2002) 'Social and psychological resources and adaptation', *Review of General Psychology*, 6 (4), 307–24.

Hobfoll, S.E. and Shirom, A. (2000) 'Conservation of resources theory: Applications to stress and management in the workplace', in R.T. Golembiewski (ed.) *Handbook of Organization Behavior* (2nd rev. edn, pp. 57–81). New York: Dekker.

Huy, Q.N. (1999) 'Emotional capability, emotional intelligence, and radical change', *Academy of Management Review*, 24, 325–45.

Isen, A.M. (2001) 'An influence of positive affect on decision making in complex situations: Theoretical issues and practical implications', *Journal of Consumer Psychology*, 11 (1), 75–85.

Isen, A.M. (2004) 'Some perspectives on positive feelings and emotions', in A.S.R. Manstead, N.H. Frijda and A. Fischer (eds) *Feelings and Emotions: The Amsterdam Symposium* (pp. 263–82). Cambridge: Cambridge University Press.

James, K., Brodersen, M. and Eisenberg, J. (2004) 'Workplace affect and workplace creativity: A review and preliminary model', *Human Performance*, 17 (2), 169–94.

Karasek, R.A. and Theorell, T. (1990) *Healthy Work*. New York: Basic Books.

Katwyk, P.T. van, Fox, S., Spector, P.E. and Kelloway, E.N. (2000) 'Using the job-related affective well-being scale (JAWS) to investigate affective responses to work stresses', *Journal of Occupational Health Psychology*, 5, 219–30.

Lane, A.M. and Lane, H.J. (2002) 'Predictive effectiveness of mood measure', *Perceptual and Motor Skills*, 94, 785–91.

Lane, A.M., Whyte, G.P., Terry, P.C. and Nevill, A.M. (2005) 'Mood, self-set goals and examination performance: The moderating effect of depressed mood', *Personality and Individual Differences*, 39 (1), 143–53.

Latham, G.P. and Pinder, C.C. (2005) 'Work motivation theory and research at the dawn of the twenty-first century', *Annual Review of Psychology*, 56: 485–516. Palo Alto, CA: Annual Reviews Inc.

Lazarus, R.S. (1999) *Stress and Emotion*. New York: Springer.

Lazarus, R.S. (2001) 'Relational meaning and discrete emotions', in K.R. Scherer, A.A. Schorr and T. Johnston (eds) *Appraisal Processes in Emotions: Theory, Research, Methods* (pp. 37–67). New York: Oxford University Press.

Lazarus, R.S. and Cohen-Charash, Y. (2001) 'Discrete emotions in organizational life', in R.L. Payne and C.L. Cooper (eds) *Emotions at Work* (pp. 21–45). Chichester: Wiley.

Lazarus, R.S. and Folkman, S. (1984) *Stress, Appraisal, and Coping*. New York: Springer.

Luthans, F. (2002) 'The need for and meaning of positive organizational behavior', *Journal of Organizational Behavior*, 23 (6), 695–706.

Lyubomirsky, S., King, L.A. and Diener, E. (in press) 'The benefits of frequent positive affect: Does happiness lead to success?', *Psychological Bulletin*, 131, 803–56.

McNair, D.M., Lorr, M. and Droppleman, L.F. (1971) *Manual: Profile of Mood States*. San Diego, CA: Educational and Industrial Testing Service.

Matthews, G., Jones, D.M. and Chamberlain, A.G. (1990) 'Refining the measurement of mood: The UWIST Mood Adjective Checklist', *British Journal of Psychology*, 81, 17–42.

Payne, R.L. (2001) 'Measuring emotions at work', in R.L. Payne and C.L. Cooper (eds) *Emotions at Work* (pp. 107–33). Chichester: Wiley & Sons.

Peterson, C. and Seligman, M.E.P. (2004) *Character Strengths and Virtues: A Handbook and Classification*. Washington, DC: American Psychological Association and Oxford University Press.

Quinn, A.M. and Fallon, B.J. (1999) 'The changes in psychological characteristics and reactions of elite athletes', *Journal of Applied Sport Psychology*, 11, 210–29.

Rafaeli, A. and Worline, M. (2001) 'Individual emotion in work organizations', *Social Science Information*, 40, 95–125.

Reich, J.W. and Zautra, A.J. (2002) 'Arousal and relationship between positive and negative affect: An analysis of the data of Ito, Cacioppo, and Lang (1998)', *Motivation and Emotion*, 26, 209–22.

Rozanski, A. and Kubzansky, L.D. (2005) 'Psychologic functioning and physical health: A paradigm of flexibility', *Psychosomatic Medicine*, 67(Supp. 1), S47–S53.

Russell, J.A. (1980) 'A circumplex model of affect', *Journal of Personality and Social Psychology*, 39, 1161–78.

Russell, J.A. (2003) 'Core affect and the psychological construction of emotion', *Psychological Review*, 110, 145–72.

Ryff, C.D. and Singer, B. (2002) 'From social structure to biology: Integrative science in the pursuit of human health and well-being', in C.R. Snyder and E.J. Lopez (eds) *Handbook of Positive Pyschology* (pp. 541–56). New York: Oxford University Press.

Ryff, C.D., Singer, B.H. and Dienberg Love, G. (2004) 'Positive health: Connecting well-being with biology', *Philosophical Transactions of the Royal Society of London Part B: Biological Science*, 359 (1449), 1383–94.

Salovey, P., Bedell, B.T., Detweiler, J.B., and Mayer, J.D. (2000) 'Current directions in emotional intelligence research', in M. Lewis and J.M. Haviland-Jones (eds) *Handbook of Emotions* (2nd edn, pp. 504–20). New York: Guilford.

Salovey, P., Rothman, A.J., Detweiler, J.B. and Steward, W.T. (2000a) 'Emotional states and physical health', *American Psychologist*, 55, 110–21.

Schaufeli, W.B. and Bakker, A.B. (2004) 'Job demands, job resources, and their relationship with burnout and engagement: A multi-sample study', *Journal of Organizational Behavior*, 25 (3), 293–315.

Seligman, M.E.P., Steen, T.A., Park, N. and Peterson, C. (2005) 'Positive psychology progress: Empirical validation of intervention', *American Psychologist*, 60 (5), 410–21.

Shirom, A. (2003) 'Job-related burnout: A review', in J.C. Quick and L.E. Tetrick (eds) *Handbook of Occupational Health Psychology* (pp. 245–65). Washington, DC: American Psychological Association.

Shirom, A. (2004) 'Feeling vigorous at work? The construct of vigor and the study of positive affect in organizations', in D. Ganster and P.L. Perrewé (eds) *Research in Organizational Stress and Well-being* (Vol. 3, pp. 135–65). Greenwich, CT: JAI Press.

Smith, C.A. and Lazarus, R.S. (1993) 'Appraisal components, core relational themes and the emotions', *Cognition and Emotion*, 7, 233–69.

Snyder, C.R. and Lopez, S.J. (eds) (2002) *Handbook of Positive Psychology*. New York: Oxford University Press.

Spector, P.E. (1986) 'Perceived control by employees: a meta-analysis of studies concerning autonomy and participation at work', *Human Relations*, 39, 1005–16.

Spector, P.E. (1998) 'A control theory of the job stress process', in C.L. Cooper (ed.) *Theories of Organizational Stress* (pp. 153–69). Oxford: Oxford University Press.

Spector, P.E. and Jex, S.M. (1991) 'Relations of job characteristics from multiple data sources with employee affect, absence, turnover intentions, and health', *Journal of Applied Psychology*, 76, 46–53.

Stanton, A.L., Parsa, A. and Austenfeld, J.L. (2002) 'The adaptive potential of coping through emotional approach', in C.R. Snyder and S.J. Lopez (eds) *Handbook of Positive Psychology* (pp. 148–58). New York: Oxford University Press.

Staw, B.M. and Barsade, S.G. (1993) 'Affect and performance: A test of the sadder-but-wiser vs. happier-and-smarter hypotheses', *Administrative Science Quarterly*, 38, 304–31.

Staw, B.M., Sutton, R.I. and Pelled, L.H. (1994) 'Employee positive emotion and favorable outcomes at the workplace', *Organization Science*, 5, 51–71.

Terry, P.C., Carron, A.V., Pink, M.J., Lane, A.M., Jones, G.J. W. and Hall, M.P. (2000) 'Perceptions of group cohesion and mood in sport teams', *Group Dynamics*, 4, 244–53.

Terry, P.C., Lane, A.M., Lane, H.J. and Keohane, L. (1999) 'Development and validation of a mood measure for adolescents: POMS-A', *Journal of Sports Sciences*, 17 (4), 861–72.

Thayer, R.E. (1989) *The Biopsychology of Mood and Arousal*. New York: Oxford University Press.

Thayer, R.E. (1996) *The Origin of Everyday Moods*. New York: Oxford University Press.

Tugade, M.M., Fredrickson, B.L. and Feldman Barrett, L.F. (2004) 'Psychological resilience and positive emotional granularity: Examining the benefits of positive emotions on coping and health', *Journal of Personality*, 72 (6), 1161–90.

Watson, D. (2002) 'Positive affectivity: The disposition to experience pleasurable emotional states', in C.R. Snyder and S.J. Lopez (eds) *Handbook of Positive Psychology* (pp. 106–20). New York: Oxford University Press.

Weiss, H. and Brief, A. (2001) 'Affect at work: A historical perspective', in R.L. Payne and C.L. Cooper (eds) *Emotions at Work* (pp. 133–73). Chichester: Wiley.

WHOQOL Group (1994) 'Development of the WHOQOL: Rationale and current status', *International Journal of Mental Health*, 23, 24–56.

Williams, S. and Cooper, C.L. (1998) 'Measuring occupational stress: Development of the Pressure Management Indicator', *Journal of Occupational Health Psychology*, 3, 306–21.

8

Ethical Leadership: A Developing Construct

Linda Klebe Treviño and Michael E. Brown

Given the many recent ethical scandals in business and other societal sectors, scholars as well as authors of popular leadership books (e.g. George, 2003) have become interested in better understanding the ethical dimension of leadership. Clearly, leaders can influence followers to behave in either an ethical or unethical direction. However, in keeping with the positive psychology perspective of this volume, we focus on *ethical* leadership and how ethical leaders can influence followers to behave ethically. First, we consider a broad conception of the ethical dimension of leadership by examining the ethical content of two leadership theories – transformational leadership and authentic leadership. Next, we offer a definition and conceptualization of a more specific ethical leadership construct based upon our qualitative and quantitative research (Brown et al., 2005; Treviño et al., 2000, 2003). We analyze the extent to which these constructs overlap and make recommendations for future research.

Leader honesty/integrity/trustworthiness has long been seen as important to perceived leader effectiveness (Craig and Gustafson, 1998; Den Hartog et al., 1999; Kouzes and Posner, 1993, Posner and Schmidt, 1992). However, until recently, little theoretical attention had been paid to the underlying reasons for this relationship or to the development of an ethical leadership construct or measure that could be theoretically and empirically linked to ethics-related outcomes in followers. Craig and Gustafson (1998) developed the Perceived Leader Integrity Scale (PLIS), but their scale items are negatively worded and appear to be more akin to abusive supervision (Tepper, 2000) than to ethical leadership. Thus, we do not find the PLIS to be consistent with a positive psychological approach.

Transformational leadership and ethics

An ethical orientation has long been incorporated into transformational leadership. Burns (1978) originally introduced transformational leadership to describe political leaders, and he distinguished transformational leadership from compliance-based, transactional approaches. According to Burns (1978), transformational leaders encourage followers to look beyond their own individual desires and needs to a broader collective purpose. Burns relied upon Kohlberg's (1969) theory of cognitive moral development, Maslow's (1954) theory of human needs, and Rokeach's (1973) theory of values to explain why transformational leaders are influential. Transformational leaders are thought to satisfy followers' lower-level existence needs, allowing them to focus on their higher-level growth needs. Burns also theorized that transformational leaders move followers to higher stages of moral development, by directing their attention to important values such as justice and equality. Developing shared values through a values internalization process was also an important element of transformational leadership for Burns, because, in his view, transformational leaders were not manipulative. Burns assumed that followers were capable of choosing among leaders and agendas and they would choose to follow those leaders whose values they shared.

Bass (1985) first applied Burns' work to leadership in business, and Bass and Avolio developed transformational leadership as a social scientific construct and measure (Bass and Avolio, 2000). They identified four types of transformational behaviors: individualized consideration, intellectual stimulation, idealized influence, and inspirational motivation. *Individualized consideration* means that transformational leaders look beyond their own needs to care about the needs and development of individual followers. With *intellectual stimulation*, transformational leaders encourage followers to challenge the status quo and question critical ideas and assumptions. Transformational leaders are also charismatic, having *idealized influence* on followers who see the leader and his or her mission as embodying moral values that are good and worthy of emulation. Finally, transformational leaders use *inspirational motivation*, offering exciting value-laden visions of the future that encourage followers to join them in their pursuit. Numerous studies have demonstrated that transformational leadership has powerful effects on followers' motivation, satisfaction, and performance, including citizenship behavior (see Lowe et al., 1996 for a review). And, recently, socialized charismatic leadership, a component of transformational leadership, has been associated with reduced employee deviance (Brown and Treviño, 2006). Thus, transformational leadership and its sub-dimensions have been related to both prosocial (citizenship) and antisocial (deviance) behaviors.

Although Burns presumed that transformational leaders were moral leaders and were not manipulative, Bass (1985) noted that transformational leaders could transform followers to do good like Gandhi or evil like Hitler, suggesting that transformational leaders might be ethical or unethical. Similarly, Howell and Avolio (1992) found evidence for the existence of both ethical and unethical charismatic leaders. Bass and Steidlmeier (1999) distinguished explicitly between 'authentic' and 'pseudo' transformational leadership, arguing that 'authentic' transformational leadership involves ethical outcomes while 'pseudo-transformational leadership' is associated with unethical outcomes. The term 'authentic transformational leader' was associated with leaders who are committed to moral values such as honesty, fairness, and human rights in contrast with pseudo transformational leaders who are self-interested, practice favoritism, and create unhealthy dependence in followers. Therefore, when we discuss leaders who 'transform' followers, it now seems essential that we consider the moral quality of that transformation, as well as the leader's motives (malevolent or altruistic) (Howell, 1988).

Price (2003) expressed concern about the 'transformation' part of transformational leadership. A leader's transformation of followers' values is contrary to philosophers' moral prohibition against 'manipulating rational agents' – even if the values are legitimate 'other-regarding' values that aim to benefit a larger group. Therefore, according to Price, it isn't enough to have good intentions or to transform followers' values in positive ways. Transforming followers' values is ethically problematic because it is manipulative. Even Bass and Steidlmeier (1999) admitted that 'authentic transformational leaders may have to be manipulative at times for what they judge to be the common good' (p. 186). Therefore, one cannot be committed to transforming others without acknowledging the underlying power relationship involved and the potential for manipulation. Further, even well-meaning authentic transformational leaders can make mistakes about moral requirements in specific situations and use their altruistic values to justify unethical actions. Price concluded by saying that 'an appeal to authenticity will not resolve whatever ethical worries we have about this normative conception of leadership' (p. 79).

The concern that transformational leaders may be creating dependence as well as empowerment was addressed in recent empirical research. Kark and colleagues (Kark et al., 2003) argued that transformational leadership includes charismatic behaviors that can create follower identification with the leader and dependence on the leader's approval. Results from a study of bank employees supported the notion that transformational leaders can simultaneously produce *both* empowerment and dependence in followers. Contrary to common belief, dependence and empowerment were not significantly correlated with each other. Employees who personally identified with their transformational leader became dependent upon the leader for direction. Those who socially identified with the department or bank branch were empowered. These results suggest that transformational leadership can create follower dependence and that the processes involved in transformational leadership are more complex than previously thought.

We are not particularly concerned that followers may become dependent on leaders. Research on cognitive moral development (Kohlberg, 1969; Treviño, 1986) makes clear that the large majority of followers will depend on others outside themselves for ethical guidance. In organizations, they look to peers and leaders for such guidance. Therefore, most followers will necessarily be dependent on *someone* for ethical guidance. In our view, it is better to acknowledge such dependence and think carefully about how leaders can influence followers in an ethical direction than to assume (wrongly) that followers are morally autonomous and, via benign neglect, leave them to follow the ethical guidance of their peers (Robinson and O'Leary-Kelly, 1998). Empirical evidence also should help to allay these concerns because transformational leadership has been found to be positively related to perceived leader integrity (Tracey and Hinkin, 1994; Parry and Proctor-Thomson, 2002) and to the leader's cognitive moral development (Turner et al., 2002), providing some support for the idea that transformational leadership (as it has traditionally been conceptualized and measured) is built upon a moral foundation and that transformational leaders will be committed to furthering moral goals such as justice and rights. Therefore, transformational leadership appears to be consistent with an ethically positive leadership style. However, as we discuss later, transformational leadership is much broader than ethical orientation (including vision, change orientation, etc.) and was not developed primarily to understand the leader's ethical influence on followers.

Authentic leadership and ethics

Luthans and Avolio (2003) introduced authentic leadership as a separate construct that lies at the intersection of positive organizational scholarship and transformational/full-range leadership. They defined it as a 'root construct' that 'could incorporate charismatic, transformational, integrity and/or ethical leadership' (p. 4). But, they also argued that these constructs could be discriminated from each other.

They proposed that authentic leaders can be developed by building upon the leader's in-born characteristics and abilities through self-awareness and self-regulation processes. They argued that authentic leadership incorporates transformational leadership, but is a bit different because, while changing followers in some fundamental way is key to transformational leadership, it is not necessary to authentic leadership. Further, authentic leaders need not be charismatic and need not be seen as charismatic or visionary by others. The definition of authentic leadership includes descriptors such as 'genuine, reliable, trustworthy, real, and veritable'. Authenticity includes '*owning* one's personal experiences' as well as '*acting* in accord with the true self'. Thus, self-awareness, openness, transparency, and consistency are at the core of authentic leadership. In addition, being motivated by positive end values and concern for others (rather than by self-interest) is key to authentic leadership and authentic leaders model positive attributes such as hope, optimism, and resiliency. Finally, authentic leaders are capable of judging ambiguous ethical issues, viewing them from multiple perspectives, and aligning decisions with moral values.

Avolio and colleagues (2004) differentiated authentic leadership from transformational leadership by noting that 'authentic leaders are anchored by their own deep sense of self, they know where they stand and with that base they stay their course and convey to others often times through actions, not just words, what they represent in terms of principles, values and ethics' (p. 6). This sense of self is the source of their confidence, hope, and optimism. These authors also explicitly included high moral character in their elaboration of the definition of authentic leadership. They proposed that authentic leaders are guided by positive moral values. The authors developed a model that explains the relationship between authentic leadership and organizational performance, relying in part upon self-concept theory to do so. According to this model, authentic leaders have the capacity to deal with complex ethical issues and they enhance their own self-awareness and followers' self-awareness of values as well. They also build trust and become role models for followers, and they build collective identification rather than identification with the leader. Thus, the influence process is based more on example setting and collective identification than on charismatic appeals.

May and colleagues (2003) further explored the moral component of authentic leadership in a complex model that includes multiple decision making steps that lead to moral action. They proposed that authentic moral leaders recognize moral dilemmas, see themselves as moral leaders, take multiple perspectives on ethical issues and evaluate multiple alternative actions in a transparent manner. Authentic moral leaders then follow through on their intentions via moral courage and sustainable action over time despite risk. The authors also focused on the development of authentic moral leaders via moral capacity, self-awareness and reflection, moral courage, efficacy and resiliency.

We find authentic leadership to be appealing, particularly as a guide to leadership training and development programs. Authentic leadership is obviously concerned with the ethical dimension of leadership. It focuses on a self-aware leader who has ethical intentions and makes good ethical decisions, becoming a role model for others in the process. However, authentic leadership combines so many capabilities and characteristics in one individual that empirical research will be needed to determine whether it is distinctive from other established constructs such as transformational leadership and the ethical leadership construct to which we turn next.

Ethical leadership

Thus far, we have discussed the broad ethical dimension of leadership as it fits within the transformational and authentic leadership domains. In this next section, we introduce a specific 'ethical leadership' construct (Treviño et al., 2000, 2003; Brown et al., 2005) we developed through qualitative and quantitative research aimed at understanding how ethical leadership is perceived from the follower's perspective and how this leadership dimension relates to ethics-related outcomes in employees.

We have defined ethical leadership as 'the demonstration of normatively appropriate conduct through personal actions and interpersonal relationships, and the promotion of such conduct to followers through two-way communication, reinforcement, and decision making' (Brown et al., 2005: 120). This means that ethical leaders model conduct that is considered to be normatively appropriate in the particular context. Second, ethical leaders promote ethical conduct by setting ethical standards, communicating with followers about those standards while providing voice and input, and holding followers accountable to those standards via the reward system. Finally, ethical leaders make normatively appropriate (principled and fair) decisions that followers can observe and emulate.

In order to develop an empirically grounded understanding of ethical leadership in business, we began with structured interviews of 20 senior executives (mostly active and retired CEOs of large American corporations) and 20 ethics/compliance officers in large American businesses. We asked these informants to describe the characteristics and behaviors of an executive 'ethical leader' with whom they had worked (without identifying the specific individual). Our purpose was to discover our informants' definition of ethical leadership. Transcription of the interviews followed by systematic content analysis of the data suggested that ethical leaders are both 'moral persons' (i.e. ethical people) and 'moral managers' (i.e. proactive leaders in the ethics arena) (Treviño et al., 2000) who stand out as socially salient in an 'ethically neutral' business environment (Treviño et al., 2003). The left column in Table 8.1 summarizes the main findings of that study.

The 'moral person' dimension identifies the motivations and personal characteristics of these leaders as described by our informants. Executive ethical leaders were described as concerned about and caring toward their people, honest and trustworthy, principled, persuasive, and committed to doing the right thing in both their personal and professional lives. They make decisions based upon moral values and ethical decision rules, and they're fair, open and ethically aware, showing concern for multiple stakeholders' interests, long-term outcomes, and means not just ends.

This description of ethical leadership overlaps substantially with May and colleagues' (2003) description of the moral component of authentic leadership. See Table 8.1 for a comparison of the conceptual content in each. May and colleagues (2003) referred to an authentic leader's concern for employees, suggesting that both constructs address the social motivation and consideration style of these leaders. In our research, ethical leaders' people focus formed the largest single response theme, suggesting that it is particularly important in the attribution of ethical leadership by observers.

Table 8.1 *Comparing the content of ethical leadership and authentic moral leadership*

Ethical leadership	Authentic leadership
MOTIVATION/PEOPLE-ORIENTATION People-focused, cares about people, treats people right, respects people, develops and mentors employees	MOTIVATION/PEOPLE-ORIENTATION Cares about employees
PERSONAL CHARACTERISTICS Walks the talk, leads by example, desires to 'do the right thing' personally and professionally, honest, trustworthy, fair, persuasive, has integrity, open	PERSONAL CHARACTERISTICS Desires to do the right thing personally and professionally, trustworthy, fair, morally courageous, genuine, open • Moral capacity • Self-awareness, authenticity, transparency • Hope, optimism, resiliency • Self-efficacy
SETTING ETHICAL STANDARDS AND ACCOUNTABILITY (TRANSACTIONAL COMPONENT) Role models, encourages ethical behavior • Sets expectations and standards • Uses rewards/punishments • Doesn't tolerate ethical lapses • Holds self and others accountable to principles and values	PERCEPTIONS OF LEADERSHIP ROLE Role models ethical behavior
ETHICAL AWARENESS/DECISION MAKING Concerned about serving the greater good, multiple stakeholder perspectives, ethically aware, also concerned about the bottom line • Concern for means, not just ends • Concern for long term, not just short term • Concern for multiple stakeholders • Uses ethical decision rules • Also concerned about the bottom line	ETHICAL AWARENESS/DECISION MAKING Recognizes moral dilemmas, takes into account multiple perspectives, stakeholder needs, evaluates multiple alternatives

Both constructs also emphasize ethical role modeling, intention to do the right thing personally and professionally, and the attributes of honesty, fairness, integrity, and openness, suggesting large overlap between the characteristics cited by the two approaches. However, our informants also said that ethical leaders are influential and persuasive (somewhat akin to transformational leadership's inspirational motivation) while Luthans and Avolio (2003) argued that authentic leaders 'do not try to coerce or even rationally persuade followers, but rather use their values, beliefs and behaviors to model the development of self and followers to make the best choices' (p. 14).

Avolio and colleagues (2004) also talked about the importance of positive psychological characteristics such as hope, resiliency, and optimism. Interestingly, none of these characterizations appeared in our empirical data. Further, in its developmental orientation, authentic moral leadership focuses on moral capacity and efficacy, self-awareness, authenticity (being genuine, real), and transparency, as well as experience with moral decision making. None of these emerged in our data either, although this may be because we interviewed observers of ethical leaders and observers would have little basis for knowing about these characteristics. Although genuineness is arguably an important part of being trustworthy, the terms genuine or real did not surface in our data.

Under the categories of ethical awareness and decision making, both authentic leadership and ethical leadership identify the leader's recognition of moral dilemmas and intention to act ethically as important. Authentic moral leaders are proposed to evaluate multiple alternative actions in a transparent manner. As noted above, transparency was not explicitly mentioned in our data, nor was the evaluation of multiple alternative actions. What was more important to our informants was the observation that ethical leaders base their decisions on moral principles as well as ethical decision rules and concern for multiple stakeholders' interests.

Perhaps most important and most different from both transformational and authentic leadership approaches, our qualitative data surfaced an aspect of ethical leadership that we termed the 'moral manager'. Our informants told us that ethical leaders proactively influence followers on ethics-related matters. They set standards explicitly and make it clear to followers that they expect ethical behavior from everyone, including themselves. They communicate their ethical standards and expectations, and they use rewards and discipline to hold followers accountable for ethical conduct. This reflects what we consider to be the 'proactive *leadership*' part of the term ethical leadership and, interestingly, it overlaps more with what we often think of as a transactional style than it does with transformational leadership. This moral manager aspect of ethical leadership is also 'manipulative' in the sense that ethical leaders unapologetically aim to influence followers' ethical conduct. Followers see them as doing this and seem to appreciate it. Thus, according to our informants, ethical leaders use influence approaches that we often think of as transactional (e.g. use of rewards and discipline) to hold followers accountable for the ethical behavior they seek. This finding is contrary to the view that transactional approaches are inconsistent with 'ethical' leadership (Kanungo and Mendonca, 1996) and this dimension of the ethical leader's role is not addressed in treatments of authentic leadership (Avolio et al., 2004) or authentic moral leadership (May et al., 2003).

It is also important to note that the executives we interviewed rarely described ethical leaders as either transformative or visionary, terms that are consistent with the transformational/charismatic leadership literatures. Further, these executives never used the term authentic to describe ethical leaders. Authenticity has mostly to do with being true to oneself. In that sense, it has a similar meaning to the word 'integrity' which means 'a state of being complete or undivided'. Our interviewees did use the term integrity, but they seemed to be using it more as a synonym for honesty. In response to an explicit question, interviewees agreed that ethical leaders behave ethically in their personal and professional lives (a part of authenticity). But, they rarely raised this issue without being prompted. Our point is that, when given the opportunity to describe an ethical leader they knew well, 40 executives said little about authenticity or self-awareness. Again, this may reflect our observer orientation. Observers cannot know whether a leader is self-aware, especially when observing executives from afar. And, they may not care. From the follower's perspective, what may be more important are the leader actions they observe and how employees are treated.

With regard to self-awareness, our informants seemed to be saying that ethical leaders are more aware of others (employees, other stakeholders) than they are of themselves. This suggests that ethical leaders may be self-aware but they are clearly not 'self interested'. Future research may wish to explore the extent to which leaders can be simultaneously self-aware and 'others aware' and how these types of awareness relate to each other.

In addition, our informants only occasionally used words like courage or risk-taking to describe ethical leaders and their behavior. Rather, the ethical leaders they described proactively led on the ethics dimension every day by role modeling ethical action, by setting high ethical standards, and by holding everyone accountable for ethical conduct. In fact, to our informants, ethical leaders were not particularly exciting or courageous. Rather, ethical leaders could simply be counted on to take care of their people, do what's right, and hold others to the same high standards.

In further work to develop the ethical leadership construct (Brown et al., 2005), we developed the ethical leadership scale (ELS), a reliable 10-item survey measure of ethical leadership that combines both the personal characteristics and behaviors (moral person dimension) with the moral leadership behaviors (moral manager dimension) (see Table 8.2). Using this measure, we found ethical leadership to be significantly correlated with related constructs such as consideration, interactional fairness,

Table 8.2   *Ethical leadership scale (ELS)*

Items are given along a 5-point response format (from 1 = strongly disagree to 5 = strongly agree). Respondents are instructed to rate their manager or supervisor.

Conducts his/her personal life in an ethical manner
Defines success not just by results but also the way that they are obtained
Listens to what employees have to say
Disciplines employees who violate ethical standards
Makes fair and balanced decisions
Can be trusted
Discusses business ethics or values with employees
Sets an example of how to do things the right way in terms of ethics
Has the best interests of employees in mind
When making decisions, asks what is the right thing to do

Source: (Brown et al., 2005)

leader honesty, trust in the leader, the idealized influence dimension of transformational leadership, and abusive supervision (negative correlation) while not being subsumed by any of them. Ethical leadership also predicted job satisfaction and dedication, perceived leader effectiveness, and employees' willingness to report problems to management beyond the effects of idealized influence.

Influence processes underlying ethical leadership

Much work remains to be done to document the underlying influence process for an ethical dimension of leadership. One of the biggest challenges tackled by transformational leadership researchers has been the documentation of the underlying psychological processes involved. For example, Shamir et al. (1993) argued that charismatic leaders influence followers through ideological/moral appeals that tie organizational goals and missions to followers' moral values and self-concepts (Gecas, 1982). They expected that charismatic leaders would rally followers to work for the benefit of the collective. However, an empirical test of this mediating mechanism was not supportive (Shamir et al., 1998). Similarly, Dvir and colleagues (Dvir et al., 2002) proposed that transformational leaders would affect performance by influencing the development of a collectivistic orientation and an internalization of moral values. Neither hypothesis was supported. In our research (Brown and Treviño, in 2006) we found some support for values congruence as a mediator. Socialized charismatic leadership (idealized influence dimension of transformational leadership) influenced employee interpersonal deviance through perceived values congruence with the leader. Bono and Judge (2003) linked transformational leadership to outcomes (satisfaction, commitment, extra-role performance) via self-concordance, the extent to which job tasks and goals express the individual's true interests and values. Much more research will be needed to understand these mediating processes.

Avolio and colleagues (2004) proposed a number of mediating influence processes for authentic leadership. For example, they proposed that authentic leaders and their followers will feel psychologically close to each other and, as a result, they will be more likely to agree about how they attribute the causes of events. This agreement about attributions is proposed to influence performance. In addition, authentic leaders and their followers are proposed to have strong psychological contracts. As a result of the ensuing trust, followers are thought to internalize the leader's values which then guide follower decision making. Further, authentic leaders are proposed to influence associates' self-efficacy and means efficacy at an individual and collective level and these then result in positive attitudes and performance. Finally, authentic leaders are proposed to influence follower identification with the leader with the purpose of developing a collective identification with the group which then also influences performance. As far as we know, no empirical tests have yet been conducted. Therefore, much remains to be learned about the processes underlying authentic leadership and its proposed effects.

In considering the underlying psychological processes that explain the relationship between ethical leadership and ethics-related outcomes such as prosocial and antisocial behavior, we have proposed a set of theoretical processes related to social learning and social exchange (Brown et al., 2005). In accordance with a social learning perspective, ethical leaders in business are visible ethical role models who stand out from an ethically neutral landscape. As moral persons, they behave ethically in their personal and professional lives, care for their employees, and make decisions based upon ethical principles and the long term interests of multiple stakeholders. We proposed that followers are likely to be attracted to and to personally identify with such visible role models of ethical conduct and to pattern their own behavior after that of the leader.

In addition, as moral managers, ethical leaders send clear messages to organizational members about expected behavior and use the reward system to hold everyone accountable to those expectations. By setting and communicating standards, and by clearly rewarding ethical conduct and disciplining unethical conduct in light of those standards, vicarious learning is more likely to take place. Followers behave ethically and refrain from unethical conduct largely because of the consequences (positive and negative) that they observe. In addition, using the reward system to support ethical conduct is consistent with followers' perceptions of organizational justice. For example, by disciplining unethical conduct, the leader is upholding organizational norms and supporting the values of those who obey the rules (Treviño, 1992).

We also proposed that ethical leadership is consistent with a social exchange perspective on leadership. In our data, ethical leaders were described as being trustworthy and as treating their people with care, concern and fairness. As such, they are likely to create social exchange relationships with their subordinates who can be expected to reciprocate this caring and fair treatment by engaging in prosocial behaviors and by refraining from antisocial conduct that is harmful to the group or organization.

At the executive level, the ethical leadership construct emphasizes the leader's salience in the social context and subsequent influence on observers. As such, executive ethical leadership is viewed as a reputational phenomenon based upon follower observations from afar. In order to be socially salient, executives must stand out as ethical leaders against an 'ethically neutral' business background (Treviño et al., 2003). And, to influence follower conduct, executive ethical leaders make proactive use of a transactional style, in addition to their personal and decision making characteristics. They become visible moral managers who develop a reputation for ethical leadership and a following among those who observe their leadership.

Discussion

Our focus on the ethical dimension of leadership has allowed us to develop a deeper understanding of this leadership dimension and how it influences employee outcomes. Clearly, significant overlap exists between our ethical leadership construct, transformational leadership, and authentic moral leadership, especially in their descriptions of the motivation involved (altruism) and many of the personal characteristics ascribed to these leaders (honesty, fairness, trustworthiness). However, substantial differences remain. Authentic moral leadership, perhaps because of its developmental focus, emphasizes the background, capabilities, and characteristics of the leader as a person with somewhat less attention to the actions of the leader that influence followers' ethical conduct. In addition, characteristics such as hope, optimism, and resiliency are emphasized in authentic moral leadership, while these are largely absent from descriptions of ethical leaders. Transformational leadership is also a broader construct that focuses on change and inspiration, characteristics that are not a part of our ethical leadership construct.

Many of the characteristics and behaviors of ethical leaders are similar to those identified by transformational (Bass and Avolio, 1993; Burns, 1978) and authentic leadership researchers (Avolio et al., 2004; May et al., 2003). Those that are most different include transactional type leader behaviors that make leaders stand out as ethical leaders and that are aimed at explicitly influencing the ethical conduct of followers. This more transactional aspect of ethical leadership raises the specter of manipulation about which Price was so concerned. But, as suggested earlier, we do not share this concern. The social scientific evidence strongly supports the idea that most employees are not autonomous moral agents. If managers act upon the myth of moral autonomy, employees will be left to fend for themselves in an atmosphere of benign ethical neglect when what they really need is strong ethical guidance from their leaders (Treviño and Brown, 2004).

So, we are convinced that ethical leaders influence followers' behavior. But, we are not as convinced that ethical leaders 'transform' followers' moral development or values. Such a transformation, if it occurs at all, would likely require explicit training oriented toward such transformation as well as a close working relationship over some significant amount of time. Would such explicit expectation of follower transformation be more or less distasteful from Price's perspective? Clearly, researchers should keep in mind Price's (2003) ethical concerns. However, it is possible that philosophers will always find notions of 'ethical leadership' morally troublesome because of the explicit influence on others' moral behavior that contrasts starkly with their assumption of moral agency (see Treviño and Weaver, 1994).

Given the overlaps in these constructs, one of the major remaining challenges will be to establish discriminant validity. Some might argue that the ethical dimension of leadership is really all about trust (Dirks and Ferrin, 2002; Kramer, 1996; Mayer et al., 1995). The initial evidence (Brown et al., 2005) indicates that ethical leadership is strongly related to yet distinct from idealized influence, the component of transformational leadership with the most overt ethical content, as well as affective trust. And, ethical leadership predicts important outcomes such as follower satisfaction with and willingness to report problems to management beyond idealized influence. Nevertheless, future research must empirically demonstrate how these constructs differ from each other and related constructs and how they contribute to knowledge and variance explained rather than simply muddying the leadership landscape with new constructs that overlap with what we already know.

Conclusion

Although recent business scandals have moved the topic of *un*ethical leadership into the forefront, in this chapter we have taken a more positive approach to ethics and leadership. Attempts to more clearly describe and define ethical leadership led us to develop the ethical leadership construct and an instrument to measure it. The preliminary evidence suggests that ethical leadership is distinct from and predicts important outcomes beyond idealized influence, the 'ethical' component of transformational leadership and that the ethical leadership scale (ELS) is a promising instrument with good initial validity and reliability. Nevertheless, construct validity is an ongoing process and we encourage others to contribute to it. Further, many unanswered questions remain about the antecedents, processes and outcomes of ethical leadership. We hope that the development of the ethical leadership construct and measure will facilitate future research and generate answers to these important questions.

Acknowledgment

Table 8.2 reprinted from *Organizational Behavior and Human Decision Processes*, 97(2), Brown, Treviño and Harrison, 'Ethical leadership: A social learning perspective for construct development and testing', *Organizational Behavior and Human Decision Processes*, 97, 117–34. Copyright 2005, with permission from Elsevier.

References

Avolio, B.J., Luthans, F. and Walumbwa F.O. (2004) 'Authentic leadership: Theory building for veritable sustained performance.' Working paper.

Bass, B.M. (1985) *Leadership and Performance beyond Expectations.* New York: Free Press.

Bass, B.M. and Avolio, B.J. (1993) *Improving Organizational Effectiveness Through Transformational Leadership.* Thousand Oaks, CA: Sage.

Bass, B.M. and Avolio, B.J. (2000) *Multifactor Leadership Questionnaire.* Redwood City, CA: Mindgarden.

Bass, B.M. and Steidlmeier, P. (1999) 'Ethics, character, and authentic transformational leadership behavior', *Leadership Quarterly*, 10, 181–217.

Bono, J.E. and Judge, T.A. (2003) 'Self-concordance at work: Toward understanding the motivational effects of transformational leaders', *Academy of Management Journal*, 46, 554–71.

Brown, M.E. and Treviño, L.K. (2006) 'Socialized charismatic leadership, values congruence, and deviance in work groups: An empirical test', *Journal of Applied Psychology*, 91, 954–62.

Brown, M., Treviño, L.K. and Harrison, D. (2005) 'Ethical leadership: A social learning perspective for construct development and testing', *Organizational Behavior and Human Decision Processes*, 97, 117–34.

Burns, J.M. (1978) *Leadership.* New York: Harper & Row.

Craig, S.B. and Gustafson, S.B. (1998) 'Perceived leader integrity scale: An instrument for assessing employee perceptions of leader integrity', *Leadership Quarterly*, 9, 127–45.

Den Hartog, D.N., House, R.J., Hanges, P.J. and Ruiz-Quintanilla, S.A (1999) 'Culture specific and cross-culturally generalizable implicit leadership theories: Are attributes of charismatic/transformational leadership universally endorsed?', *Leadership Quarterly*, 10, 219–56.

Dirks, K.T. and Ferrin, D.L. (2002) 'Trust in leadership: Meta-analytic findings and implications for research and practice', *Journal of Applied Psychology*, 87, 611–28.

Dvir, T., Eden, D., Avolio, B.J. and Shamir, B. (2002) 'Impact of transformational leadership on follower development and performance: A field experiment', *Academy of Management Journal*, 45, 735–44.

Gecas, V. (1982) 'The self concept', in R.H. Turner and J.F. Short (eds) *Annual Review of Sociology*, 8 (pp. 1–33).

George, B. (2003) *Authentic Leadership: Rediscovering the Secrets to Creating Lasting Value*. San Francisco, CA: Jossey-Bass.

Howell, J.M. (1988) 'Two faces of charisma: Socialized and personalized leadership in organizations', in J.A Conger and R.N. Kanungo (eds) *Charismatic Leadership* (pp. 213–236). San Francisco, CA: Jossey-Bass.

Howell, J.M. and Avolio, B.J. (1992) 'The ethics of charismatic leadership: Submission or liberation?', *Academy of Management Executive*, 6, 43–54.

Kanungo, R.N. and Mendonca, M. (1996) *Ethical Dimensions of Leadership*. Thousand Oaks, CA: Sage.

Kark, R., Shamir, B. and Chen, G. (2003) 'The two faces of transformational leadership: Empowerment and dependency', *Journal of Applied Psychology*, 88, 246–55.

Kohlberg, L. (1969) 'State and sequence: The cognitive-development approach to socialization', in D. Goslin (ed.) *Handbook of Socialization Theory and Research* (pp. 347–480). Chicago: Rand-McNally.

Kouzes, J.M. and Posner, B.Z. (1993) *Credibility*. San Francisco: Jossey-Bass.

Kramer, R.M. (1996) 'Divergent realities and convergent disappointments in the hierarchical relation: Trust and the intuitive auditor at work', in R.M. Kramer and T.R. Tyler (eds) *Trust in Organizations: Frontiers of Theory and Research* (pp. 216–45). Thousand Oaks, CA: Sage.

Lowe, K.B., Kroeck, K.G. and Sivasubramaniam, N. (1996) 'Effectiveness correlates of transformational and transactional leadership: A meta-analytic review of the MLQ literature', *Leadership Quarterly*, 7, 385–425.

Luthans, F. and Avolio, B. (2003) 'Authentic leadership: A positive development approach', in K.S. Cameron, J.E. Dutton and R.E. Quinn (eds) *Positive Organizational Scholarship*. San Francisco: Berrett-Koehler.

Maslow, A. (1954) *Motivation and Personality*. New York: Harper Brothers.

May, D.R., Chan, A.Y.L., Hodges, T.D. and Avolio, B.J. (2003) 'Developing the moral component of authentic leadership', *Organizational Dynamics*, 32, 247–60.

Mayer, R.C., Davis, J.H. and Schoorman, F.D. (1995) 'An integrative model of organizational trust', *Academy of Management Review*, 20, 709–34.

McClelland, D.C. (1985) *Human Motivation*. Glenview, IL: Scott Foresman.

Parry, K.W. and Proctor-Thomson, S.B. (2002) 'Perceived integrity of transformational leaders in organizational settings', *Journal of Business Ethics*, 35, 75–96.

Posner, B.Z. and Schmidt, W.H. (1992) 'Values and the American manager: An update updated', *California Management Review*, Spring, 80–94.

Price, T. (2003) 'The ethics of authentic transformational leadership', *The Leadership Quarterly*, 14, 67–81.

Robinson, S. and O'Leary-Kelly, A. (1998) 'Monkey see, monkey do: The influence of work groups on the antisocial behavior of employees', *Academy of Management Journal*, 41, 658–72.

Rokeach, M. (1973) *The Nature of Human Values*. New York: The Free Press.

Rotter, J.B. (1966) 'Generalized expectancies for internal versus external control of reinforcement', *Psychological Monographs: General and Applied*, 80, 1–28.

Schminke, M., Ambrose, M.L. and Neubaum, D.O. (2005) 'The effect of leader moral development on ethical climate and employee attitudes', *Organizational Behavior and Human Decision Processes*, 97, 135–51.

Shamir, B., House, R. and Arthur, M.B. (1993) 'The motivation effects of charismatic leadership: A self-concept based theory', *Organization Science*, 4, 1–17.

Shamir, B., Zakay, E., Breinin, E. and Popper, M. (1998) 'Correlates of charismatic leader behavior in military units: Subordinates attitudes, unit characteristics, and superior's evaluation of leader's performance', *Academy of Management Journal*, 43, 387–409.

Tepper, B. (2000) 'Consequences of abusive supervision', *Academy of Management Journal*, 43, 178–90

Tracey, J.B. and Hinkin, T.R. (1998) 'Transformational leadership or effective managerial practices?', *Group and Organization Management*, 23, 220–36.

Treviño, L.K. (1986) 'Ethical decision making in organizations: A person-situation interactionist model', *Academy of Management Review*, 11, 601–17.

Treviño, L.K. (1992) 'The social effects of punishment in organizations: A justice perspective', *Academy of Management Review*, 17, 647–76.

Treviño, L.K. and Brown, M.E. (2004) 'Managing to be ethical: Debunking five business ethics myths', *Academy of Management Executive*, 18, 69–81.

Treviño, L.K. and Weaver, G.R. (1994). 'Business ETHICS/BUSINESS ethics: One field or two?', *Business Ethics Quarterly*, 4, 113–28.

Treviño, L.K. and Youngblood, S.A. (1990) 'Bad apples in bad barrels: A causal analysis of ethical decision-making behavior', *Journal of Applied Psychology*, 75, 378–85.

Treviño, L.K., Brown, M. and Hartman, L.P. (2003) 'A qualitative investigation of perceived executive ethical leadership: Perceptions from inside and outside the executive suite', *Human Relations*, 55, 5–37.

Treviño, L.K., Hartman, L.P. and Brown, M. (2000) 'Moral person and moral manager: How executives develop a reputation for ethical leadership', *California Management Review*, 42, 128–42.

Turner, N., Barling, J., Epitropaki, O., Butcher, V. and Milner, C. (2002) 'Transformational leadership and moral reasoning', *Journal of Applied Psychology*, 87, 304–11.

Weaver, G., Treviño, L.K. and Agle, B. (in press) 'Somebody I look up to: Ethical role modeling in business', *Organizational Dynamics*.

9

The Positive Role of Political Skill in Organizations

Pamela L. Perrewé, Gerald R. Ferris, Jason S. Stoner,
and Robyn L. Brouer

Organizations have long been considered political arenas and the study of organizational politics has been a popular topic for a great number of years (e.g. Mintzberg, 1983; Ferris et al., 1989, 2002). Mintzberg (1983) defined politics as an individual or group behavior that is typically disruptive, illegitimate and not approved of by formal authority, accepted ideology, or certified expertise. However, more recently researchers have conceptualized politics as neither an inherently bad or good phenomenon, but rather one to be observed, analyzed, and comprehended in order to gain a more informed understanding of organizations and how they operate (Ferris and Brouer, in press).

Politics can be conceptualized as the informal ways people try to exercise influence in organizations through the management of shared meaning (Sederberg, 1984; Ferris and Brouer, in press). Organizational research suggests that organizational politics is a fundamental truism of organizational life. Further, given the uncertainty that surrounds the contemporary organizational context, politicking in organizations is a phenomenon that is likely to remain.

The question is not if organizations are inherently political, but rather, how do individuals manage the politics of organizational life? We believe that those individuals who are successful at navigating through the politics within organizations, and who are adept at interpersonal influence, possess political skill. Further, we argue that political skill encompasses a skill set that not only is positive, but also essential in today's workforce (Ferris et al., 2005a). We begin our discussion with an overview of the role of political skill within the contemporary organizational context.

The contemporary organizational context

Organizational redesign and restructuring

The changing nature of jobs and work, which have been re-configured in newly designed and structured organizations, has created environments that maximize social interaction as a main feature of work. The changes we have seen take place in organizations have made us reconsider the way we define the meaning of 'job'. The static sets of duties and responsibilities that we have referred to as 'jobs' are giving way to more dynamic, fluid, and constantly changing sets of roles needed to adapt to turbulent contexts (Cascio, 1995). Consequently, we are seeing work organized within teams, where individuals work collaboratively and interdependently to produce products and services. Thus, the knowledge, skills, and abilities required to be effective in these settings increasingly are social and political skills.

New generation employees

Levine (2005) has suggested that young people today who are getting ready to enter the work world are simply not ready. He claims they lack the ability to delay gratification, the capacity to start at entry level and work their way up the ladder, they lack political skill and are amazingly unprepared to deal with organizational politics. He argued, 'To succeed, it is not sufficient to know a lot, work hard, and turn out quality products or services. You have to make yourself liked, and you have to show you like the people you want to like you. That's politics' (p. 192). Sanders (2005) echoed this notion in his recent book, *The Likeability Factor*. Thus, not only are organizational structures increasingly being designed to maximize interactions with others, but also the new generation of workers appear to be inept at successfully managing these interactions.

The focus on positive aspects of work contexts and behavior

We have seen several forces combine today to focus interest in positive behavior in organizations, which would suggest the importance of possessing qualities, skills, and characteristics that can further such interests. Sanders' (2005) likeability factor is one manifestation of that positive trend. Another is the positive psychology movement, which was stimulated several years ago by Martin Seligman and his colleagues (e.g. Seligman, 1998; Seligman and Csikszentmihalyi, 2000), was extended to positive organizational behavior by Fred Luthans (Luthans, 2002a, 2002b), and is reflected in the recent work on positive organizational scholarship by Cameron and colleagues (2003).

We argue that political skill is a fundamental building block for success given the movement toward positivity in organizations. In sum, because of the emphasis on team-based approaches within organizations, the younger generation of workers' lack of political skill and knowledge of organizational politics, and the movement toward organizational positivity, now is the time to consider the positive role of political skill.

Political skill defined

We define political skill as the ability to effectively understand others at work, and to use such knowledge to influence others to act in ways that enhance one's personal and/or organizational goals. Politically skilled individuals are socially astute, and keenly aware of the need to deal differently with different situations and people. Therefore, they have the capacity to adjust their behavior to different and changing situational demands in a sincere and trustworthy manner. Despite the sometimes negative connotations made of the term 'organizational politics', we have argued for many years not only that politics does not have to be viewed in an exclusively pejorative light, but also that there are some quite positive qualities associated with the ability to be effective in such organizations; and we believe that political skill captures these positive qualities.

Politically skilled individuals exude self-confidence that is both attractive and comforting to others. However, this self-confidence never goes too far so as to be perceived as arrogance, but is always properly measured and maintains a positive character. Although self-confident, those high in political skill are not self-absorbed, because their focus is outward toward others, not inward and self-centered. This allows politically skilled individuals to maintain a proper balance and perspective, and also to ensure that they are accountable to others as well as to themselves.

We suggest that people high in political skill not only know precisely when and what to do in different social situations at work, but how to do it in a manner that disguises any self-serving motives, thus, appearing to be sincere. Furthermore, we see political skill as independent from intelligence or cognitive ability, because it is a different sort of competency, and does not depend, for its effectiveness, on being mentally smart. So, it is possible to be highly politically skilled without possessing an unusually high IQ.

At the same time, it certainly is possible to possess modest or even below average intelligence, and still be very politically skilled (Ferris et al., 2005a). In terms of its derivation, we believe there are aspects of political skill that are dispositional or inherited, but we see other aspects that can be developed or shaped through a combination of formal and informal training and developmental experiences (Perrewé et al., 2000).

The dimensionality of political skill

Political skill is thought to consist of four dimensions: social astuteness, interpersonal influence, networking ability, and apparent sincerity. Social astuteness refers to individuals' abilities to accurately understand social situations, including the behaviors of both themselves and others (Ferris et al., 2005a). Interpersonal influence refers to the ability of the politically skilled to both influence those around them and to adapt and adjust their behaviors to changing environmental demands (Ferris et al., 2005a).

The third dimension, networking ability, is what enables politically skilled individuals to develop connections, friendships, and alliances. This ability creates social capital, which equips the politically skilled with more resources to use toward goal attainment. The last dimension of political skill is apparent sincerity. Researchers have argued that influence attempts will only be successful if the influencers are perceived as possessing no concealed motives (Jones, 1990). Politically skilled individuals inspire high levels of trust and reputations of integrity by appearing to be sincere and genuine (Ferris et al., 2005a).

Political skill is not only a positive skill set in and of itself, it leads to the acquisition of other positive assets. Indeed, political skill gives individuals a calm sense of self-confidence, personal security, and control. Furthermore, the networking ability aspect of political skill builds social capital and social support. These positive assets lead politically skilled individuals to be viewed more favorably by others, which, in turn, can increase their reputation and status (Ferris et al., 2005a).

Positive impact of political skill in organizations

Political skill and job performance

Researchers have long investigated the influence of stable dispositional variables in predicting job performance. For instance, research on the 'Big 5' personality traits (Mount and Barrick, 1995) has noted that individuals who are diligent, persistent, and detail-oriented tend to have higher performance than individuals who are emotionally unstable and behave erratically. Likewise, general mental ability has been linked to job performance (Schmidt and Hunter, 1998). Although these and similar constructs have been shown to correlate with job performance, the statistical relationships have been modest in magnitude (e.g. Barrick and Mount, 1991). Judge and colleagues (2004) suggested that perhaps charisma and social skill are more important determinates of leader effectiveness than intelligence.

We suggest, and research supports the notion, that political skill is a valid predictor of job performance and performance ratings. In terms of job performance, political skill plays an integral part in employee success in today's work environments. With constant threats of layoffs and corporate restructuring, the work environment today is filled with ambiguity and constant change. Individuals who have political skill are socially astute, thus being able to observe the changing workplace, adapt to their current surroundings, and adjust and re-calibrate their behavior (Ferris et al., 2005a).

Furthermore, in terms of performance ratings, research has shown that individuals with political skill have an advantage over those who lack political skill. For instance, Ferris et al. (2005b) found a direct, positive relationship between political skill and performance ratings in a sample of branch managers from a financial services institution. Similarly, in a sample from an Australian motor manufacture, Semadar, Robins and Ferris (2006) found political skill was a stronger predictor of positive performance ratings than emotional intelligence, leadership self-efficacy, and self-monitoring.

Not only does political skill influence performance ratings by aiding individuals' job performance, but also individuals with political skill are able to effectively manage impressions of their effort and high job performance. For instance, Frink and Ferris (1998) noted that individuals who set higher goals tend to have higher performance ratings because they are able to transmit the impression of being ambitious, energetic, hardworking, and committed. Furthermore, research has noted that individuals are rated higher when raters perceive themselves to be similar to the employee (e.g. Wayne and Liden, 1995). Individuals with political skill are able to mange their employer's perceptions that they appear to be similar to the employer, and thus reflect a good fit with the organization, culture, and/or workgroup.

Lastly, individuals with political skill are masters of interpersonal influence and apparent sincerity (Ferris et al., 2005a). As such, politically skilled individuals are able to communicate with employers in a way that will highlight their positive behaviors and downplay their negative behaviors. In sum, politically skilled employees gain high, positive performance ratings due to their ability to manage their image and likeability in the mind of the performance rater.

Leader political skill

Leadership is the ability to influence an individual or a group toward the achievement of some predetermined goals. Therefore, possessing the skill set that arms one with the ability to understand others at work and the willingness to use this understanding to influence these others is essential to effective leadership. Leaders need to be able to manage meanings to construct a reality for their followers, and political skill will enable them to do that effectively (Fairhurst and Starr, 1996).

Without political skill, both leaders and managers likely would fail. Ciampa (2005) found that 40 percent of new CEOs fail within their first 18 months on the job. Caimpa contended that because CEOs are unlikely to receive systematic feedback, they must not only understand the political climate of the organization, but also they must be politically skilled. Furthermore, House and Aditya (1997) suggested that leadership researchers need to begin to address the style in which leaders express behaviors. These authors argued that this style is a critically important factor in leadership success. Leader political skill (LPS) is essentially a reflection of a leader's style. In fact, Douglas and Ammeter (2004) found that leadership effectiveness was predicted by perceptions of leader political skill.

Also, Treadway et al. (2004) examined the relationship between leader political skill and perceived organizational support. Specifically, they found that leader political skill was positively related to perceptions of organizational support. Perceptions of organizational support were then related positively to job satisfaction and negatively to organizational cynicism. Additionally, job satisfaction was positively related to organizational commitment, and organizational cynicism was negatively related to organizational commitment. This suggests that a leader's political skill might be an important factor in garnering support and commitment to goals that are necessary in order for a team and organization to be successful.

Ahearn and colleagues (2004) stated that because organizations are changing, the role of a manger is changing to that of a leader, and there is more of a focus on team-work. These authors argued that political skill is a critical component of successful leadership today. In fact, these authors found that leader political skill produced significant incremental variance in team effectiveness scores beyond other team and leader variables. Moreover, Semadar et al. (2006) examined not only political skill, but also emotional intelligence, leadership self-efficacy, and self-monitoring, and found that political skill had the strongest effect on managerial effectiveness, and was what distinguished top performers from others.

Finally, Douglas and colleagues (2005) argued for the important role of leader political skill in authentic leadership. Authentic leaders were described as individuals who hold true to their fundamental moral character and values. However, because leadership is a social phenomenon, they argued that leader political skill is an essential component in the study of authentic leadership because politically skilled leaders inspire trust, confidence, and authenticity as mechanisms to incur follower motivation, commitment, and productive work behavior.

Political skill, reputation, and career success

Ferris et al. (2005a) defined reputation as 'a form of identity made of a complex combination of perceived characteristics and accomplishments, demonstrated behaviors, and intended images presented over a period of time' (p. 92). Reputations consist of human capital (i.e. knowledge, skills, and credentials), political capital (i.e. networking ability, intelligence, and personality), and social capital (i.e. availability of networks). Political skill is an integral factor in developing, maintaining, and defending one's reputation. Specifically, political skill is a key component of political capital, which aids one's compilation of social capital.

When developing a reputation, individuals with political skill are able to manage their first impressions effectively. Because of their social astuteness, ability to influence others, and appear sincere in their actions, in new situations, politically skilled individuals present themselves in a way that is viewed positively. Secondly, political skill helps maintain one's reputation. Politically skilled individuals are astute and thus keenly aware of their reputation. Therefore, they are able to act in a manner that is consistent with the reputation.

Lastly, political skill aids in protecting individuals' reputations (i.e. reputation defense). Politically skilled individuals are able to build and maintain networks, which, in turn, are important in reputation defense. By possessing extensive networks, politically skilled individuals are able to call upon influential others for support and coalition building if and when their reputation is being threatened.

In addition to its role in reputation, political skill is influential in career success in several ways. First, in terms of just surviving in today's tumultuous times, as de Botton (2004) pointed out (cited in Levine, 2005: 192), 'the path to promotion or its opposite may have an apparently haphazard relationship to performance. The successful alpinists of organizational pyramids may not be employees who are best at their tasks, but those who have mastered a range of political skills in which ordinary life does not offer instruction.' Perrewé and Nelson (2004) suggested that, because organizations are political arenas, political skill is essential to survival. In other words, it is not necessarily employee performance that leads to keeping one's job. Politically skilled employees are able to demonstrate that they have important competencies valued by the organization during times of corporate restructuring and downsizing.

Furthermore, political skill may be positively related to higher compensation. Research on impression management and social influence has noted that certain influence attempts will be more effective in achieving higher salary. For instance, ingratiation (Gould and Penley, 1984), tactical impression management (Kipnis and Schmidt, 1988) and positive emotions (Staw et al., 1994) all have been positively linked with salary increases. As such, politically skilled individuals are more likely to be able to successfully implement influence efforts, and do so in a positive manner. Thus, political skill can be influential in securing increased compensation.

In terms of promotions, political skill again plays an important, essential role. As suggested by signaling theory (Spence, 1974), employers are looking for a 'fit' between employees and employers when making promotion decisions, because 'fit' can be perceived as an indicator of organizational commitment and identity. Political skill allows individuals to present a positive image that they fit well with the organization. Furthermore, individuals who are politically skilled are more likely to be able to effectively influence their supervisors, which can lead to increased chances for promotions (Wright, 1979). Lastly, networks have been shown to be important in career success (Seibert et al., 2001). As noted earlier, individuals with political skill are able to form and maintain networks with influential individuals, thus enabling career success.

Political skill as antidote to stress

Research in the organizational sciences has long shown the negative effects of stress on individuals (Kahn and Byosiere, 1992). When individuals perceive a stressor as causing them harm, they experience strain in the form of behavioral (e.g. increases turnover intentions and absences), physiological (e.g. increases in heart rate and blood pressure), and/or psychological outlets (e.g. feelings of tension, dissatisfaction). The financial burden of having strained employees is astronomical as organizations pay for things such as increases in medical coverage and losses in productivity. It has been proposed that political skill can be effective in mitigating the negative effects of stress in one of two ways (e.g. Brouer et al., 2006; Perrewé et al., 2000). First, it is proposed that political skill actually insulates employees from stress, and second, political skill facilitates stress coping mechanisms for employees.

Classic stress theories (e.g. Lazarus, 1968) propose that individuals assess new situations and stimuli to determine if they constitute stressors. Often stressors are perceived to be present if the new situation or stimulus leaves individuals with a feeling of a loss of control (e.g. Karasek, 1979). It has been noted that political skill gives employees a feeling of control (Brouer et al., 2006; Perrewé et al., 2004). As such, Perrewé et al. (2000) posited that executives who possess political skill would be less likely to perceive their environment as stressful. In general, when individuals with political skill encounter new situations, they do not feel as though they have lost control because of their ability to accurately assess the situation and behave accordingly. Thus, political skill should be negatively related to perceptions of stressors.

Second, researchers (e.g. Folkman and Lazarus, 1985) have posited that felt strain is really a consequence of the misfit between perceived stressors and ability to cope with said stressors. Political skill could moderate the relationship between stressors and strain by acting as a form of coping (Perrewé et al., 2000, 2004). That is, once stressors are perceived to be present, political skill facilitates coping by giving individuals a feeling of interpersonal control. They will be able to look at their situation and take appropriate action to reduce felt strain.

Empirical research supports the moderating effect of political skill. Treadway and colleagues (2005) found that employees with low political skill engaging in political activity reported high levels of emotional labor. Conversely, these researchers also found that employees with high political skill did not report high levels of emotional labor when engaging in political behaviors. Furthermore, Kolodinsky and colleagues (2004) found that individuals with moderate levels of political skill reported high levels of job satisfaction and low levels of job tension. Finally, Perrewé et al. (2004) found that political skill moderated the relationship between role conflict and psychological and physiological strain. Specifically, when employees perceived themselves to have role conflict at work, those with high political skill had lower psychological anxiety, fewer somatic complaints, and lower heart rate and blood pressure levels than those low in political skill.

Future directions and managerial implications

This chapter has highlighted some of the positive aspects of political skill. Specifically, we examined how political skill can have positive effects on job performance and ratings, leader effectiveness, reputation, and career success. Furthermore, we illustrated how political skill can reduce experienced stress in the workplace.

Given its potentially positive aspects, we recommend additional research examining the role of political skill within organizations. For instance, layoff situations are stressful times for employees due to increases in job insecurity. Could political skill moderate this relationship such that savvy employees see the elimination of co-workers as opportunities rather than threats, as fewer individuals are around to compete for organizational positions?

Secondly, the positive aspects of political skill have implications for practicing professionals. Specifically, given the importance political skill plays in career success, perhaps human resource management departments should place emphasis on developing the social astuteness, influence tactics, sincerity, and networking abilities of employees. Ferris and colleagues (1993) proposed an alternative view for why diversity programs sometimes do not reach full potential. Essentially, they proposed that part of career success is being able to play the political game, of which majority group members are often well educated. In order for diversity programs to be truly integrated into the workforce, human resources departments could provide some training in political skill to minority group members so that they are more knowledgeable about the rules of the political game, and therefore, how to be effective at work.

Researchers have suggested that political skill can be developed through training programs (Ferris et al., 2000) and practice (Perrewé et al., 2005). Given the significant role of political skill within organizations, efforts designed to develop the political skill of managers and employees appear to be critical for success.

References

Ahearn, K.K., Ferris, G.R., Hochwarter, W.A., Douglas, C. and Ammeter, A.P. (2004) 'Leader political skill and team performance', *Journal of Management*, 30, 309–27.

Barrick, M. and Mount, M. (1991) 'The big five personality dimensions and job performance: A meta-analysis', *Personnel Psychology*, 44, 1–26.

Brouer, R.L., Ferris, G.R., Hochwarter, W.A., Laird, M.D. and Gilmore, D.C. (in press). 'The strain-related reactions to perceptions of organizational politics as a workplace stressor: Political skill as a neutralizer', in E. Vigoda-Gadot and A. Drory (eds) *Handbook of Organizational Politics*. Northampton, MA: Edward Elgar Publishing, Inc.

Cameron, K.S., Dutton, J.E. and Quinn, R.E. (eds) (2003) *Positive Organizational Scholarship: Foundations of a New Discipline*. San Francisco: Berrett-Koehler.

Cascio, W.F. (1995) 'Whither industrial and organizational psychology in a changing world of work', *American Psychologist*, 50, 928–39.

Ciampa, D. (2005) 'Almost ready: How leaders move', *Harvard Business Review*, January, 46–53.

De Botton, A. (2004) *Status Anxiety*. New York: Vintage Books.

Douglas, C. and Ammeter, A.P. (2004) 'An examination of leader political skill and its effect on ratings of leader effectiveness', *The Leadership Quarterly*, 15, 537–50.

Douglas, C., Ferris, G.R. and Perrewé, P.L. (2005) 'Leader political skill and authentic leadership', in W.L. Gardner, B.J. Avolio and F.O. Walumbwa (eds) *Authentic Leadership: Origins, Development, and Effects* (Vol. 3, pp. 139–54, *Monographs in Leadership Management* series, J.G. Hunt, ed.). Oxford: Elsevier Science.

Fairhurst, G.A. and Starr, R.A. (1996) *The Art of Framing: Managing the Language of Leadership*. San Francisco: Jossey-Bass.

Ferris, G.R. and Brouer, R.L. (in press) 'Organizational politics', in S.G. Rogelberg (ed.) *The Encyclopedia of Industrial and Organizational Psychology*. Thousand Oaks, CA: Sage.

Ferris, G.R., Adams, G., Kolodinsky, R.W., Hochwarter, W.A. and Ammeter, A.P. (2002) 'Perceptions of organizational politics: Theory and research directions', in F.J. Yammarino and F. Dansereau (eds) *Research in Multi-level issues, Volume 1: The Many Faces of Multi-level Issues* (pp. 179–254). Oxford: JAI Press/Elsevier Science.

Ferris, G.R., Davidson, S.L. and Perrewé, P.L. (2005a) *Political Skill at Work: Impact on Work Effectiveness*. Palo Alto, CA: Davies-Black Publishing.

Ferris, G.R., Frink, D.W. and Galang, M.C. (1993) 'Diversity in the workplace: The human resources management challenges', *Human Resource Planning*, 16, 41–52.

Ferris, G.R., Perrewé, P.L., Anthony, W.P. and Gilmore, D.C. (2000) 'Political skill at work', *Organizational Dynamics*, 28, 25–37.

Ferris, G.R., Russ, G.S. and Fandt, P.M. (1989) 'Politics in organizations', in R.A. Giacalone and P. Rosenfeld (eds) *Impression Management in the Organization* (pp. 143–70). Hillsdale, NJ: Lawrence Erlbaum.

Ferris, G.R., Treadway, D.C., Kolodinsky, R.W., Hochwarter, W.A., Kacmar, C.J., Douglas, C. and Frink, D.D. (2005b) 'Development and validation of the political skill inventory', *Journal of Management*, 31, 126–52.

Folkman, S. and Lazarus, R.S. (1985) 'If it changes it must be a process: Study of emotion and coping during three stages of a college examination', *Journal of Personality and Social Psychology*, 48, 150–70.

Frink, D.D. and Ferris, G.R. (1998) 'Accountability, impression management, and goal setting in the performance evaluation proces', *Human Relations*, 51, 1259–83.

Gould, S. and Penley, L.E. (1984) 'Career strategies and salary progression: A study of their relationship in municipal bureaucracy', *Organizational Behavior and Human Performance*, 34, 244–65.

House, R.J. and Aditya, R.N. (1997) 'The social scientific study of leadership: quo vadis?', *Journal of Management*, 23, 409–73.

Jones, E.E. (1990) *Interpersonal Perception*. New York: W.H. Freeman.

Judge, T.A., Colbert, A.E. and Ilies, R. (2004) 'Intelligence and leadership: A quantitative review and test of theoretical propositions', *Journal of Applied Psychology*, 89, 542–52.

Kahn, R.L. and Byosiere, P. (1992) 'Stress in organizations', in M.D. Dunnette and L.M. Hough (eds) *Handbook of Industrial and Organizational Psychology* (2nd edn, Vol. 2, pp. 571–650). Palo Alto, CA: Consulting Psychology Press.

Karasek, R.A. Jr (1979) 'Job demands, job decision latitude, and mental strain: Implications for job redesign', *Administrative Science Quarterly*, 24, 285–310.

Kipnis, D. and Schmidt, S.M. (1988) 'Upward influence styles: Relationships with performance evaluations, salary, and stress', *Administrative Science Quarterly*, 33, 528–42.

Kolodinsky, R.W., Hochwarter, W.A. and Ferris, G.R. (2004) 'Nonlinearity in the relationship between political skill and work outcomes: Convergent evidence from three studies', *Journal of Vocational Behavior*, 65, 294–308.

Lazarus, R.S. (1968) 'Emotions and adaptation: Conceptual and empirical relations', in W.J. Arnold (ed.) *Nebraska Symposium on Motivation* (pp. 175–266). London, NE: University of Nebraska Press.

Levine, M. (2005) *Ready or Not, Here Life Comes*. New York: Simon and Schuster.

Luthans, F. (2002a) 'Positive organizational behavior: Developing and managing psychological strengths for performance improvement', *Academy of Management Executive*, 16, 57–75.

Luthans, F. (2002b) 'The need for and meaning of positive organizational behavior', *Journal of Organizational Behavior*, 23, 695–706.

Mintzberg, H. (1983) *Power in and Around Organizations*. Englewood Cliffs, NJ: Prentice-Hall.

Mount, M.K. and Barrick, M.R. (1995) 'The Big Five personality dimensions: Implications for research and practice in human resources management', in G.R. Ferris (ed.) *Research in Personnel and Human Resource Management* (Vol. 13, pp. 153–200). Greenwich, CT: JAI Press.

Perrewé, P.L. and Nelson, D.L. (2004) 'Gender and career success: The facilitative role of political skill', *Organizational Dynamics*, 33, 366–78.

Perrewé, P.L., Ferris, G.R., Frink, D.D. and Anthony, W.P. (2000) 'Political skill: An antidote for workplace stressors', *Academy of Management Executive*, 14, 115–23.

Perrewé, P.L., Zellars, K.L., Ferris, G.R., Rossi, A.M., Kacmar, C.J. and Ralston, D.A. (2004) 'Neutralizing job stressors: Political skill as an antidote to the dysfunctional consequences of role conflict stressors', *Academy of Management Journal*, 47, 141–52.

Perrewé, P.L., Zellars, K.L., Rossi, A.M., Ferris, G.R., Kacmar, C.J., Liu, Y., Zinko, R. and Hochwarter, W.A. (2005) 'Political skill: An antidote in the role overload – strain relationship', *Journal of Occupational Health Psychology*, 10, 239–50.

Sanders, T. (2005) *The Likeability Factor*. New York: Crown Publishers.

Schmidt, F.L. and Hunter, J.E. (1998) 'The validity and utility of selection methods in personnel psychology: Practical and theoretical implications of 85 years of research findings', *Psychological Bulletin*, 124, 262–74.

Sederberg, P.C. (1984) *The Politics of Meaning: Power and Explanation in the Construction of Social Reality*. Tuscon, AZ: University of Arizona Press.

Seibert, S.E., Kraimer, M.L. and Liden, R.C. (2001) 'A social capital theory of career success', *Academy of Management Journal*, 44, 219–37.

Seligman M.E.P. (1998) 'Building human strengths: Psychology's forgotten mission', *APA Monitor*, January, 2.

Seligman M.E.P. and Csikszentmihalyi M. (2000) 'Positive psychology', *American Psychologist*, 55, 5–14.

Semadar, A., Robins, G. and Ferris, G.R. (2006) 'Comparing the effects of multiple social effectiveness constructs on managerial performance', *Journal of Organizational Behavior*, 27, 443–61.

Spence, A.M. (1974) *Market Signaling: Informational Transfer in Hiring and Related Screening Processes*. Cambridge, MA: Harvard University Press.

Staw, B., Sutton, R. and Pelled, L. (1994) 'Employee positive emotions and favorable outcomes at the workplace', *Organizational Science*, 5, 51–71.

Treadway, D.C., Hochwarter, W.A., Ferris, G.R., Kacmar, C.J., Douglas, C., Ammeter, A.P. and Buckley, M.R. (2004) 'Leader political skill and employee reactions', *The Leadership Quarterly*, 15, 493–513.

Treadway, D.C., Hochwarter, W.A., Kacmar, C.J. and Ferris, G.R. (2005) 'Political will, political skill, and political behavior', *Journal of Organizational Behavior*, 26, 229–45.

Wayne, S.J. and Liden, R.C. (1995) 'Effects of impression management on performance ratings: A longitudinal study', *Academy of Management Journal*, 38, 232–60.

Wright, J.P. (1979) *On a Clear Day You Can See General Motors*. New York: Avon Book.

10

Forgiveness in Organizations

Kim S. Cameron

The examination of forgiveness in organizations has emerged from the new field of study called Positive Organizational Scholarship (POS) (Cameron et al., 2003). POS advocates the investigation of what goes right in organizations rather than what goes wrong, what is life-giving rather than life-depleting, what is experienced as good rather than bad, what is inspiring rather than distressing, and what brings joy and inspiration rather than anxiety and stress. It seeks to balance the traditional emphases in organizational studies toward factors such as competition, problem solving, reciprocity, adversarial negotiation, uncertainty, resistance to change, legal contracting, or financial capital as the key indicator of worth with more positive, elevating dynamics. It seeks to understand the highest potentiality of human systems.

Of course, positive phenomena often cannot be understood without also understanding their opposites, and positive and negative dynamics are frequently correlated. Human excellence and flourishing are often products of difficult and challenging circumstances rather than idyllic and pleasurable circumstances. Thus, the study of positive phenomena is not wholly one-sided, because the positive and the negative are often causally intertwined. This is certainly the case with the study of forgiveness in organizations. Forgiveness is not a relevant phenomenon unless negative events have occurred and harm has been produced. For example, when organizations downsize and eliminate the jobs of employees, or when tragic events occur such as a mine disaster or an airplane crash, forgiveness becomes an important consideration in whether organizations heal and move forward or whether they languish and become mired in retribution. Understanding the negative, in these cases, is a prerequisite to investigating the positive.

Whereas forgiveness is a commonly practiced virtue, its definition is oft-misunderstood, so this chapter first discusses the definition of forgiveness and differentiates it from other terms with which it is frequently confused. Next, empirical research examining the effects of forgiveness on organizational performance is summarized, and finally, some leadership prescriptions are offered for facilitating forgiveness in organizations that have experienced trauma or injury.

An inattention to organizational forgiveness

Forgiveness is one of the relatively few universal human virtues (Peterson and Seligman, 2004), meaning that it represents a fundamental moral good. All of the world's major religious traditions – Buddhism, Christianity, Hinduism, Islam, Judaism – consider forgiveness a virtue to which human beings should aspire (McCullough and Worthington, 1999; Rye et al., 2000). At the same time, forgiveness is among the least understood virtues and one of the most difficult to develop. On the one hand, because minor abrasions occur in almost all human interactions, most people are practiced forgivers of small offenses. In most interpersonal interactions, forgiveness is commonplace. People regularly overlook and move beyond minor abrasions and petty offenses that arise in the course of everyday interactions. In organizations, however, forgiveness is less common, less understood, less advocated, and less valued. Justice, retribution, and triumph are far more prized values in the competitive world of economic and social exchange, and the institutionalization of collective forgiveness in most organizational settings is not customary.

One reason is because forgiveness has often been treated as exclusively an intrapsychic phenomenon (Enright and Coyle, 1998; Worthington et al., 2000). It is claimed to occur only within a single individual and is not a social phenomenon at all. Collective forgiveness is said to be fiction. The abandonment of anger and retribution is a personal cognitive and emotional change – that is, forgiveness requires abandoning negative affect and a desire for retribution – but, it is argued, a social component is not present. An individual can forgive, for example, without re-establishing a relationship with the offender or without interacting with another at all. Forgiveness is mental and emotional, not social.

On the other hand, other scholars have highlighted the social components of forgiveness, and they have argued that internal changes are frequently interrelated with behavioral changes. Forgiveness involves individual change to be sure, but it also involves a change in relationships. Interpersonal relationships may be altered after an offense independent of any cognitive or affective change that might occur.

In a nutshell, forgiveness may be best understood as having two distinct dimensions: It is both an internal mental/emotional state and an interpersonal act. It can be a process that goes on entirely inside the mind of the victim, or it can be a transaction that occurs between two people, even without much in the way of inner processing. (Baumeister et al., 1998: 86)

Another reason for inattention to organization level forgiveness is because of its different manifestations. Bright's (2005) research on forgiveness in a transportation company argued that all people carry with them certain expectations regarding how the world should work, how people should treat one another, how organizational policies should function, what constitutes appropriate language, what moral or ethical codes should be practiced, and so on. The operative word is 'should', in that these expectations relate to what is right and wrong, appropriate and inappropriate. So long as experiences conform to expectations, no offense occurs. However, when a violation of normative expectations transpires, the immediate reaction is negativity, and it is often demonstrated by reactions such as anger, defensiveness, retaliation, or frustration. This 'dissonance and distress' (Yamhure Thompson and Shahen, 2003: 407) is a normal outgrowth of a mismatch between expectations and experiences.

Upon experiencing initial negativity, Bright (2005) found that people tend to respond in one of three ways – begrudging, neutralizing, or transcendence. Begrudging means that people continue to feel hostile, expect retribution, and foster negative feelings – which is not a forgiving response at all. Neutralizing refers to abandoning negative feelings and putting aside the sense of offense. This was labeled 'pragmatic' forgiving by Bright, usually pursued for a utilitarian reason. The third response replaces negative feelings with positive feelings, and a sense of injury is replaced by a sense of empathy and even love. Bright referred to this alternative as 'transcendent' forgiveness. People attempt to identify what good can come from the offense, positivity replaces negativity, and harmful events become interpreted as an opportunity for learning.

Forgiveness occurs, in other words, when resentment, negative judgment, bitterness, and indifferent behavior are abandoned. But when those negative emotions, attitudes, and behaviors are replaced by positive emotions, affirmative motivations, and prosocial behavior toward the offender, forgiveness becomes an uplifting and inspirational experience, not merely a neutral state (Cameron and Caza, 2002; McCullough and Witvliet, 2002). Most writing regarding forgiveness heretofore has focused on a neutralizing response to offense – abandoning negative feelings – so less is known about a positive or transcendent response to forgiveness.

A third reason for inattention to organizational forgiveness is that it is not differentiated from other related, but conceptually distinct, concepts such as pardoning, condoning, excusing, forgetting, denying, minimizing, or trusting (Enright and Coyle, 1998; McCullough et al., 2000). Forgiveness is distinct from pardoning, for example, because pardoning refers to sparing an offender from legal penalties. Forgiving a perpetrator of an offense is independent of whether or not the justice system acts against the offender. Forgiveness may be present even as penalties are assessed for the damage done. Likewise, forgiveness is distinct from condoning and excusing, which imply that those who have been harmed accept or justify the offense. To decide that the damage or injury was not the fault of the perpetrator or that a reasonable provocation accounted for the harm is to condone or excuse the offense. Responsibility for producing harm is removed from the offender by assuming that real offense has not occurred. Overlooking, excusing, and condoning are theoretically not forms of forgiveness at all since the perpetrator of harm is determined to have done nothing wrong.

Forgiveness is also distinct from forgetting. One need not erase the memory of the offense in order to offer forgiveness. In fact, Smedes (1984: 60, 35) argued that forgetting, 'may be a dangerous way to escape the inner surgery of the heart that we call forgiving'. Nor is forgiveness the same as denial that harm was done. Denial occurs when an offended party refuses to acknowledge the gravity of the harm, reduces the severity of the offense, suppresses anger, or diminishes the significance of the experienced trauma. These mechanisms are often used to avoid the effort involved in facing the consequences of the offense squarely, but they are not required for forgiveness to occur (Fitzgibbons, 1986). Offended parties may experience anger, even rage, aimed at the transgressor. Yet, forgiveness may ensue as emotions, attitudes, and behaviors are transformed over time, and, importantly, forgiveness usually does take time. Finally, forgiveness is distinct from *trusting*. Offenders need not be trusted just because they are forgiven. Abandoning negative emotions does not require that trust be re-established, even though a social relationship is renewed. Victims may not be sure that the offender will not do harm again, but offering forgiveness to an offender now does not depend on the offender's future behavior.

A definition of forgiveness in organizations

Forgiveness in organizations occurs, then, when emotional, attitudinal, cognitive, and behavioral changes transpire after harm or wrong-doing has been experienced. Negative feelings, bitterness, resentment, desire for revenge, or retaliatory behavior are abandoned and replaced by a neutralized position at a minimum, and by an increase in positive emotions, affirmative motivations, and prosocial behavior in the ideal. Forgiveness occurs in organizations when the collective group reframes an offense such that they adopt a positive, prosocial, learning oriented response to the violation. The organization and its members are able to move past the trauma and pursue an optimistic and positive future.

Despite misconceptions associating forgiveness with weakness or timidity, experiencing full forgiveness is an indication of remarkable strength and discipline. Forgiveness is anything but a display of frailty or lack of resolve. Acquiring full forgiveness is difficult because it involves a transformation – new mindsets and new behavioral patterns – not just a minor adjustment in cognition and conduct (Cameron and Caza, 2002). It may involve abandoning what is deeply felt, habitual, and previously embraced as a way of life. Organizational culture change may be required.

> To let go of justified anger and hurt, to think about the betrayal and the betrayer in a new light, to give up the well-deserved right to hurt back – all of these call for change at many levels: cognitive, affective, relational, behavioral, volitional, and spiritual. (Pargament and Rye, 1998: 63)

Forgiveness is not an all-or-nothing, present-or-absent phenomenon. Rather, it may vary in the form that it takes in organizations. For example, Enright and the Human Development Study Group (1994) pointed out that forgiveness may be manifest in stages similar to those proposed in Kohlberg's (1981) moral development model. Following Kohlberg's logic, a progression from stage 1 through stage 6 represents a progression from a less comprehensive stage of forgiveness to a stage where a more complete transformation has been experienced. Specifically, the first two stages of forgiveness are based on revenge and restitution. 'We will forgive only if the offender is punished, suffers the same kind of pain we experienced, and is required to submit restitution.' The third and fourth stages are based on societal expectation and authority. 'We will forgive if others (e.g. stakeholders) expect it or if a superordinate authority (e.g., the bankruptcy court) indicates that we should. The fifth and sixth stages are based on social relationships and on love. We will forgive if it will re-establish good relationships and restore peace or tranquility. Or, we will forgive because of our ability to love the offender, regardless of conditions, requests, attitudes, or behaviors of that offender.' The first five stages all are dependent on external conditions (e.g. retribution, justice, external expectations), so that forgiveness is a reactive response motivated by external factors. Only in the sixth stage does forgiveness take place because of the internal attributes of the forgiver. Hence, whereas a transformation may eventually occur in each stage, only in the sixth stage is the transformation unconditional, proactive, and a product of internalized virtuousness (Cameron et al., 2004).

One more distinction should be made regarding the concept of forgiveness in organizations. It relates to the difference between a single forgiving response and the internalized attribute of forgiveness. Forgiveness of a single offense, for example, may not indicate a capacity for or a disposition toward forgiveness in an organization. A forgiving response is more likely, for instance, when three conditions exist: (1) the offender asks for forgiveness or expresses contrition; (2) the effects of the offense are not severe; and (3) the offense is unintentional (Sandage et al., 2000). A disposition toward forgiveness exists, however, regardless of these external conditions, and it is demonstrated even in the presence of severe, intentional damage, and where no remorse is demonstrated. It is the attribute of forgiveness – or dispositional forgiveness – rather than a single forgiving response, that is of interest when studying forgiveness in organizational settings.

Dispositional forgiveness, in other words, is a stable characteristic, consistent across context and time. In organizations, it is an institutionalized capacity to move beyond trauma and harm and to adopt a positive orientation. In theory, almost any organization could demonstrate forgiveness of a single misfortune or injury (as is the case in interpersonal interactions) by not dwelling on the past offense and by excusing the perpetrators. On the other hand, few organizations have developed the virtue of forgiveness which is demonstrated more comprehensively and universally. Investigating such organizations is an important area of interest in the field of Positive Organizational Scholarship.

Forgiveness and performance

The effects of forgiveness have been quite widely studied in the field of Positive Psychology, but much less is known about forgiveness in organizations. For the most part, the presence of forgiveness has a favorable impact on individuals and organizations. For example, at the individual level, a growing body of evidence has linked chronic states of *unforgiveness* (including anger, hostility, resentment, and fear) to adverse health outcomes (Kaplan, 1992; Williams, 1989). Thoreson et al. (2000) found that when people are unforgiving, allostatic load (the body's stress response) increases along with the accompanying negative physiological effects over time. Witvliet et al. (2002) reported that unforgiving responses are associated with significantly more depression, anger, and anxiety as well as cardiovascular problems and immune system compromise. Unforgiving responses (e.g. rehearsing the hurt) eroded health by activating intense cardiovascular and sympathetic nervous system reactivity. Moreover, unforgiving responses of blame, anger, and hostility were found to be associated with coronary heart disease and premature death (Affleck et al., 1987; Tennen and Affleck, 1990). Acute and chronic stress (Kiecolt-Glaser et al., 1998) and poor immune system functioning and cardiovascular disease were also found to be associated with unforgiveness (Ader et al., 1991).

Forgiving responses, on the other hand, have been found to buffer ill-health by decreasing allostatic load and by promoting physiological and psychological healing (Thoreson et al., 2000). Interventions that emphasized forgiveness were found to reduce coronary problems as well as improve mental health (Al-Mabuk et al., 1995; Coyle and Enright, 1997; Freedman and Enright, 1996; Friedman et al., 1986). Evidence also suggests that forgiving another enhances cardiovascular fitness, emotional stability, mental health, learning behavior, creativity, and life happiness (McCullough et al., 2000; Sandage et al., 2000). Berry and Worthington (2001) reported that stressful interpersonal relationships are associated with alterations in the endocrine systems, the pituitary glands, and the adrenal hormones, and that forgiveness serves a buffering function in minimizing the harmful effects of these kinds of stress. They found that the quality of social relationships was significantly predicted by two dispositional attributes: unforgiveness (trait anger) and forgiveness (love and empathy). The more the relationship is characterized by forgiveness, the healthier it is.

Forgiveness is further associated with long-term benefits to social adjustment, physical health, and mental health (Kaplan, 1992; Thoresen et al., 2000; Williams, 1989). Emotional and social stability are positively correlated with dispositional forgiveness, as is greater life satisfaction, self-esteem, and more complete recovery from disease (Ashton et al., 1998). Moreover, forgiveness is negatively correlated with detrimental personality factors such as neuroticism, worry, anxiety, depression, and hostility and is negatively correlated with physical illness (McCullough et al., 2000). In brief, developing the virtue of forgiveness has been shown to have benefits to physical, mental, emotional, and social health in individuals.

At the organizational level, the importance of forgiveness is dramatically illustrated by a quotation from Nobel laureate, Desmond Tutu (1998: xiii). Describing post-apartheid South Africa, he commented on the critical role of collective forgiveness:

> Ultimately, you discover that without forgiveness, there is no future. We recognize that the past cannot be remade through punishment ... There is no point in exacting vengeance now, knowing that it will be the cause for future vengeance by the offspring of those we punish. Vengeance leads only to revenge. Vengeance destroys those it claims and those who become intoxicated with it ... therefore, forgiveness is an absolute necessity for continued human existence.

Glynn (1994) observed that one explanation for the successful formation of the European Economic Union is forgiveness. Collectively speaking, the French, Dutch, and British forgave the Germans for the atrocities of the Second World War as did other damaged nations. Likewise, the reciprocal forgiveness demonstrated by the United States and Japan after the Second World War helps explain the flourishing economic and social interchange that developed in subsequent decades. Contrariwise, the lack of peace in certain war-torn areas of the world can be explained at least partly by the refusal of collectivities to forgive one another for past trespasses (Helmick and Petersen, 2001).

Forgiveness in organizations has been investigated empirically very sparsely, but forgiveness in small organizations such as families and therapy groups provides evidence that it is associated with collective outcomes such as higher morale and satisfaction, and greater social capital, trust, humanness, and caring relationships in organizations (McCullough et al., 2000). Moreover, since organizational forgiveness is manifested by a collective abandonment of grudges, bitterness, and blame, and the adoption of positive, forward-looking approaches in response to harm or damage, it is particularly relevant when organizations have experienced harm or unjust treatment, as in the case of downsizing.

Extensive research has shown that a large majority of organizations report a sense of injustice, personal and organizational injury, and irreparable damage as a result of cutbacks (Cameron, 1998). Almost all post-downsizing organizations develop negative internal attributes such as deteriorating morale, communication, trust, innovation, participative decision making, and flexibility. Increases in conflict, rigidity, scapegoating, secretiveness, politicking, fear, and short-term focus also occur. Because of these internal dysfunctions, organizational performance in areas such as employee turnover, quality, and productivity almost always suffer as well. Recovery from downsizing in spite of negative events would seem to be associated with the capacity of the organization to collectively forgive the perceived harm, to move forward optimistically, and to set aside negative emotions and attributions.

One study that explored this association measured six organizational virtues and three performance outcomes in organizations that had recently experienced downsizing and were suffering from its negative effects (Cameron et al., 2004). The six organizational virtues included dispositional forgiveness, restoration forgiveness, hope, compassion, respect, and integrity. The outcomes, measured via company records, included employee turnover, quality, and productivity. Findings from this study indicated that organizational forgiveness is significantly associated with improvements in productivity after downsizing as well as lower voluntary employee turnover. In the aftermath of downsizing, in other words, when most firms deteriorate in performance (Cameron et al., 1987), forgiveness appears to buffer negative effects and fosters the capability to move forward, to put aside feelings of injustice and harm, and to view the organization positively. Forgiveness appears to be a positive predictor of desired outcomes.

The positive effects of forgiveness on organizational performance can be explained by its buffering and amplifying benefits. That is, as one of the fundamental human virtues, forgiveness carries the buffering and amplifying benefits of virtuousness that have been uncovered in other studies of organizations. Virtuousness tends to buffer the organization from harm, and it amplifies positive effects (Cameron, 2003; Bright et al., 2006).

For example, a *buffering* effect is evident when organizations are more resilient to challenging circumstances, or when they are able to withstand stressful, difficult events. Virtuousness has been found to buffer the organization from the negative effects of downsizing, crises, or wrong-doing by enhancing three capabilities: resiliency, commitment, and a sense of efficacy (Dutton et al., 2002; Masten and Reed, 2002). Fostering virtuousness during prosperous times deepens and enhances resiliency, or the ability to absorb threat and trauma and to bounce back from adversity (Fredrickson, 2000). This occurs through enhancing the preservation of social capital and collective efficacy (Sutcliffe and Vogus, 2003). Resilience, healing, and restoration to former conditions are more likely.

Forgiveness also creates an *amplifying* effect within organizations (Cameron, 2003). This amplifying effect occurs in the following ways. First, observing virtuous behaviors such as forgiving responses produces positive emotions, leading to a replication of virtuousness and an elevation in positive well-being (Fredrickson, 2003). Because forgiveness transforms negative to positive emotions, it can lead to a contagion effect (Barsade, 2002), in which one person expresses forgiveness making others more likely to forgive. This, in turn, leads to a replication of virtuousness and an elevation in positive well-being (Fredrickson, 2003). In turn, positive emotions build high-quality relationships and increase social connections among organization members (Dutton and Heaphy, 2003). In addition, forgiving responses foster prosocial behavior. When people observe demonstrations of virtuousness, they feel compelled to join with and build upon their contributions causing a virtuous spiral of increasingly positive benefit in an organization (Feldman and Khademian, 2003).

Forgiveness and leadership

In addition to the positive effects of forgiveness on the performance of organizations and individuals, forgiveness is also an important attribute of leaders because it buffers them against the potential harm and distraction that can result from the mistakes, misdeeds, and offenses of others (Bright, 2005). Forgiveness functions as a lubricant to the friction that occurs during the natural course of human interaction in which the potential for inflicting or experiencing offense in an organization is an inherent possibility. Indeed, forgiveness is central to the establishment, preservation and maintenance of human relationships that make up and sustain organizations (Aquino et al., 2003).

Cameron (2001) summarized a set of leadership roles and responsibilities that emerged from investigations of high performing organizations that were characterized by institutionalized forgiveness and other virtues. In fostering and enabling forgiveness, these leaders were described as providing meaning, vision, legitimacy, and support.

1. Leaders acknowledged the trauma, harm, and injustice that their organization members experienced, but they defined the occurrence of hurtful events as an opportunity to move forward. A new target for action was identified.
2. Leaders associated the outcomes of the organization (e.g. its products and services) with a higher purpose that provided personal meaning for organization members. This higher purpose helped replace a focus

on self (e.g. a need for personal retribution) with a focus on a higher objective.
3. High standards of performance were not compromised. Forgiveness was not synonymous with tolerance of error. Forgiving mistakes did not mean excusing them or lowering expectations. Instead, forgiveness facilitated excellence, growth, and improvement rather than inhibiting it.
4. Leaders communicated that human development and human welfare were as important in organizational priorities as was the financial bottom line. Even when budgets were tight and resources constrained, support was given to human capital. When employees experienced understanding and support, as well as positive developmental experiences, they caught a vision of an avenue for moving past the injury. This support provided the foundation upon which positive financial performance could be re-built.
5. Since forgiveness was usually offered in partnership with other virtues, the common language used by leaders included the use of virtuous terms such as forgiveness, compassion, humility, courage, and love. Public expressions using virtuous language made it visible and legitimate for employees as well as external stakeholders to feel and behave virtuously.
6. Virtuous actions were highlighted, celebrated, and amplified through reinforcing structures, systems, and networks. Stories and scripts that define the core values of the organization contained examples of forgiveness and virtuousness. Organizational resources were made available to support expressions of success in moving past the trauma.

These leadership roles and responsibilities led to 10 prescriptions for leaders who aspire to enable and engender forgiveness when traumatic events occur. These prescriptions are not empirically based but merely flow logically from the leadership attributes listed above (Cameron, 2001). In facilitating forgiveness:

1. Acknowledge anger and resentment. Recognize that forgiveness does not occur quickly. Allow time for grieving.
2. Clarify the target of forgiveness. Identify the human beings involved – both offenders and victims. The target of forgiveness is people, not objects.
3. Provide opportunities for interaction and conversation. Forgiveness usually requires opportunities for verbal expressions, empathetic listening, and human support.
4. Demarcate the end of the hurtful or victim phase from the beginning of the healing and restoration phase, often with a symbolic event. Provide visible avenues to help people begin to move toward desirable objectives.
5. Provide opportunities to develop and display positive affect, often by doing good as well as doing well. Find ways for victims to serve others. Allow people to practice giving.

6. Honor justice and equity. Work toward justice for offenders as well as restoration for those harmed. Most people have difficulty forgiving in the absence of justice, apology, or restitution.
7. Create positive memories. Celebrate the best of the past, and move on. Hold a 'funeral' to memorialize victims, but articulate a bright, new future.
8. Provide reinforcement and resources for activities that help organization members progress toward meaningful, instrumental objectives. Foster an optimistic climate and a sense of hope.
9. Maintain leadership visibility and accessibility to those harmed in order to inspire confidence, clarify vision, and reinforce concern.
10. Gather and record stories and examples of virtuousness. Recount incidents where the organization fostered virtue.

Summary

The investigation of forgiveness in organizational life has largely been neglected. Systematic and rigorous studies of the development and demonstration of virtues such as forgiveness have been all but absent in organizational studies. This chapter defines forgiveness and distinguishes it from other related concepts, but, most importantly, it highlights the potential impact of forgiveness on employee behavior and its effects on organizational outcomes such as productivity and quality. Under conditions of organizational injury or trauma (such as when organizations downsize or tragic events occur), leaders have an especially important role to play in fostering and enabling forgiveness. Leadership roles and responsibilities emerging from an investigation of high performing, forgiving organizations are offered as guidelines.

References

Ader, R., Felten, D.L. and Cohen, N. (1991) *Psychoneuroimmunology*. San Diego: Academic Press.
Affleck, G., Tenen, H., Croog, S. and Levine, S. (1987) 'Causal attribution, perceived benefit, and morbidity after a heart attack: An eight-year study', *Journal of Consulting and Clinical Psychology*, 55, 29–35.
Al-Mabuk, R.H., Enright, R.D. and Cardis, P.A. (1995) 'Forgiving education with parentally love-deprived late adolescents', *Journal of Moral Education*, 24, 427–44.
Aquino, K., Grover, S.L., Goldman, B. and Folger, R. (2003) 'When push doesn't come to shove: Interpersonal forgiveness in workplace relationships', *Journal of Management Inquiry*, 12 (3), 209–16.
Ashton, M.C., Paunonen, S.V., Helmes, E. and Jackson, D.N. (1998) 'Kin altruism, reciprocal altruism, and the Big Five personality factors', *Evolution and Human Behavior*, 19, 243–55.
Barsade, S.G. (2002) 'The ripple effect: Emotional contagion and its influence on group behavior', *Administrative Science Quarterly*, 47 (4), 644–75.

Bauemeister, R.F., Exline, J.J. and Sommer, K.L. (1998) 'The victim role, grudge theory, and two dimensions of forgiveness', in E.L. Worthington (ed.) *Dimensions of Forgiveness: Psychological Research and Theological Perspectives* (pp. 9–28). Philadelphia, PA: Templeton Foundation Press.

Berry, Jack W. and Worthington, E.L. (2001) 'Forgivingness, relationship quality, stress while imagining relationship events, and physical and mental health', *Journal of Counseling Psychology*, 48, 447–55.

Bright, David S. (2005) 'Forgiveness and change: Begrudging, pragmatic, and transcendent responses to discomfiture in a unionized trucking company. Unpublished dissertation, Case Western Reserve University, Cleveland, OH (Dissertation Abstractions International).

Bright, D.S., Cameron, K.S. and Caza, A. (2006) 'The amplifying and buffering effects of virtuousness in downsized organizations', *Journal of Business Ethics* (in press).

Cameron, K.S. (1998) 'Strategic organizational downsizing: An extreme case', *Research in Organizational Behavior*, 20, 185–229.

Cameron, K.S. (2001) 'Leadership through organizational forgiveness', *Leading in Trying Times*. University of Michigan Business School, http://www.bus.umich. edu/le...p_Through_Organizational_Forgiveness.htm

Cameron, K.S. (2003) 'Organizational virtuousness and performance', in K.S. Cameron, J.E. Dutton and R.E. Quinn (eds) *Positive Organizational Scholarship: Foundations of a New Discipline* (pp. 48–65). San Francisco: Berrett-Koehler.

Cameron, K. and Caza, A. (2002) 'Organizational and leadership virtues and the role of forgiveness', *Journal of Leadership and Organizational Studies*, 9 (1), 33–48.

Cameron, K.S., Bright, D.S. and Caza, A. (2004) 'Exploring the relationships between organizational virtuousness and performance', *American Behavioral Scientist*, 47 (6), 766–90.

Cameron, K.S., Dutton, J.E. and Quinn, R.E. (eds) (2003) *Positive Organizational Scholarship: Foundations of a New Discipline*. San Francisco: Berrett-Koehler.

Cameron, K.S., Kim, M.U. and Whetten, D.A. (1987) 'Organizational effects of decline and turbulence', *Administrative Science Quarterly*, 32, 222–40.

Coyle, C. and Enright, R.D. (1997) 'Forgiveness intervention with post-abortion men', *Journal of Consulting and Clinical Psychology*, 65, 1042–46.

Dutton, J.E., Frost, P.J., Worline, M.C., Lilius, J.M. and Kanov, J.M. (2002) 'Leading in times of trauma', *Harvard Business Review*, 80, 54–61.

Dutton, J.E. and Heaphy, E.D. (2003) 'The power of high-quality connections', in K.S. Cameron, J.E. Dutton and R.E. Quinn (eds) *Positive Organizational Scholarship: Foundations of a New Discipline* (pp. 263–78). San Francisco: Berrett-Koehler.

Enright, R.D. and Coyle, C. (1998) 'Researching the process model of forgiveness within psychological interventions', in E.L. Worthington (ed.) *Dimensions of Forgiveness* (pp. 139–61). Philadelphia: Templeton Foundation Press.

Enright, R.D. and the Human Development Study Group (1994) 'Piaget on the moral development of forgiveness: Identity and reciprocity', *Human Development*, 37, 63–80.

Feldman, M.S. and Khademian, A.M. (2003) 'Empowerment and cascading vitality', in K.S. Cameron, J.E. Dutton and R.E. Quinn (eds) *Positive Organizational Scholarship: Foundations of a New Discipline* (pp. 343–58). San Francisco: Berrett-Koehler.

Fitzgibbons, R.P. (1986) 'The cognitive and emotive uses of forgiveness in the treatment of anger', *Psychotherapy*, 23, 629–33.

Fredrickson, B.L. (2000) 'Why positive emotions matter in organizations: Lessons from the broaden-and-build theory', *The Psychologist – Manager Journal*, 4, 131–42.

Fredrickson, B.L. (2001) 'The role of positive emotions in positive psychology: The broaden-and-build theory of positive emotions', *American Psychologist*, 56, 218–26.

Fredrickson, B.L. (2003) 'Positive emotions and upward spirals in organizations', in K.S. Cameron, J.E. Dutton and R.E. Quinn (eds) *Positive Organizational Scholarship: Foundations of a New Discipline* (pp. 163–75). San Francisco: Berrett-Koehler.

Freedman, S.R. and Enright, R.D. (1996) 'Forgiveness as an intervention with incest survivors', *Journal of Consulting and Clinical Psychology*, 64, 983–92.

Friedman, M., Thoreson, C., Gill, J., Ulmer, D., Powell, L.H., Price, V.A., Brown, B., Thompson, L., Rabin, D., Breall, W.S., Bourg, W., Levy, R. and Dixon, T. (1986) 'Alteractions of Type A behavior and its effects on cardiac recurrence in post myocardial infarction patients: Summary results of the coronary prevention recurrence project', *American Heart Journal*, 112, 653–65.

Glynn, Patrick (1994) 'Toward a politics of forgiveness', *American Enterprise*, 5, 48–53.

Helmick, R.G. and Petersen, R.L. (2001) *Forgiveness and Reconciliation: Religion, Public Policy, and Conflict*. Philadelphia: Templeton Foundation Press.

Kaplan, B.H. (1992) 'Social health and the forgiving heart: The Type B story', *Journal of Behavioral Medicine*, 15, 3–14.

Kiecolt-Glaser, K.J., Glaser, R., Cacioppo, J.T. and Malarkey, W.B. (1998) 'Marital stress: Immunological, neuroendocrine, and autonomic correlates', in S.M. McCann and J.M. Lipton (eds) *Annuals of the New York Academy of Sciences, Volume 840: Neuroimmunomodulation: Molecular Aspects, Integrative Systems, and Clinical Advances* (pp. 656–63). New York: New York Academy of Sciences.

Kohlberg, L. (1981) *Essays in Moral Development*. New York: Harper Row.

Masten, A.S. and Reed, G.J. (2002) 'Resilience in development', in C.R. Snyder and S.J. Lopez (eds) *Handbook of Positive Psychology* (pp. 74–88). New York: Oxford University Press.

McCullough, M.E. and Witvliet, C.V. (2002) 'The psychology of forgiveness', in C.R. Snyder and S.J. Lopez (eds) *Handbook of Positive Psychology* (pp. 446–58). London: Oxford University Press.

McCullough, M.E. and Worthington, E.L. (1999) 'Religion and the forgiving personality', *Journal of Personality*, 67, 1141–64.

McCullough, M.E., Pargament, K.I. and Thoreson, C. (2000) *Forgiveness: Theory, Research, and Practice*. New York: Guilford.

Pargament, K.I. and Rye, M.S. (1998) 'Forgiveness as a method of religious coping', in E.L. Worthington (ed.) *Dimensions of Forgiveness: Psychological Research and Theological Perspectives* (pp. 59–78). Philadelphia: Templeton Foundation Press.

Peterson, C. and Seligman, M.E.P. (eds) (2004) *Character Strengths and Virtues: A Handbook and Classification*. New York: Oxford University Press.

Quinn, R.E. and Cameron, K.S. (1988) *Paradox and Transformation: Towards a Theory of Change in Organizations*. Cambridge, MA: Ballinger.

Rye, M.S., Pargament, K.I., Ali, M.A., Beck, G.L., Dorff, E.N., Hallisey, C., Narayanan, V. and Williams, J.G. (2000) 'Religious perspectives on forgiveness', in M.E. McCullough, K.I., Pargament and C. Thoreson, *Forgiveness: Theory, Research, and Practice* (pp. 17–40). New York: Guilford.

Sandage, S.J., Worthington, E.L., Hight, T.L. and Berry, J.W. (2000) 'Seeking forgiveness: Theoretical context and initial empirical study', *Journal of Psychology and Theology*, 28, 21–35.

Smedes, L.B. (1984) 'Stations on the journey from forgiveness to hope', in E.L. Everett (ed.) *Dimensions of Forgiveness: Psychological Research and Theological Perspectives* (pp. 341–54). Philadelphia: Templeton Foundation Press.

Sutcliffe, K.M. and Vogus, T.J. (2003) 'Organizing for resilience', in K.S. Cameron, J.E. Dutton and R.E. Quinn (eds) *Positive Organizational Scholarship: Foundations of a New Discipline* (pp. 94–110). San Franciso: Berrett-Koehler.

Tennen, H. and Affleck, G. (1990) 'Blaming others for threatening events', *Psychological Bulletin*, 108, 209–32.

Thoresen, C.E., Harris, A.H. and Luskin, F. (2000) 'Forgiveness and health: An unanswered question', in M.E. McCullough, K.I. Pargament and C. Thoreson, *Forgiveness: Theory, Research, and Practice* (pp. 163–190), New York: Guilford.

Tutu, D (1998) 'Without forgiveness there is no future', in R.D. Enright and J. North (eds) *Exploring Forgiveness*. Madison: University of Wisconsin Press.

Tutu, D. (1999) *No Future without Forgiveness*. New York: Doubleday.

Williams, R. (1989) *The Trusting Heart*. New York: Random House.

Witvliet, C V.O., Ludwig, T. E. and Vander Laan, K.L. (2001) 'Granting forgiveness or harboring grudges: Implications for emotion, physiology, and health', *Psychological Science*, 12, 117–23.

Worthington, E.L., Kurusu, T.A., Collins, W., Berry, J.W., Ripley, J.S. and Baier, S.N. (2000) 'Forgiveness usually takes time: A lesson learned by studying interventions to promote forgiveness', *Journal of Psychology and Theology*, 28, 3–20.

Yamhure Thompson, L. and Shahen, P.E. (2003) 'Forgiveness in the workplace', in R.C. Giacalone and C.L. Jurkiewicz (eds) *Handbook of Spirituality and Organizational Performance* (pp. 405–20). New York: M.E. Sharpe.

11

Self-Engagement at Work

Thomas W. Britt, James M. Dickinson, Tiffany M. Greene-Shortridge, and Eric S. McKibben

As individuals go to work and carry out various tasks, there will be times when they are invested in the quality of their work and feel responsibility for and commitment to superior job performance. There will also be times when they feel disengaged from their work or from certain aspects of their job, consequently withdrawing or disconnecting from a given area of performance. In the present chapter we argue that engaging the self in work serves to commit an individual to superior performance, and that such engagement has consequences for motivation, affect, and performance. Although most prior authors have viewed engagement in work as having primarily positive consequences, we present a more complex analysis, ultimately arguing that engaging the self in work can have positive consequences when the employee has the resources and aptitudes necessary for successful performance, but may have negative consequences when substantial impediments exist to effective performance.

In the present chapter we will first address issues in the conceptualization and operationalization of job engagement. We spend some time on these issues, because researchers have conceptualized and measured job engagement in different ways, and we hope to bring some integrative order to these viewpoints. We then address the predictors of engagement in work. Researchers examining employees in a variety of occupations and organizations have consistently shown specific variables to be predictive of job engagement. We then summarize research on the consequences of job engagement for health and performance. The final section of our chapter addresses areas in need of future research. Throughout this chapter we hope to show that engagement in work is a construct that falls within the purview of positive organizational behavior (Luthans, 2002; Wright, 2003), in that job engagement is a desirable motivational state to possess at work. However, we also note the importance of understanding that even 'positive' variables such as job engagement can have maladaptive consequences under certain conditions, and that models of positive organizational behavior need to integrate these conditions into comprehensive theories.

The conceptualization and measurement of engagement at work

Different conceptualizations of job engagement

My (TWB) interest in job engagement emerged out of a more general interest in the determinants of responsibility. Schlenker and colleagues (1994) developed the Triangle Model of Responsibility to address issues of accountability, including what it means to hold one another responsible for conduct in a way that leads to social evaluation and sanctioning. The theory integrated prior approaches to responsibility and has been used to predict when people will hold others responsible for their conduct, as well as the types of information people seek when they need to draw conclusions about an individual's level of responsibility (Schlenker et al., 1994). The model has recently been used to understand when an individual will be engaged in particular tasks and domains (Britt, 1999, 2003a; see also Schlenker, 1997). Britt and his colleagues have defined job engagement as feeling responsible for and committed to superior job performance, so that job performance 'matters' to the individual (Britt, 1999, 2003b; Britt and Bliese, 2003).

Because employees who are engaged in their work feel a sense of personal responsibility for their job performance, the outcomes that occur at work have greater implications for their identity. Therefore, to be engaged in work is also to care about and be committed to performing well. Britt et al. (2005) used a political analogy to further illustrate this approach toward defining job engagement. US presidents are sometimes judged on the basis of their level of engagement toward a particular policy or issue. For example, a president may be accused of not being engaged in the Middle East peace process, or in a crisis occuring in another continent. Presidents who are criticized for a lack of engagement in particular issues are often seen as not taking personal responsibility for the outcome of a particular challenge and thus not appearing to care about the issue. On the other hand, a president who is engaged in a particular issue is often viewed as taking on responsibility for solving the problem and being committed to reaching a solution. In a similar manner, our approach to job engagement emphasizes employees feeling personally responsible for and caring about their job performance outcomes. Given the above definition, we have measured job engagement as a variable with items assessing perceived responsibility for job performance, commitment to job performance, and whether performance matters to the individual (Britt, 1999, 2003b; Britt and Bliese, 2003; Britt et al., 2001, 2005). These items assess a single construct with demonstrated reliability, with Cronbach Alpha's typically approaching or exceeding .90.

Most other researchers have viewed engagement in work as a multi-faceted construct consisting of two or more separate components (Harter et al., 2003; May et al., 2004; Rothbard, 2001; Schaufeli et al., 2002). Many of these prior authors developed models of job engagement based on the seminal work of Kahn (1990). In fact, this paper can be seen as jump-starting interest in the construct of job engagement. Using a qualitative, interview-based method, Kahn (1990) explored the conditions that lead to 'moments' of engagement and disengagement at work. Kahn laid out a carefully planned methodology, including the examination of two very different samples: counselors at a children's summer camp and employees of a thriving architectural firm. He chose these two settings because of their dissimilarities, in order to maximize the generalizability of his findings. Kahn observed these two groups of workers, interviewed them, and explored archival data to discover the indicators of engagement at work. Kahn defined engagement in work as self-employment and expression physically, cognitively, and emotionally during role performances, and asked employees to recall the conditions under which they experienced this state. Kahn found that engagement in work had the ability to fluctuate frequently within an individual, decreasing the potential for it to be fully accounted for by individual differences.

Rothbard (2001) examined engagement in both work and family roles, and whether engagement in one role either depletes or enhances engagement in a second role. In this work, Rothbard conceptualized engagement as two distinct, though interrelated, factors. The first factor was that of attention, operationalized as 'time spent thinking and concentrating on a role'. The second factor was labeled absorption, operationalized as 'losing track of time and becoming engrossed in role performance' (Rothbard, 2001: 665), and can be considered similar to Csikszentmihalyi's (1990) construct of flow. The use of these two factors came from recommendations by Kahn (1990). Rothbard distinguished engagement from other similar constructs, explaining that engagement represents a level of psychological presence in an activity, whereas other constructs such as role identification and role commitment are potential reasons for becoming engaged.

May et al. (2004) conducted a quantitative study of engagement in work also based on Kahn's (1990) ethnographic work. May et al. (2004) first made clear the distinction between job engagement and the related constructs of job involvement (Brown and Leigh, 1996) and flow. First, they explained that job involvement is focused on the degree to which a job is tied to one's self-image, whereas engagement is concerned with the ways in which a person invests in performing a job. Second, while flow has been considered a peak cognitive state during an activity, engagement concerns cognitive, emotional, and physical investment in work.

Therefore, May et al. (2004) defined engagement as Kahn did, as self-employment and expression physically, cognitively, and emotionally during role performances (Kahn, 1990: 694). They conducted their study with administrative employees of an insurance company, and attempted to measure engagement as three separate cognitive (e.g. 'Performing my job is so absorbing that I forget about everything else'), emotional (e.g. 'I really put my heart into my job'), and physical ('I exert a lot of energy performing my job') factors. However, a factor analysis of survey responses did not converge to this three-factor solution, so scores were averaged across these three dimensions to form a single measure of engagement.

Yet another approach to the conceptualization and measurement of engagement has grown out of research on job burnout. Maslach et al. (2001) have argued that job engagement can be seen as the opposite of job burnout, and is characterized by high levels of energy, involvement in work, and a sense of personal efficacy at work. These authors see job burnout and job engagement as opposite ends of a single continuum, rather than as two separate dimensions. However, Schaufeli et al. (2002) argued that job engagement and job burnout should be conceptualized and assessed as two independent, but correlated, constructs. These authors argued that engagement at work is characterized by vigor, dedication, and absorption, and provided evidence through structural equation modeling for separate constructs of burnout and engagement.

Finally, Harter et al. (2003) have recently defined employee engagement as 'a combination of cognitive and emotional antecedent variables in the workplace' (p. 206). These authors proposed that employee engagement is best assessed by a diverse set of 12 items addressing such factors as knowing what is expected at work, having the necessary resources to do well, receiving recognition or praise, and having fellow employees who are committed to doing quality work. Although the authors argue that these variables are the antecedents of employee engagement, no evidence is presented to show these variables contribute to an independent assessment of engagement.

Integrating the theoretical perspectives on job engagement

Although there are clearly diverse conceptualizations and assessments of job engagement, these viewpoints share important commonalities. For example, Britt (1999, 2003a), May et al. (2004), Maslach et al. (2001), and Schaufeli et al. (2002) all emphasize that job engagement entails the individual being dedicated to successful performance through emotional investment in performance. Beyond this commonality, there clearly exist differences of opinion regarding which additional factors and measures are necessary to adequately capture job engagement. These differences stem from what we see as a lack of differentiating the outcomes and predictors of job engagement from the assessment of job engagement itself. For example, our conceptualization of job engagement emphasizes individuals feeling responsible for job performance and caring about the outcomes of performance (Britt, 1999, 2003b; Britt et al., 2005). Therefore, engagement is a motivational state created by beliefs of personal responsibility and caring. We see such components as vigor, physical exertion, attention, effort, and absorption as immediate outcomes of being engaged in work that have implications for the more distal outcomes of job performance and health.

Furthermore, we believe some of the constructs offered by other researchers as indicators of engagement should actually be considered antecedents of engagement. For example, we see efficacy at work (Maslach et al., 2001) as a predictor of job engagement. In addition, we see many items used by Harter et al. (2003) as addressing predictors of job engagement (e.g. knowing what is expected at work, having the resources necessary to do well). Recognizing these distinctions will become especially important later in the chapter when we address the consequences of job engagement. As we shall see, viewing job engagement as involving the investment of the self-system in performance has implications for the effects that engagement in work will have on health and performance.

In addition, we believe that using multiple measures addressing different constructs to assess job engagement will invariably lead to confusion regarding which aspects of job engagement are related to important outcomes (see Carver, 1989). For example, imagine that researchers conduct a study examining the relationship between job engagement and ratings of job performance where job engagement is assessed through separate measures of vigor, absorption, and dedication. How do the researchers test the relationship between job engagement and job performance? Do they perform separate correlations between the predictors and job performance? Do they combine the three dimensions, and then examine the correlation? Do they conduct structural equation modeling where the three subscales assess a higher order construct of job engagement, and then relate this to job performance? Do they conduct a multiple regression showing that each sub-dimension predicts variance in performance ratings? All these strategies leave open the possibility that one or more of the sub-dimensions are more important than the others in explaining the predictive power of the overall construct.

For this reason and because of the reasons outlined above, we have chosen to measure job engagement with a single scale, and to clearly distinguish between the assessment of engagement itself and the predictors and consequences of job engagement. However, in discussing the predictors and consequences of job engagement below, we also review research by the authors described above. Interestingly, researchers using different conceptualizations and assessments of job engagement have found similar sets of variables that predict engagement in work. Figure 11.1 provides a model that will serve to guide our discussion of the predictors and consequences of job engagement. This model specifies those conditions hypothesized to give rise to job engagement, and how immediate outcomes of job engagement, such as absorption and effort, and conditions of the work environment, are hypothesized to influence health and job performance.

Predictors of engagement in work

Job-related attributes

Britt (1999, 2003b) used the Triangle Model of Responsibility (Schlenker, 1997; Schlenker et al., 1994) to predict when soldiers would become personally engaged in their jobs in different settings. According to the Triangle Model, felt responsibility for any given event or performance domain is a function of relationships between the event or domain itself, the prescriptions or rules that describe what is required for superior performance, and the identity images possessed by the actor that may or may not be relevant to the event or domain. Personal responsibility, and therefore job engagement, should be high when a set of clear guidelines governs performance in the event or domain (high job clarity), the individual feels a strong sense of personal control and contribution for their performance (high job control), the individual feels the performance domain is relevant to central aspects of his or her identity and/or training (high relevance of job to identity), and when the performance or event in question has important consequences (high job importance). These predictors of job engagement are shown in Figure 11.1.

Britt (1999) examined job engagement among soldiers on a military operation and at their home base, and found that job clarity, job control, and identity-relevance independently predicted job engagement in two different samples. The ability of these three variables to independently predict job engagement was also replicated in a study of US Army Rangers (Britt, 2003b). In addition, job importance has been found to predict job engagement (Britt et al., 2001). Britt (1999) also found evidence for the utility of the Triangle Model in predicting job engagement by examining differences in engagement between units deployed to Saudi Arabia. All units were Patriot Air Defense Artillery companies trained to fire patriot missiles to intercept scud missiles. However, one of these units was assigned to do a much different task (basically perform the mission of an infantry unit) and was given little control over their job. However, the requirements for their job were clear. Britt (1999) found that this unit scored lower than the other units on job relevance and job control, but not on job clarity. Furthermore, this unit scored lower than the other units on job engagement. Finally, the differences between the units on job engagement were reduced to non-significance when controlling for job control and job relevance, supporting these components of the model as determinants of the unit differences in job engagement.

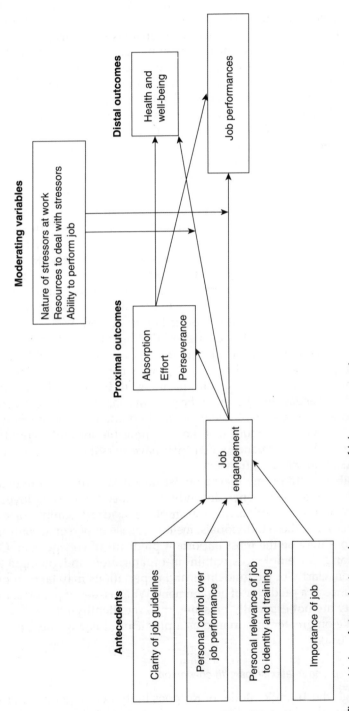

Figure 11.1   *Antecedents and consequences of job engagement*

May et al. (2004) also conducted a comprehensive evaluation of predictors of job engagement. Building on the qualitative work of Kahn (1990), these authors argued that the proximal determinants of job engagement would be perceiving work as personally meaningful, feeling confident at being able to meet demands at work, and feeling safe at being oneself at work. The first two of these proximal predictors are best considered job-related attributes. May et al. (2004) also examined correlates of these proximal predictors. Meaningfulness of work was hypothesized to be predicted by having an enriching job and sensing that the job fit with the employee's identity; confidence at meeting work demands was hypothesized to be predicted by having emotional resources at work, being low in self-consciousness, and being involved in many outside activities. Using path analysis, the authors found support for most of their hypothesized relationships. Most importantly for the present chapter, being involved in personally meaningful work and feeling confident at being able to execute performance were related to job engagement. Furthermore, Bakker et al. (2003) found that autonomy was a predictor of engagement in work (see also Maslach and Leiter, 1997). Finally, some of the items viewed by Harter et al. (2003) to be antecedents of employee engagement emphasize both job control/autonomy (e.g. 'At work, I have the opportunity to do what I do best everyday') and job clarity (e.g. 'I know what is expected of me at work').

Taken together, these studies suggest that high levels of engagement in work are associated with clear job guidelines, personal control/autonomy over job performance, and performing work consistent with one's identity, which is therefore personally meaningful. In line with the primary model of job engagement used in the present chapter, all of these variables serve to engage the self-system of the individual in job performance. That is, individuals should feel more responsible for and committed to successful job performance when they have personal control over clear and personally meaningful work.

It is also worth noting that the most potent job attribute predictive of job engagement may change depending on aspects of the employee sample or working conditions. For example, consider a sample of elderly employees. For these individuals, feeling a sense of personal control over their work may be the most important predictor of engagement. On the other hand, for employees within an organization undergoing a major transition, clarity of job guidelines and expectations may take on greater importance as a predictor of engagement. When issues of personal control or clarity are not especially pressing, then the identity-relevance of a job may take on greater importance as a predictor of engagement (see Britt, 1999, 2003a).

Leadership and relationships with co-workers

Although the Triangle Model of Responsibility does a good job of specifying the job-related predictors of engagement, it does not adequately address the leadership and interpersonal factors that may directly or indirectly predict engagement. Kahn's (1990) qualitative work suggested that employees were more likely to feel engaged in work when they experienced a sense of 'psychological safety', which he defined as 'feeling able to show and employ one's self without fear of negative consequences to self-image, status, or career' (p. 708). Kahn determined that relationships with co-workers, positive group dynamics, and a supportive and clarifying leadership style contributed to the condition of psychological safety that gave rise to higher levels of engagement. In a similar vein, Harter et al. (2003) argued that most of their antecedents of job engagement can be influenced by managers through actions that influence the job-related predictors of engagement described above.

Even though leadership and co-worker relationships should influence job engagement, it is informative that in research conducted to date these variables have been found to relate to job engagement through the job-related attributes of engagement described above. In the study described earlier, May et al. (2004) found that relationships between supervisors and co-workers predicted psychological safety, which then predicted engagement in work. Leadership and co-worker perceptions did not directly relate to job engagement apart from their association with being oneself at work. Similar findings were obtained by Britt and Bliese (1998), who examined perceptions of leader consideration and initiating structure as predictors of job engagement among soldiers deployed on a peacekeeping mission to Bosnia. These authors found that perceptions of leader behaviors (especially providing structure) predicted job engagement through their association with the job-related attribute of having clear guidelines for job performance. For these reasons, aspects of leadership and co-worker relations are not indicated in Figure 11.1 as direct predictors of job engagement. However, it is clear that leadership relates to the job-related antecedents of high job engagement. It remains to be seen whether there are specific categories of leader or co-worker relations that directly predict job engagement apart from their association with the proximal job-related antecedents that predict engagement.

Consequences of job engagement

More research has been conducted on the assessment and predictors of job engagement than on the consequences of job engagement for health and performance. In the model we provide in Figure 11.1, we believe it is important to distinguish between the proximal, immediate consequences arising from being personally engaged in work (e.g. increased effort and absorption), and the more distal consequences of job engagement (e.g. performance and well-being). As discussed by prior authors, engagement should lead to increased effort to perform well, absorption in the work-related aspects of one's existence, and perseverance (May et al., 2004;

Rothbard, 2001; Schaufeli et al., 2002). With these immediate consequences, one would expect job engagement to be an inherently positive motivational state that would always produce adaptive consequences. In fact, most of the researchers examining job engagement focus on the positive consequences of job engagement for psychological health and performance. We agree that job engagement is a desirable state that managers should strive to induce. However, we do not expect job engagement to always have positive consequences.

Because job engagement reflects feelings of personal responsibility for and commitment to superior performance, the outcomes of performance should have greater implications for the individual's identity (see Britt, 1999; Britt et al., 2005). Therefore, when the individual has the necessary resources and abilities for successful performance, being highly engaged in work should motivate the individual to excel and to feel personally fulfilled. Under such conditions engagement in work might actually buffer individuals from stressors not relevant to job performance, because the individual is capable of becoming absorbed in meaningful work activities (Britt and Bliese, 2003). However, consider a situation where the employee does not have access to necessary resources or have the aptitudes necessary for effective performance (e.g. Peters and O'Connor, 1980). Under such circumstances where successful performance is doubtful or even unlikely, feeling personally responsible for and committed to job performance may have negative consequences for the individual (Britt, 2003c; Britt et al., 2006). These types of moderating variables are depicted in Figure 11.1.

This same kind of dynamic may occur when employees are experiencing poor or abusive supervision (see Tepper, 2000). Experiencing abusive supervision that detracts from the ability to perform effectively may be especially troubling for people personally engaged in their work. Individuals who are disengaged from their jobs can respond to abusive supervision by further withdrawing effort and resources, but this method of avoidant coping will be difficult for highly engaged workers to adopt. Below we discuss research that has examined the role of job engagement in the stressor–strain relationship, and then turn to research examining the association between engagement and performance.

Job engagement and the stressor–strain relationship

Britt and his colleagues (Britt, 1999; Britt and Bliese, 2003; Britt et al., 2005) have examined job engagement as a moderator of the relationship between different types of stressors and outcomes. As indicated above, job engagement should serve to motivate the individual to perform well, channeling the individual's efforts and attention into job performance (May et al., 2004; Schaufeli et al., 2002). The net effect of such absorption and dedication should be that job engagement buffers individuals from the negative consequences of stressors that do not impede job performance.

Britt and Bliese (2003) examined job engagement as a buffer against stressors among soldiers deployed to Bosnia on a peacekeeping mission. Using hierarchical linear modeling to control for unit-level influences, these authors found that those soldiers high in job engagement reported lower levels of psychological symptoms and health symptoms in comparison to soldiers low in job engagement while under high levels of environmental, family, or unit stress. The authors hypothesized that being engaged in work led to decreased resources for processing the negative implications of stressors occurring outside the immediate work environment.

Britt et al. (2005) replicated these findings in a longitudinal study of soldiers stationed overseas. Soldiers completed measures of job engagement, objective workload (hours worked per day in the past week, training days in the past 6 months) and subjective work overload (e.g. 'I have so much work to do I cannot do everything well'), and physical and psychological health at Time 1 and then completed the same measures 3 to 4 months later (Time 2). The authors found that after controlling for Time 1 measures of physical and psychological health, job engagement buffered soldiers from the negative effects of work hours (for physical symptoms only) and a high numbers of training days (for both psychological and physical symptoms). Soldiers who were highly engaged in their work at Time 1 reported fewer symptoms at Time 2 when working long hours or spending many days away training at Time 1.

The authors hypothesized that highly engaged workers may likely interpret objective work demands differently. Employees who are highly engaged in their work will see longer hours and more training as giving them the skills they need to perform well. However, employees who are relatively disengaged from their jobs will see these objective work demands as causing them to spend more time in areas that do not connect with their self-concept. This research contributed to the literature on the relationship between work hours and health symptoms. Prior research had found a relatively weak overall relationship between work hours and health (see Sparks et al., 1997). The results of Britt et al. (2005) showed that disengaged workers may be likely to show a stronger positive relationship between work hours and health.

Although high job engagement buffered soldiers from the objective indicators of workload, a different pattern emerged for the subjective perception of work overload. Feeling one has too much work to do anything well should be especially troubling to individuals engaged in their work, because such a stressor is likely to prevent superior performance. In fact, Britt et al. (2005) found that high job engagement at Time 1 exacerbated the relationship between subjective work overload at Time 1 and physical symptoms at Time 2. Only among individuals high in job engagement did subjective work overload predict increases in physical health symptoms from Time 1 to Time 2. These findings suggest that obstacles to successful performance may be especially difficult for highly engaged workers (see also Britt, 2003c).

Britt (1999) discovered a conceptually similar finding in a study investigating the relationship between job engagement, perceptions of job success, and stress and depression. He found that job engagement magnified the relationship between perceptions of success and stress and depression. That is, the relationships between perceptions of succeeding versus failing at work and stress and depression were stronger when soldiers reported higher levels of engagement in their job. These results further support the argument that a downside to job engagement is that impediments to successful performance or the realization one is not performing well may be accompanied by heightened stress and depressive symptoms when individuals feel personally engaged in performance.

In summarizing the research on job engagement as a moderator of the stressor/strain relationship, it would appear that job engagement can be a double-edged sword, protecting workers from the negative effects of stressors that do not impede job performance, but enhancing the negative relationship between performance-impeding stressors and outcomes. Although this would be an accurate characterization, it is also important to consider the potential benefits of 'being stung' by the inability to perform effectively. Long ago, Epstein (1973) pointed out that one way individuals discover what is important to them is by observing their emotional reactions to events. Employees may not realize how engaged they are in their jobs until they encounter obstacles to performing well.

As detailed below, more longitudinal research is needed to examine the process by which highly engaged workers deal with impediments to performance. It may be the case that highly engaged employees go through a process of initial stress and disappointment when encountering such obstacles, but they are also especially effective at ultimately overcoming these obstacles and contributing to enhanced organizational development. Although disengaged workers may initially respond better to performance impediments, they are also unlikely to develop innovative solutions to such impediments. Such a scenario seems reasonable in the context of dealing with obstacles that are changeable through the employee's actions. However, engaged employees may respond differently to impediments that are not changeable. The presence of uncontrollable impediments that continuously hinder performance may result in highly engaged workers looking elsewhere for investing their energies (see Britt, 2003c).

Job engagement and performance

Surprisingly little research has investigated the relationship of engagement at work with different aspects of job performance. However, recent research has examined the relationship between the antecedents of employee engagement and performance. Harter et al. (2003) examined consequences of what they refer to as 'employee engagement', using the measure of 12 different perceptions described earlier. Although these authors did not measure engagement specifically, they did show that antecedents of job engagement were predictive of important outcomes at the business unit level. Harter et al., performed a meta-analysis on a database consisting of 7939 business units that contained 198,514 participants. The authors examined the correlation between both the composite score and the individual predictors that made up the composite score with business outcomes. They found positive correlations between the composite score of engagement and customer satisfaction, productivity, profitability, and reduced employee turnover. This research supported a connection between the antecedents of job engagement and performance. Future research will be necessary to determine if job engagement is responsible for this relationship.

Britt et al. (2006) recently examined engagement in a training course as a predictor of rated performance at the end of the course. In addition, these authors examined a potential moderator of the engagement–performance relationship: whether an individual has doubts about possessing the skills necessary for effective performance. These authors studied ROTC (Reserve Officer Training Corps) cadets who were participating in a leadership training course. The cadet's level of engagement in the camp, perception of whether he or she possessed the skills to be a leader, and conscientiousness were assessed during the training camp. The cadet's leadership performance was rated by experts at the end of the camp. The authors found that engagement in the course was positively related to rated leadership performance, even after controlling for conscientiousness. Doubts about possessing leadership skills were also negatively related to performance ratings. An interaction between the two variables also emerged, showing that the negative relationship between doubts about possessing leadership skills and rated performance was stronger for cadets who were highly engaged in the course. Therefore, engagement not only magnified the relationship between performance-impeding stressors and health, but also between performance-impeding stressors and performance.

Future directions

Many exciting areas exist for future research on engagement at work. Perhaps one of the most pressing areas is the explicit recognition of levels of engagement with different aspects of one's job. Much of the research conducted on job engagement has focused on assessing overall engagement in the job. However, individuals can be highly engaged in particular areas of their job, and disengaged from others. Future research should examine how differential engagement within areas or tasks contributes to specific outcomes within those domains. Consider an academic who is highly engaged in the research component of her job, but is relatively disengaged from teaching and service activities. This differential engagement should be related to different performance in the given areas.

In addition, interesting hypotheses could be tested regarding what happens when the level of psychological engagement in a given area of work is inconsistent with the weight assigned to that area in the overall performance evaluation. In the above example, a high level of psychological engagement in the domain of research should result in mostly positive consequences when research is given a large weight in the academic's overall performance evaluation, but may cause problems if teaching performance is weighted more strongly. This information would be lost if only overall engagement in work were examined.

Another promising area of future research involves temporal fluctuations in job engagement. For example, Sonnentag (2003) recently argued that an employee's level of job engagement may fluctuate on a daily basis, and that the extent to which individuals experienced a sense of recovery from the work day would predict engagement in work on the following day. Sonnentag (2003) found support for this relationship even after controlling for overall job engagement, and also showed that daily fluctuations in job engagement mediated the relationship between work recovery and proactive behaviors at work. This research suggests that engagement in work does fluctuate, and that such fluctuations are meaningfully related to important outcomes.

Future research on levels and temporal fluctuations in engagement in work illustrates the importance of examining the underlying processes responsible for engagement within different areas and how engagement relates to important outcomes. More diary-type studies examining engagement over time would lead to a better understanding of how engagement in different work areas develops, and the process by which individuals disengage from particular tasks and their overall job. For example, what is the temporal process by which disengagement or engagement occurs? How easy is it to rebound from disengagement to engagement in a given area following interventions designed to increase job clarity, control, and relevance? These types of questions can only be addressed using longitudinal research designs.

Concluding thoughts

Lazarus (2003) wrote a critique of the positive psychology movement shortly before his death. He offered many criticisms of the approach, including the difficulty of identifying a priori strengths that were universally positive and the failure of the positive psychology movement to recognize prior work on stress and coping as 'positive'. Although many of his criticisms were challenged by other authors, two points seemed to resonate with a number of researchers: the difficulty of completely separating the study of positive from negative constructs, and recognizing that many positive psychological constructs can be associated, under particular conditions, with negative consequences (see Tennen and Affleck, 2003, for an expanded account of these issues).

As discussed above, we view engagement in work as a positive psychological construct, in that engagement is associated with increased caring about performance outcomes, and contributes to meaning that individuals assign to their work (Britt et al., 2001). However, we are also aware that under certain kinds of conditions (e.g. lack of critical resources, work overload), engagement in work may have negative consequences for the individual (Britt, 2003c; Britt et al., in press). We would argue that most constructs falling under the purview of positive psychology have the capacity for negative consequences under specific conditions, and we would encourage researchers to study the processes leading to these consequences in order to provide a complete account of how positive psychological states at work contribute to adaptive functioning.

References

Bakker, A.B., Demerouti, E., Taris, T.W., Schaufeli, W.B. and Schreurs, P.J.G. (2003) 'A multigroup analysis of the job demands-resources model in four home care organizations', *International Journal of Stress Management*, 10, 16–38.

Britt, T.W. (1999) 'Engaging the self in the field: Testing the Triangle Model of Responsibility', *Personality and Social Psychology Bulletin*, 25, 696–706.

Britt, T.W. (2003a) 'Motivational and emotional consequences of self engagement: Dynamics in the 2000 presidential election', *Motivation and Emotion*, 27, 339–58.

Britt, T.W. (2003b) 'Aspects of identity predict engagement in work under adverse conditions', *Self and Identity*, 2, 31–45.

Britt, T.W. (2003c) 'Black Hawk Down at work: When your most motivated employees can't do their job, get ready for an exodus', *Harvard Business Review*, 81, 16–17.

Britt, T.W., Adler, A.B. and Bartone, P.T. (2001) 'Deriving benefits from stressful events: The role of engagement in meaningful work and hardiness', *Journal of Occupational Health Psychology*, 6, 53–63.

Britt, T.W. and Bliese, P. (1998) 'Leadership, perceptions of work, and the stress-buffering effects of job engagement.' Colloquium presented at the Center for Creative Leadership as winner of the Walter F. Ulmer Applied Research Award.

Britt, T.W. and Bliese, P.B. (2003) 'Testing the stress-buffering effects of self engagement among soldiers on a military operation', *Journal of Personality*, 72, 245–65.

Britt, T.W., Castro, C.A. and Adler, A.B. (2005) 'Self engagement, stressors, and health: A longitudinal study', *Personality and Social Psychology Bulletin*, 31, 1475–86.

Britt, T.W., Thomas, J.T. and Dawson, C.R. (2006) 'Domain engagement magnifies the relationship between qualitative overload and performance in a training setting', *Journal of Applied Social Psychology*, 36, 2100–14.

Brown, S.P. and Leigh, T.W. (1996) 'A new look at psychological climate and its relationship to job involvement, effort, and performance', *Journal of Applied Psychology*, 81, 358–68.

Carver, C.S. (1989) 'How should multi-faceted personality constructs be tested? Issues illustrated by self-monitoring, attributional style, and hardiness', *Journal of Personality and Social Psychology*, 56, 577–85.

Csikszentmihalyi, M. (1990) *Flow: The Psychology of Optimal Experience*. New York, NY: Harper & Row.

Epstein, S. (1973) 'The self-concept revisited: Or a theory of a theory', *American Psychologist*, 28, 404–16.

Harter, J.K., Schmidt, F.L. and Keyes, C.L.M. (2003) 'Well-being in the workplace and its relationship to business outcomes: A review of the Gallup studies', in C. Keyes and J. Haidt (eds) *Flourishing: Positive Psychology and the Life Well-lived* (pp. 205–24). Washington, DC: American Psychological Association.

Kahn, W.A. (1990) 'Psychological conditions of personal engagement and disengagement at work', *Academy of Management Journal*, 33, 692–724.

Lazarus, R.L. (2003) 'Does the positive psychology movement have legs?', *Psychological Inquiry*, 14, 93–109.

Luthans, F. (2002) 'The need and meaning of positive organizational behavior', *Journal of Organizational Behavior*, 23, 695–706.

Maslach, C. and Leiter, M.P. (1997) *The Truth About Burnout: How Organizations Cause Personal Stress and What to Do About It*. San Francisco, CA: Jossey-Bass.

Maslach, C., Schaufeli, W.B. and Leiter, M.P. (2001) 'Job burnout', *Annual Review of Psychology*, 52, 397–422.

May, D.R., Gilson, R.L. and Harter, L. (2004) 'The psychological conditions of meaningfulness, safety, and availability and the engagement of the human spirit at work', *Journal of Organizational and Occupational Psychology*, 77, 11–37.

Peters, L.H. and O'Connor, E.J. (1980) 'Situational constraints and work outcomes: The influences of a frequently overlooked construct', *Academy of Management Review*, 5, 391–7.

Rothbard, N.P. (2001) 'Enriching or depleting? The dynamics of engagement in work and family roles', *Administrative Science Quarterly*, 46, 655–84.

Schaufeli, W.B., Salanova, M., Gonzalez-Roma, V. and Bakker, A.B. (2002) 'The measurement of engagement and burnout: A two sample confirmatory factor analytic approach', *Journal of Happiness Studies*, 3, 71–92.

Schlenker, B.R. (1997) 'Personal responsibility: Applications of the Triangle Model', in L.L. Cummings and B. Staw (eds) *Research in Organizational Behavior* (Vol. 19, pp. 241–301). Greenwich, CT: JAI.

Schlenker, B.R., Britt, T.W., Pennington, J., Murphy, R. and Doherty, K. (1994) 'The triangle model of responsibility', *Psychological Review*, 101, 632–52.

Sonnentag, S. (2003) 'Recovery, work engagement, and proactive behavior: A new look at the interface between nonwork and work', *Journal of Applied Psychology*, 88, 518–28.

Sparks, K., Cooper, C., Fried, Y. and Shirom, A. (1997) 'The effects of hours of work on health: A meta-analytic review', *Journal of Occupational and Organizational Psychology*, 70, 391–408.

Tennen, H. and Affleck, G. (2003) 'While accentuating the positive, don't eliminate the negative or Mr. In-between', *Psychological Inquiry*, 14, 163–69.

Tepper, B.J. (2000), 'Consequences of abusive supervision', *Academy of Management Journal*, 43, 178–90.

Wright, T.A. (2003) 'Positive organizational behavior: An idea whose time has truly come', *Journal of Organizational Psychology*, 24, 437–42.

12

The Benefits and Possible Costs of Positive Core Self-Evaluations: A Review and Agenda for Future Research

Timothy A. Judge and Charlice Hurst

In any analysis of the source of positive psychological states and behavior in work and applied psychology, one must consider the strong possibility that some individuals are born with predispositions toward positive feelings and behaviors. In a 1997 conceptual article, Judge and colleagues (1997) introduced the concept of core self-evaluations. According to Judge et al. (1997), core self-evaluations is a broad concept representing the fundamental evaluations that people make about themselves and their functioning in their environment. Individuals with positive core self-evaluations appraise themselves in a consistently positive manner across situations; such individuals see themselves as capable, worthy, and in control of their lives. Individuals with negative core self-evaluations, in contrast, tend to view themselves as less worthy than others, dwell on their failures and deficiencies, and see themselves as victims of their environment. According to Judge et al. (1997, 1998a), the concept of core self-evaluations is indicated by four widely-studied traits: self-esteem, locus of control, neuroticism, and generalized self-efficacy. Judge et al. (2002) have presented evidence that the first three of these traits are the most widely studied in psychology. As these authors note, however, very little research has examined the commonalities and overlap among these traits. Although neuroticism has been considered a broad trait even by those researchers who do not endorse the five-factor model (Eysenck, 1990), study upon study continues to treat self-esteem and locus of control as individual, isolated traits. As we will show, consideration of these traits in isolation leads to underprediction and semantic confusion (Dewey, 1974).

In this chapter, we will review the evidence on core self-evaluations. We first review evidence for the construct validity of the concept. We also briefly discuss the measurement of core self-evaluations. Then, as an exemplar of a positive trait, we consider the benefits and possible costs of positive core self-evaluations. Finally, we lay out an agenda for future research based on the foregoing review.

Construct validity of core self-evaluations

Following Schwab (1980), in reviewing the construct validity of core self-evaluations, we consider four questions: (1) *Convergent validity* – do the four core traits (self-esteem, locus of control, neuroticism, and generalized self-efficacy) share sufficient covariance to indicate a common concept?; (2) *Lack of discriminant validity of core traits* – do the core traits display similar patterns of relationships with other variables, which would suggest that the core traits lack discriminant validity relative to each another?; (3) *Discriminant validity relative to other traits* – is the core concept distinct from other traits, such as the Big Five (excluding emotional stability, of course, which is also part of the Big Five)?; (4) *Incremental validity* – does the broad core factor predict criteria better than the isolated core traits or beyond other traits (such as the Big Five traits)? Let us consider each of these questions in turn.

Convergent validity

Research has consistently shown that the four core traits are substantially interrelated. For example, in the Judge et al. (2002) meta-analysis, the average correlation among the traits was .64, which is as high as the correlations among alternative measures of the Big Five traits (see Ones, 1993). Moreover, factor analyses – using both exploratory and confirmatory methods – have consistently shown that the four core traits load on a common factor (Erez and Judge, 2001; Judge et al., 1998a, 2000). Although evidence suggests that locus of control tends to correlate less strongly with the other three traits than these three traits correlate with each other, overall, it appears that measures of the four core traits converge to indicate a higher-order core self-evaluations concept.

Lack of discriminant validity of core traits

Some might argue that the four core traits are in fact distinct because they correlate differently with relevant outcomes. This, of course, is an empirical question. In correlating the individual core traits with three important applied criteria (subjective well-being, job satisfaction, and job performance), the results tend to show that the individual core traits show a very similar pattern of correlations with other variables (Judge et al., 2002). For example, with respect to job satisfaction and job performance, Judge and Bono's (2001) meta-analysis revealed that, with the exception of the correlation between generalized self-efficacy and job satisfaction (which was boosted by a single strong correlation in one large sample study), the credibility intervals all overlap. Thus, it appears that the core traits do not display much discriminant validity in terms of their correlations with the three outcomes.

Discriminant validity relative to other traits

Some researchers have argued that core self-evaluations is not a new concept. Schmitt (2004: 352) questions the degree to which core self-evaluations is separate from the Big Five, noting that core self-evaluations 'is a broader concept indicated by a composite of three Big Five traits', Judge et al.'s (2002) study revealed that self-esteem, generalized self-efficacy, and locus of control displayed an average correlation of .44 with extraversion and .46 with conscientiousness. These correlations are far from trivial; however, the correlations of these traits with the Big Five traits tend to be similar to the correlations of neuroticism with the other Big Five traits (see Judge et al., 2004). Moreover, these core traits correlate much more strongly with neuroticism than with either conscientiousness or extraversion.

Incremental validity

Perhaps the 'acid test' of the distinctiveness and usefulness of core self-evaluations is to determine whether the broad core trait predicts broad criteria better than the individual traits, and predicts criteria controlling for the five-factor model traits. Erez and Judge (2001) have addressed this issue explicitly in terms of the relationship of core self-evaluations to motivation and job performance. They found that the overall core concept always predicted motivation and performance, whereas the individual traits did so inconsistently. Judge et al. (2002) also demonstrated that the core factor better predicted criteria (job satisfaction, life satisfaction) than did the individual core traits. Moreover, both of these studies showed that core self-evaluations predicted criteria controlling for all or some of the Big Five traits. Thus, it appears that the overall concept is a more consistent predictor of outcomes than are the individual traits, and provides incremental validity over the five-factor model.

Measurement of core self-evaluations

Despite support for the concept of core self-evaluations, one limiting issue is the measurement of the trait. In the past, Judge and colleagues measured core self-evaluations with a combination of measures of the specific core traits. The resulting measure was long, containing 37 items. Because most trait measures are substantially shorter than this, and to avoid some of the limitations of indirect measures (see Judge et al., 2004), Judge et al. (2003) developed and validated a direct measure of core self-evaluations, the Core Self-Evaluations Scale (CSES). The CSES is provided in Table 12.1. Judge et al. (2003) demonstrated the validity of this measure across four independent samples. In each sample, the CSES was reliable ($\alpha \geq .80$). Confirmatory factor-analyses of the 12 items suggested that they indicate a single dimensional construct. Furthermore, the CSES showed convergent validity, as evidenced by its correlations with the four core traits, was

Table 12.1   *Core Self-Evaluations Scale (CSES)*

Instructions: Below are several statements about you with which you may agree or disagree. Using the response scale below, indicate your agreement or disagreement with each item by placing the appropriate number on the line preceding that item.

1	2	3	4	5
Strongly disagree	Disagree	Neutral	Agree	Strongly agree

1. ____ I am confident I get the success I deserve in life.
2. ____ Sometimes I feel depressed. (r)
3. ____ When I try, I generally succeed.
4. ____ Sometimes when I fail I feel worthless. (r)
5. ____ I complete tasks successfully.
6. ____ Sometimes, I do not feel in control of my work. (r)
7. ____ Overall, I am satisfied with myself.
8. ____ I am filled with doubts about my competence. (r)
9. ____ I determine what will happen in my life.
10. ____ I do not feel in control of my success in my career. (r)
11. ____ I am capable of coping with most of my problems.
12. ____ There are times when things look pretty bleak and hopeless to me. (r)

Note: r = reverse-scored.
Source: Judge et al. (2003)

significantly correlated with job satisfaction, life satisfaction, and supervisory ratings of job performance, and displayed incremental validity in predicting these criteria controlling for the core self-evaluations factor as well as the traits from the five-factor model.

The possible benefits of positive core self-evaluations

Having introduced the CSE concept, described construct validity evidence, and presented information in its measurement, we now turn to the possible implications of positive core self-evaluations. First, we review positive effects of positive core self-evaluations.

Happy feelings: Core self-evaluations and subjective well-being

Research on core self-evaluations has consistently revealed positive relationships with job satisfaction (Best et al., 2005; Heller et al., 2002; Judge et al., 2000, 2002, 2004, 2005; Judge and Bono, 2001; Piccolo et al., 2005; Rode, 2004) and life satisfaction (Heller et al., 2002; Judge et al., 1998a, 2002; Piccolo et al., 2005; Rode, 2004). In a meta-analysis of the four components of CSE and job satisfaction, Judge and Bono (2001) demonstrated that each of the traits was significantly correlated with job satisfaction. The average corrected correlation was .32. Furthermore, the correlation increased to .41 when the traits were aggregated. Likewise, Judge et al. (1998a) found significant relationships between each of the traits and both job and life satisfaction, rated by focal participants and their significant others, in three samples (physicians in the United States, graduates of an East Coast business school, and employed Israeli students). Structural equation estimates revealed that a single core self-evaluations factor had moderately strong, significant effects on these outcomes.

More recent findings have supported the positive effects of CSE across cultures. In separate samples of Dutch and Spanish students and employees, Judge et al. (2004) found that the psychometric properties of the CSE scale were similar to those of US samples. The CSE-job satisfaction relationship was investigated in the Dutch sample, resulting in a strong, positive correlation ($r = .56$, $p < .01$). In an exploration of the validity of the CSE construct in Japan, a culture even more divergent from that of the US, Judge et al. (2005) found that the four component traits loaded on one higher order factor. This factor, in turn, was significantly positively correlated with job satisfaction ($r = .49$, $p < .05$), life satisfaction ($r = .52$, $p < .05$), and happiness ($r = .67$, $p < .05$).

In addition to establishing that a meaningful relationship exists, researchers have sought to illuminate processes underlying the link between CSE and satisfaction. Several mechanisms have been suggested. Judge et al. (1998b) argued that, consistent with self-verification theory, individuals with high CSE should attend to and process information about their work environment in a manner that leads to positive conclusions while individuals with low CSE should do the opposite, influencing job satisfaction. In addition, based on Locke's (1976) part–whole hypothesis, Judge et al. (1998b) reasoned that an increase in job satisfaction would lead to a commensurate increase in life satisfaction. As expected, Judge, et al., found that the relationship between core self-evaluations and job satisfaction was partially mediated by perceptions of job characteristics. While core self-evaluations had a direct effect on life satisfaction, it also bore indirect effects via perceptions of work characteristics and job satisfaction.

Best et al. (2005) recently presented further evidence for the influence of CSE on job satisfaction via appraisals of the work environment. In a study of Veterans Administration employees in a wide range of positions, the authors found that core self-evaluations was negatively related to perceptions of organizational obstacles to goal fulfillment (perceived organizational constraint; $\beta = -.32$, $p < .05$). Perceived organizational constraint mediated between CSE and burnout, which negatively predicted job satisfaction ($\beta = -.44$, $p < .05$). CSE, furthermore, had a direct negative effect on burnout ($\beta = -.31$, $p < .05$). These results suggest that employees high in CSE are less likely to view their job tasks and organizational environment as stressful, shielding them from burnout and its deleterious effects on job satisfaction.

Studies that focus only on perceptual measures of job characteristics make it impossible to distinguish whether high-CSE individuals simply hold a rosier picture of objective attributes or whether they actually select into jobs with better attributes. To address this drawback in earlier research, Judge et al. (2000) examined the mediating role of objective job complexity, ascertained by coding job titles, as well as subjective job characteristics. They found that both subjective and objective indicators of job complexity were partial mediators of the relationship between CSE measured in childhood and early adulthood and later job satisfaction for individuals between the ages of 41–50. These results suggest that core self-evaluations influence not only how favorably people view their jobs, but also the actual level of complexity of the jobs they obtain.

In addition to selecting more challenging jobs, people with high CSE may find their work more satisfying because they choose personally meaningful goals. Self-concordance theory posits that goals pursued for fun or on the basis of personally relevant values increase subjective well-being and goal attainment (Sheldon and Elliot, 1998). Judge et al. (2005) proposed that individuals with positive self-concept should be less vulnerable to external pressures and, therefore, more likely to set self-concordant goals. In longitudinal studies of college students and employees of several different firms, participants disclosed goals they had set for the following two months and answered questions that captured the level of self-concordance of each goal. In both studies, self-concordant goals partially mediated between core self-evaluations and life satisfaction and between core self-evaluations and goal attainment. It appears that core self-evaluations do lead to the pursuit of self-concordant goals, which increases life satisfaction and goal attainment. However, the influence of goal attainment on life satisfaction was mixed. The authors concluded that core self-evaluations 'may serve more like a trigger than an anchor. People with positive core self-evaluations strive for "the right reasons," and therefore "get the right results"' (p. 266).

While initial studies of the CSE construct assumed that job satisfaction mediated its relationship with life satisfaction (Judge et al., 1998), Heller et al. (2002) argued that the job–life satisfaction link might be spurious due to dispositional influences on both. In a longitudinal study of university employees, they found that, controlling for CSE, the correlations between various combinations of self and significant other ratings of job and life satisfaction decreased by 33–51 percent. In most cases, the partial correlation between job satisfaction and life satisfaction remained significant. Thus, while the job–life satisfaction link is partially spurious, there may also be situational influences on subjective well-being. This finding was significant for its contribution to the specification of future models of the link between core self-evaluations and satisfaction. CSE may affect life satisfaction partially through job satisfaction, but it may also affect both job and life satisfaction through mutual or independent pathways, in concert with situational influences.

But does it matter to the bottom line?

The evidence that CSE influences satisfaction seems convincing, but what about performance effects? Judge and Bono (2001) found that the average corrected correlation of the four core self-evaluations traits with job performance was .23 and that the validity of the aggregated traits was .30. Judge et al. (1998b) argued that CSE should affect performance via its influence on motivation. High-CSE individuals should be more likely to persist in the face of setbacks, believe in their capabilities, feel that they can control outcomes, and experience less fear and anxiety in novel or challenging situations. This hypothesized mediating role of motivation was supported by Erez and Judge (2001) in a laboratory study with a sample of undergraduate students and a field study of salespeople at a *Fortune 500* company. In both cases, motivation partially mediated the relationship between CSE and performance. In the lab study, CSE positively influenced motivation, which was measured as persistence on the task and as subjective task motivation. In the field study, CSE directly affected sales productivity and supervisor-rated performance while also exerting an indirect influence via goal-setting motivation.

Bono and Colbert (2005) offered additional insight into the CSE–motivation–performance relationship via a longitudinal field study examining the effects of CSE on responses to multi-source feedback. As predicted, they found that high-CSE individuals were more satisfied with multi-source feedback and were more committed to goals set as a result of the feedback process. Furthermore, people with high CSE were more committed to goals when there were discrepancies between their self-ratings and the ratings of others. Low-CSE individuals' commitment was higher when self- and other-ratings were mutually consistent, and moderate-CSE individuals were most committed when their ratings from others were high, regardless of self-ratings. The results of this study suggest that high-CSE individuals are more likely than others to benefit from feedback that differs from their own self-perceptions.

The influence of CSE on persistence and commitment was explored in an entirely different context by Wanberg et al. (2005), who found that unemployed high-CSE individuals demonstrated greater job search intensity over the course of several months. The authors warned, however, that the effect of CSE was 'quite small' (HLM coefficient = .51, $p < .01$) relative to some of the study's control variables such as occupation (HLM coefficient = –4.71 to –11.40, $p < .01$) and gender (HLM coefficient = –6.47, $p < .01$). Still, their finding is indicative that positive self-concept may give individuals on the job market an edge due to their stronger motivation, particularly when taken with Judge et al.'s (2004) finding that CSE was moderately correlated with career ambition ($r = .29$, $p < .01$). Future research might explore whether job search persistence and career ambition can explain why high-CSE individuals obtain more complex jobs.

CSE may also be an important asset for the many individuals whose work carries them into unfamiliar environments. Johnson et al. (2003) reported that, controlling for extraversion, CSE had a positive effect on social ties of expatriate employees with host country nationals and with other expatriates

(β = .30 in both cases, p < .05). Social ties, in turn, mediated between CSE and adjustment to work. Together, the Wanberg et al. (2005) and Johnson et al. (2003) findings suggest that positive core self-evaluations may be particularly beneficial under circumstances of insecurity and change. This may be especially critical in an era of increasingly unstable employment contracts and distributed work arrangements.

In sum, the evidence gathered to date directly disputes the idea that positive self-concept is unimportant or, even, dangerous. Certainly, it is no panacea for all that ails. Yet, there is ample evidence that individuals with high CSE view their circumstances more optimistically, set more difficult and self-concordant goals, persist longer in pursuit of those goals, deal constructively with feedback and disappointments, and adapt well to new environments. These behaviors may, in turn, lead to their obtaining more complex jobs, finding greater fulfillment in those jobs, and performing more effectively.

The possible costs of positive core self-evaluations

It appears that positive core self-evaluations have a number of important benefits to individuals and to organizations. However, every concept has potential limitations, and core self-evaluations is no exception. Now, we turn to the possible negative side-effects of core self-evaluations.

The costly pursuit of a positive self-concept

In Western society, it is generally considered 'good' (desirable) to think positively of oneself and 'bad' (undesirable) to think poorly of oneself. One might expect, then, for people to pursue or strive toward a positive self-concept. Indeed, Crocker and Park (2004) argue that when people seek to raise their levels of self-esteem, there are short-run benefits but long-term costs. The key to this argument is how people seek to raise their self-esteem. These authors argue that people pursue self-esteem by attempting to 'validate their abilities or qualities in the domains in which self-worth is invested' (Crocker and Park, 2004: 393). Thus, for example, an employee might pursue self-esteem by seeking to validate their self-worth through effective job performance. So what is wrong with this? These authors argue that to make self-esteem contingent in this way is costly in terms of autonomy (people work because they feel they have to rather than want to), loss of relationships (people become focused on themselves at the expense of others), and increased risk of depression (when people fail, it undermines their global sense of self-worth). These arguments are controversial, and the evidence marshaled in support of them is often indirect and sketchy. However, they do raise an interesting perspective – whether society's pressures to be positive have, in a sense, created a monster that is manifested in the pursuit of self-esteem.

Can one be too positive?

Is it possible to be too positive? Is there a risk of creating a 'Stepford Organization'? The benefits, and costs, of positiveness continue to be debated in the literature (Baumeister et al., 2003; Colvin et al., 1995; Taylor et al., 2003; Taylor and Sherman, 2004). In one camp are researchers who claim that positive thinking and even positive illusions are beneficial. They argue that positive people, even those with a false positive self-concept, are better adjusted (happier) and more motivated (Taylor et al., 2003). In the other camp are those who argue that those who have an unrealistically positive self-concept are viewed as exploitive by their peers, and actually have lower levels of well-being (Colvin et al., 1995). Although whether the *illusion* of self-esteem is helpful is debatable, others have argued that either self-esteem itself has few benefits (Baumeister et al., 2003), or the pursuit of self-esteem is harmful (Crocker and Park, 2004).

On this former point, we think the evidence is clear that self-esteem is positively but moderately related to various criteria that people would view as important. People with high self-esteem tend to be more satisfied with their jobs and their lives, and tend to perform better at their jobs. It is true that the correlations are not strong, so that one cannot say that self-esteem is some magic ingredient for life success. But, at the same time, we believe it a misreading of the literature to conclude that self-esteem has no or few benefits.

Another means of looking at an overly positive self-concept is to consider narcissism. Narcissists are individuals who have a high opinion of themselves, are self-centered, given to grandiose fantasies, and interpersonally manipulative. One could scarcely think of a more biting insult than to label someone a narcissist; yet the advantages and disadvantages of narcissism continue to be debated. There is little dispute that narcissists tend to derogate others when their self-concept is threatened, to emphasize winning over relationships, to be repelled by intimacy, and to be highly susceptible to the self-serving bias (tendency to make internal attributions for success and external attributions for failure). Yet, at the same time, it is far from clear that narcissists are unhappy. Indeed, a team of researchers recently conducted several studies showing that narcissists tend to be happier, largely because they have higher levels of self-esteem (Sedikides et al., 2004). Thus, whether narcissism is good or bad may depend on one's perspective: what is good for the narcissist may be bad for the people who are objects of the narcissist's attention.

Settlement of the debates surrounding the benefits and drawbacks of narcissism may, after all, bear little relevance to CSE. At first glance, narcissism may seem to be simply an extreme form of positive self-concept. However, further probing suggests that narcissism and CSE are quite distinct, given both differences in their conceptualization and in their patterns of relationships with various criteria. For instance, narcissists react defensively against negative feedback (see Sedikides and Gregg, 2001), a characteristic that is clearly inconsistent with findings that people with high CSE react more proactively to negative feedback that is discrepant with their own self-perceptions (Bono and Colbert, 2005). Moreover, correlations vary widely between narcissism and self-esteem, which is typically the highest loading of the four component traits on the second-order CSE factor in confirmatory factor analyses (Judge et al., 1998a; Erez and Judge, 2001). Brown and Zeigler-Hill (2005) provided evidence that these variations are grounded in the fact that self-esteem measures differ in the extent to which they emphasize attitudes of superiority and dominance as opposed to the attitude that one is simply 'as good as' or 'not inferior to' others. Indeed, Campbell and colleagues (2001) reported findings that narcissism seemed to encompass only agentic, ego-centered conceptions of the self (i.e. intellect, extraversion) while self-esteem seemed to comprise a balance of agentic and communal self-perceptions (i.e. conscientiousness, empathy). Finally, there is virtually no conceptual overlap between the dimensions of the most widely-used narcissism measure (the Narcissistic Personality Inventory, or NPI; Raskin and Hall, 1981) and the dimensions of CSE.

Recently, Hiller and Hambrick (2005) suggested that executives can reach such a high level of CSE that it taints their decision making. They proposed that 'hyper-CSE' would be a useful measure of executive hubris, an assertion that recalls the debate over the relationship between high self-esteem and narcissism. Hiller and Hambrick (2005) argued that CSE is not likely related to 'unhealthy reactive narcissism' but should be positively related to 'healthy narcissism', which they understand to be based on secure self-esteem. Some theorists view narcissism as occurring along a continuum with overlap between 'adaptive narcissism' and healthy self-esteem. However, Hiller and Hambrick (2005) argued that CSE becomes inflated because of the power inherent in an executive's position. However, CSE is more likely a stable characteristic. Even for executives with positive CSE, the negative outcomes predicted seem more characteristic of the narcissism construct.

Is positive self-concept associated with violence and antisocial behavior?

In an influential article, Baumeister and colleagues (1996) argued that aggression results from threats to self-esteem and, therefore, that many high self-esteem individuals may be predisposed to violent or antisocial behavior. In supporting this view, Baumeister et al. (1996) argue that psychopaths often have inflated self-views. Whether this is true or not, as we shall note shortly, a positive self-view is not necessarily isomorphic with an inflated self-view. As with many psychopathologies, the mental structures necessary to commit violent acts are probably complex, even conflicted, and may depend on the nature of the crime (the causes of rape are unlikely to be identical to the causes of terrorist acts). Overall, as

Baumeister et al. (2003: 22) noted: 'Many researchers have sought to link self-esteem to violence, aggression, and antisocial tendencies. The results are mixed at best.' Thus, if we can generalize from the self-esteem literature, we doubt there is any simple connection between positive core self-evaluations and violent, antisocial, or deviant behavior.

Benefits of negative thinking

Remember the retort 'I'm not cynical, I'm just realistic'? There actually is some evidence that depressed people are more realistic in estimating contingencies of actions such that they are more accurate in judging the consequences of their actions (Alloy and Abramson, 1979). Thus, when making accurate decisions is important, being positive may actually be bad. On the other hand, depressed people also exhibit memory decay to a greater degree than nondepressed individuals, especially when people are put under 'cognitive load' (mental strain). Thus, it is not that depression represents a vast cognitive advantage to individuals. Rather, it simply may be that depressed people, or negative people more generally, are in fact sadder but wiser in making certain judgments.

Future research

Pursuit of positive self-concept at work

Because work is a major source of identity to most individuals (consider the number of surnames in English and other languages that define a family in terms of an occupation; Hulin, 2002), it is reasonable to expect that most of us derive at least some sense of self-worth from our work. Crocker has raised questions about the functionality of such contingencies in self-worth. So, the questions become: Do people base their core self-evaluations on occupational success? Is it 'healthy' to do so? Does it matter what specifically it is based on (e.g. is it 'healthier' to base one's self-concept on interpersonal closeness, or popularity within a social network, or earnings, etc.)?

Stability of core self-evaluations

Research by Kernis (2005) has suggested that variability in self-esteem is important. Consistent with this idea that self-concept may vary within persons, Schinkel et al. (2004) conceptualized CSE as a state-based construct. Judge et al.'s (2003) Core Self-Evaluations Questionnaire was used as the measurement instrument in a laboratory study with Dutch undergraduates who took bogus job tests. Participants who received detailed performance feedback experienced a significant decrease in CSE (from 3.64 at Time 1 to 3.58 at Time 2) while CSE of those in the condition without feedback actually increased. Furthermore, procedural fairness interacted with feedback such that CSE increased for those in the no-feedback condition who perceived high procedural fairness while it remained basically unchanged for those who perceived low procedural fairness. These findings, in concert with Kernis' work, indicate that there is some merit to the idea that the stability of an individual's CSE, as well as the general level, influences the appraisal processes believed to link CSE to outcomes.

Effects on creativity

With the exception of Judge and Bono (2001) and Erez and Judge (2001), there has been little study of the effects of core self-evaluations on domains of job performance other than task performance. There is good reason to believe, however, that core self-evaluations may play a key role in creative action in organizations. According to Amabile's influential 'componential model' (1996), intrinsic motivation is a key antecedent to creativity. While creativity researchers have devoted considerable attention to factors that may influence intrinsic motivation, little attention has been paid to the role of personality. Rather, they have tended to focus on contextual characteristics. However, given the finding by Judge et al. (2005) that CSE positively predicts the pursuit of self-concordant goals, it's very likely that people with positive CSE are more intrinsically motivated.

Self-control

Another potentially fruitful area of inquiry is the relationship of CSE to self-control. Recently, Tangney et al. (2004) proposed that self-control predicts a broad range of positive outcomes (i.e. secure attachment style, empathy, constructive conflict resolution, low levels of psychopathology) and seems not to possess any serious drawbacks. In their study, controlling for socially desirable responding, self-control was positively correlated with emotional stability ($r = .42$, $p < .001$) and negatively correlated with depression ($r = -.34$, $p < .001$), anxiety ($r = -.33$, $p < .001$) and hostility ($r = -.27$, $p < .01$). It would seem, however, that self-control is not a conceptual replacement for self-concept but, rather, a consequence of self-concept. After all, locus of control is a major component of CSE, and it seems likely that people who believe they can exercise control will make more of an effort to do so.

Interpersonal relationships

The findings by Johnson et al. (2003) point to the potential for a significant role for core self-evaluations in interpersonal relationships at work. Though the influence of personality on social ties at work is a fairly under-examined area, there is evidence that it may be an important avenue for further research. For instance, Klein et al. (2004) found that neuroticism was negatively associated with centrality in friendship ($\beta = -.26$, $p < .01$) and advice networks ($\beta = -.40$, $p < .01$) and positively associated with centrality in adversarial networks ($\beta = .31$, $p < .05$) of teams five months after their formation. When all of the study's other control variables were introduced, none of the other Big Five traits (extraversion, agreeableness, conscientiousness, and openness to experience) predicted advice network centrality. Other than neuroticism, only openness predicted friendship network centrality ($\beta = -.43$, $p < .01$), while openness ($\beta = .27$, $p < .05$), agreeableness ($\beta = -.30$, $p < .05$) and extraversion ($\beta = .33$, $p < .001$) were significantly associated with adversarial network centrality. The Big Five are often considered the most useful personality traits for predicting work outcomes. However, in both Johnson et al. (2003) and Klein et al. (2004), CSE and one of its major components, neuroticism (e.g. emotional stability), predicted variance beyond extraversion.

Most of the research on self-concept in relationships has focused on romantic attachments. This literature may provide a starting point for building a model of the role of CSE in relationships at work. For instance, Murray and Rose (2005) argue that high self-esteem promotes relationship health, in part, because it leads to more accurate perceptions of relationship partners' positive regard and affections. Furthermore, they cite evidence that high self-esteem individuals may hold an approach orientation to relationships while low self-esteem individuals are avoidant, focused on protecting themselves from getting hurt rather than promoting intimacy and trust. Applied to a work context, high CSE individuals may be more likely to establish trust with co-workers and, because they are less concerned with the potential for harm, may engage in fewer political behaviors. Moreover, since CSE is a multi-faceted construct, it may predict relationship behaviors and outcomes better than any of its components alone, as has been found in research on CSE and other criteria such as job satisfaction and performance.

Conclusion

Within the realm of positive psychology, core self-evaluations is an important emergent concept. It is an integrative trait that may bring together disconnected streams of research. It is related to a host of outcomes that are important to individuals and organizations. However, we have also reviewed areas where positive core self-evaluations might have limitations. Future research would benefit from further study of the benefits of, limits to, and possible costs of, positive core self-evaluations.

References

Alloy, L.B. and Abramson, L.Y. (1979) 'Judgment of contingency in depressed and nondepressed students: Sadder but wiser?', *Journal of Experimental Psychology: General*, 108, 441–85.

Amabile, T. (1996) *Creativity in Context: Update to the Social Psychology of Creativity*. Boulder, CO: Westview Press.

Baumeister, R.F., Campbell, J.D., Krueger, J.I. and Vohs, K.D. (2003) 'Does high self-esteem cause better performance, interpersonal success, happiness, or healthier lifestyles?', *Psychological Science in the Public Interest*, 4, 1–44.

Baumeister, R.F., Smart, L. and Boden, J.M. (1996) 'Relation of threatened egotism to violence and aggression: The dark side of high self-esteem', *Psychological Review*, 103, 5–33.

Best, R.G., Stapleton, L.M. and Downey, R.G. (2005) 'Core self-evaluations and job burnout: The test of alternative models', *Journal of Occupational Health Psychology*, 10, 441–51.

Bono, J.E. and Colbert, A.E. (2005) 'Understanding responses to multi-source feedback: The role of core self-evaluations', *Personnel Psychology*, 58, 171–203.

Brown, R.P. and Zeigler-Hill, V. (2005) 'Narcissism and the non-equivalence of self-esteem measures: A matter of dominance?', *Journal of Research in Personality*, 38, 585–92.

Campbell, W.K., Rudich, E.A. and Sedikides, C. (2001) 'Narcissism, self-esteem, and the positivity of self-views: Two portraits of self-love', *Personality and Social Psychology Bulletin*, 28, 358–68.

Colvin, C.R., Block, J. and Funder, D.C. (1995) 'Overly positive self-evaluations and personality: Negative implications for mental health', *Journal of Personality and Social Psychology*, 68, 1152–62.

Crocker, J. and Park, L.E. (2004) 'The costly pursuit of self-esteem', *Psychological Bulletin*, 130, 392–414.

Dewey, R. (1974) 'Six pillars of the social sciences' Tower of Babel', *Etc.: A Review of General Semantics*, 31, 239–47.

Erez, A. and Judge, T.A. (2001) 'Relationship of core self-evaluations to goal setting, motivation, and performance', *Journal of Applied Psychology*, 86, 1270–9.

Eysenck, H.J. (1990) 'Biological dimensions of personality', in L.A. Pervin (ed.) *Handbook of Personality* (pp. 244–76). New York: Guilford Press.

Heller, D., Judge, T.A. and Watson, D. (2002) 'The confounding role of personality and trait affectivity in the relationship between job and life satisfaction', *Journal of Organizational Behavior*, 23, 815–35.

Hiller, N. and Hambrick, D.C. (2005) 'Conceptualizing executive hubris: The role of (hyper-) core self-evaluations in strategic decision-making', *Strategic Management Journal*, 26, 297–319.

Hulin, C.L. (2002) 'Lessons from industrial and organizational psychology', in J.M. Brett and F. Drasgow (eds) *The Psychology of Work: Theoretically Based Empirical Research* (pp. 3–22). Mahwah, NJ: Lawrence Erlbaum.

Johnson, E.C., Kristof-Brown, A.L., van Vianen, A.E.M, de Pater, I.E. and Klein, M.R. (2003) 'Expatriate social ties: Personality antecedents and consequences for adjustment', *International Journal of Selection and Assessment*, 11, 277–88.

Judge, T.A. and Bono, J.E. (2001) 'Relationship of core self-evaluations traits – self-esteem, generalized self-efficacy, locus of control, and emotional stability – with job satisfaction and job performance: A meta-analysis', *Journal of Applied Psychology*, 86, 80–92.

Judge, T.A., Bono, J.E., Erez, A. and Locke, E.A. (2005) 'Core self-evaluations and job and life satisfaction: The role of self-concordance and goal attainment', *Journal of Applied Psychology*, 90, 257–68.

Judge, T.A., Bono, J.E. and Locke, E.A. (2000) 'Personality and job satisfaction: The mediating role of job characteristics', *Journal of Applied Psychology*, 85, 237–49.

Judge, T.A., Erez, A. and Bono, J.E. (1998b) 'The power of being positive: The relation between positive self-concept and job performance', *Human Performance*, 11, 167–88.

Judge, T.A., Erez, A., Bono, J.E. and Thoresen, C.J. (2002) 'Are measures of self-esteem, neuroticism, locus of control, and generalized self-efficacy indicators of a common core construct?', *Journal of Personality and Social Psychology*, 83, 693–710.

Judge, T.A., Erez, A., Bono, J.E. and Thoresen, C.J. (2003) 'The Core Self-Evaluations Scale (CSES): Development of a measure', *Personnel Psychology*, 56, 303–31.

Judge, T.A., Locke, E.A. and Durham, C.C. (1997) 'The dispositional causes of job satisfaction: A core evaluations approach', *Research in Organizational Behavior*, 19, 151–88.

Judge, T.A., Locke, E.A., Durham, C.C. and Kluger, A.N. (1998a) 'Dispositional effects on job and life satisfaction: The role of core evaluations', *Journal of Applied Psychology*, 83, 17–34.

Judge, T.A., Van Vianen, A.E.M. and De Pater, I.E. (2004) 'Emotional stability, core self-evaluations, and job outcomes: A review of the evidence and an agenda for future research', *Human Performance*, 17, 325–46.

Kernis, M.H. (2005) 'Measuring self-esteem in context: The importance of stability of self-esteem in psychological functioning', *Journal of Personality*, 73, 1569–1605.

Klein, K.J., Lim Beng-Chong, Saltz, J.L. and Mayer, D.M. (2004) 'How do they get there? An examination of the antecedents of centrality in team networks', *Academy of Management Journal*, 47, 952–63.

Locke, E. A. (1976) 'The nature and causes of job satisfaction', in M.D. Dunnette (ed.) *Handbook of Industrial and Organizational Psychology* (pp. 1297–1343). Chicago: Rand McNally.

Murray, S. and Rose, P. (2003) 'Optimal self-esteem may promote relationship defense', *Psychological Inquiry*, 15, 55–8.

Ones, D.S. (1993) *'The construct validity of integrity tests.'* Unpublished doctoral dissertation, University of Iowa.

Piccolo, R.F., Judge, T.A., Takahashi, K., Watanabe, N. and Locke, E.A. (2005) 'Core self-evaluations in Japan: Relative effects on job satisfaction, life satisfaction, and happiness', *Journal of Organizational Behavior*, 26, 965–84.

Raskin, R. and Hall, C.S. (1981) 'The narcissistic personality inventory: Alternative form reliability and further evidence of construct validity', *Journal of Personality Assessment*, 45, 159–63.

Rode, J.C. (2004) 'Job satisfaction and life satisfaction revisited: A longitudinal test of an integrated model', *Human Relations*, 57, 1205–29.

Schinkel, S., van Dierendonck, D. and Anderson, N. (2004) 'The impact of selection encounters on applicants: An experimental study into feedback effects after a negative selection decision', *International Journal of Selection and Assessment*, 12, 197–205.

Schmitt, N. (2004) 'Beyond the Big Five: Increases in understanding and practical utility', *Human Performance*, 17, 347–57.

Schwab, D.P. (1980) 'Construct validity in organizational behavior', *Research in Organizational Behavior*, 2, 3–43.

Sedikides, C. and Gregg, A.P. (2001) 'Narcissists and feedback: Motivational surfeits and motivational deficits', *Psychological Inquiry*, 12, 237–9.

Sedikides, C., Rudich, E.A., Gregg, A.P., Kumashiro, M. and Rusbult, C. (2004) 'Are normal narcissists psychologically healthy?: Self-esteem matters', *Journal of Personality and Social Psychology*, 87, 400–16.

Sheldon, K.M. and Elliot, A.J. (1998) 'Not all personal goals are personal: Comparing autonomous and controlled reasons for goals as predictors of effort and attainment', *Personality and Social Psychology Bulletin*, 24, 546–57.

Tangney, J.P., Baumeister, R.F. and Boone, A.L. (2004) 'High self-control predicts good adjustment, less pathology, better grades, and interpersonal success', *Journal of Personality*, 72, 271–322.

Taylor, S.E. and Sherman, D.K. (2004) 'Positive psychology and health psychology: A fruitful liaison', in. P.A. Linley and S. Joseph (eds) *Positive Psychology in Practice* (pp. 305–19). Hoboken, NJ: John Wiley & Sons.

Taylor, S.E., Lerner, J.S., Sherman, D.K., Sage, R.M. and McDowell, N.K. (2003) 'Portrait of the self-enhancer: Well adjusted and well liked or maladjusted and friendless?', *Journal of Personality and Social Psychology*, 84, 165–76.

Wanberg, C.R., Glomb, T.M., Song, Z. and Sorenson, S. (2005) 'Job-search persistence during unemployment: A 10-wave longitudinal study', *Journal of Applied Psychology*, 90, 411–30.

PART THREE

METHODOLOGICAL ISSUES IN POB RESEARCH

13

A Look at Two Methodological Challenges for Scholars Interested in Positive Organizational Behavior

Thomas A. Wright

Since the measuring device has been constructed by the observer ... we have to remember that what we observe is not nature in itself but nature exposed to our method of questioning.

Werner Karl Heisenberg, *Physics and Philosophy* (1958)

A number of applied scholars, drawing on the impetus of the various 'positive' movements – Positive Psychology, Positive Organizational Behavior (POB), and Positive Organizational Scholarship (POS) – have clearly called for an increased emphasis on positive processes and behaviors in organizational research. In the applied sciences, this proactive and positive approach has been alternatively termed Positive Organizational Behavior (POB) by Luthans (2002a, 2002b, 2003) and Positive Organizational Scholarship (POS) by Cameron et al. (2003). Disregarding these semantic differences for the moment, this chapter is about the challenge of conducting positive-based research in a rigorous, methodologically sound manner. To be sure, as with research purporting to measure the more 'negative' aspects of organizational life, there are a number of methodological concerns of which positive organizational scholars should be well aware. Space limitations necessitate that I limit my discussion to two such challenges.

The first addresses the core conceptual and methodological challenge facing positive organizational scholars: providing further clarification to the ambiguity surrounding the widely assumed, but rarely measured, temporal distinction between POB and POS. Simply stated, this challenge involves deciding whether the particular variable or concept of interest is best considered as a state and in the domain of POB or is best considered as a trait and in the domain of POS. The second challenge is twofold in nature. Following the admonition of the various positive movements, I suggest that cardiovascular research focus on not only the negative or cost-related aspects of cardiovascular disease, but also on the positive aspects of cardiovascular health. Relatedly, and to assist researchers in better focusing on the positive, I propose that positive organizational research consider the use of such composite cardiovascular measures as pulse product and pulse pressure in addition to the more commonly used systolic and diastolic blood pressure. But first, I direct our attention to the important, but invariably neglected, role of time or timing in positive organizational research. Incorporating time as a 'main effect' variable, I next define and provide the basis for a temporal distinction between POB and POS.

POB and POS defined

POB is primarily concerned with those human strengths and psychological capacities that lend themselves to developmental approaches specifically designed to enhance workplace performance (Luthans, 2003). Concerned with temporary or state-like characteristics, POB focuses on those psychological and behavioral processes that are conducive to more immediate, short-term strategies of change intervention. Luthans and Avolio (2003) proposed confidence, hope and optimism as three prime examples of this POB emphasis on more situational, state-like positive capacities. Alternatively, as I read the literature, POS is more concerned with processes considered to have stable or trait-like qualities (Cameron et al., 2003; Pratt and Ashforth, 2003). In particular, POS focuses on such processes as excellence, thriving, flourishing, abundance, resilience, and growth, each of which are assumed to more meaningfully and dynamically unfold and develop over much longer periods of time. Considered together, these positive-based approaches significantly overlap and emphasize the need for applied research to focus on building human strengths and virtues (Luthans, 2002a; Wright, 2003), or what has been termed the 'health' approach to the study of organizational behavior (Wright and Cropanzano, 2000). However, the positive organizational movement (and OB research in general) would undoubtedly greatly benefit from a clearer temporal distinction regarding exactly what constitutes the domain of POB vs. POS. Fortunately, the methodological basis exists for scholars interested in providing better clarification of the distinction between state-like and trait-like. Using research on the positive-based construct of psychological well-being (PWB), we now examine how one can methodologically determine whether PWB, or any other psychological (and physiological) process, exhibits more state-like (POB) or trait-like (POS) qualities.

The role of time in positive organizational research

While the variable of time is acknowledged a central theoretical role regarding many aspects of human behavior (McGrath and Rotchford, 1983), time or timing has not played a significant practical role in research on organizational issues (Ancona and Chong, 1996; Wright, 1997). Nowhere is this lack of awareness more evident than in the failure to provide a legitimate temporal distinction between what constitutes a state as opposed to a trait. In fact, outside of being integral to such topics as the escalation of commitment (Ross and Staw, 1986; Staw and Ross, 1987), research on time or timing has received miniscule attention in the applied sciences (Ancona and Chong, 1996). In particular, at best, issues surrounding time are usually accorded secondary roles, either as moderating variables, or as merely an afterthought.

This second class status is highly unfortunate as a number of scholars (e.g. Alpert, 1995; Wright, 1997) have noted that an increased attention to 'time' as a main effect variable will greatly assist in providing a more comprehensive understanding of a wide range of organizational topics. More specifically, a primary reason for the continued controversy surrounding state vs. trait explanations for organizational behaviors in general, and the POB vs. POS temporal distinction in particular, involves the fact that past research has not adequately accounted for the role of time. The following example will be useful in demonstrating the relevance of considering time in applied research.

Wright (1997) noted that pragmatism primarily drives design in much organizational research and that far different results might be obtained in many studies depending on just *when* variable measures are actually taken. For example, Helmreich et al. (1986) found that the effects of personality on job performance varied considerably over time. They labeled the obtained delayed impact of personality on job performance the 'honeymoon effect'. While the relationship between personality and performance was not significant after three months, the relationship was significant after both 6 and 8 months. Helmreich et al. could not theoretically justify their time choices (3, 6, and 8 months) as appropriate periods to provide. In generalizing their results to the field at large, these authors correctly concluded that the predictive value of personality has been prematurely dismissed in much research because of the failure to specifically consider the 'main effect' role of time.

A prime example of this failure to adequately consider the role of time can be found in the positive movements' (Positive Psychology, POB, and POS) renewed interest in employee PWB. Historically, PWB has been considered as both a disposition/trait, *and* as a state/mood (Diener, 1984). As a trait, PWB is viewed as a 'context-free' or global construct, one not tied to any particular situation (Warr, 1987, 1990). However, a thorough consideration of PWB as a trait requires that we actually determine the relative contribution of the more variable (state) vs. the more stable (trait) components of the measure. To date, the exact temporal demarcation between exactly what constitutes a state (i.e. 'at this moment','currently', 'today' etc.) versus a trait (i.e. 'during the past month', 'during the past year', 'in general' etc.) dimension is far from clear-cut (George, 1991; Wright, 1997). Certainly, the need for a more specific temporal distinction between state and trait has been well evidenced in personality theory (cf. Pervin, 1989; Watson et al., 1988). Unfortunately, as with organizational research, personality theory has not provided us with the necessary hard and fast temporal distinction between state and trait (cf. Allen and Potkay, 1981). I propose that a clear temporal distinction is especially warranted in the positive approaches to organizational research as interest continues to rapidly grow. Fortunately, a rudimentary basis for a temporally based state/trait distinction exists in the literature (Wright, 1997).

Generally speaking, personality research typically considers person characteristics as dispositional or trait-like if they have some measure of temporal continuity and if they are capable of influencing subsequent behavior. Based upon these requirements, and in a purely arbitrary manner, Wright (1997) proposed that 6 months be considered as the temporal demarcation between state and trait measures. Certainly, one might argue that 6 months for a state is too long. In fact, in conversations with me on the subject, at least one prominent management scholar, Russell Cropanzano, current editor of the *Journal of Management*, suggested that a state or mood is most accurately operationalized when narrowly measured 'at this moment' or 'today'. I see merit in this line of reasoning. Certainly, as noted earlier, the need to provide an adequate temporal distinction between state and trait is especially noteworthy in the positive organizational movements when one considers that 'state' is considered to be, by definition (e.g. Luthans, 2002a; Luthans and Avolio, 2003), in the domain of POB and 'trait' in the domain of POS. As a result, there is a dire need for the positive movements to reach a conceptual consensus regarding exactly what temporal period constitutes a state and what constitutes a trait. Of course, once we have conceptually identified an appropriate temporal state/trait distinction, to be validated as a trait, one must be confident in the stability of the measure over time.

PWB measurement stability over time

Historically, the state vs. trait distinction has been of special interest to scholars concerned with examining the contribution of situational and dispositional influences on organizational behavior (Davis-Blake and Pfeffer, 1989; Newton and Keenan, 1991; Staw et al., 1986; Staw and Ross, 1985). Essential to any discussion regarding this distinction between state vs. trait influences is the question of whether behavior is caused by the 'person' or the 'situation', a debate central to organizational behavior research (Arvey et al., 1989; George, 1992; Gerhart, 1987; Staw and Ross, 1985). For example, consider positive-based approaches that have recently (re)established a link between PWB and job performance (Wright, 2005). If PWB is, as many believe, a dispositional or trait-like variable exhibiting acceptable levels of stability over time, then organizations may well be able to improve their overall effectiveness by increasing levels of employee PWB through the careful selection, training and development, and placement of workers who demonstrate high dispositional levels of PWB. In addition, employee well-being also has significant implications for employee health as well (Wright, 2005).

Traditionally, the determination of the dispositional or trait-like nature of PWB (among other variables) has been addressed in organizational research through the reliance on test–retest correlational analysis. To that end, measures of well-being have been shown to demonstrate substantial levels of test–retest consistency. For example, Chamberlain and Zita (1992) found that measures of well-being were correlated at .69 when taken 6 months apart. Headley and Wearing (1989) found associations in the .50–.60 ranges up to 6 years later. Likewise, Cropanzano and Wright (1999), in a 5-year study, established a 6-month correlation of .76, a 4-year correlation of .68, and a 5-year correlation of .60. However, as I will now discuss, and consistent with previous research (Cropanzano and Wright, 1999; Newton and Keenan, 1991), I propose that these significant test–retest correlations cannot, solely at face value, be taken as sufficient proof of PWB stability because test–retest correlations, as noted by Newton and Keenan (1991: 781), 'reveal only the relative, not absolute, positions of individuals in a group'. The methodological importance of this 'relative' vs. 'absolute' distinction can be best explained through the use of a simple example.

Suppose that for the purposes of either selection, training and development, or placement, an organization is very interested in determining the level of temporal stability of employee PWB, measured on a 10-point scale, over a 2-year period. Further suppose that at Time 1, every employee had scores clustering around 5 on the 10-point scale, while at Time 2, every employee had PWB scores clustering around 9 on the 10-point scale. Using test–retest correlational analysis as the sole determinant of PWB stability, the customary procedure in organizational research, one would undoubtedly conclude that the PWB measure was highly stable because the test–retest correlation was very high. However, this distribution of scores over Times 1 and 2 indicates that there was also considerable measurement change over time. More specifically, while the high test–retest correlations do indicate a similarity in PWB score *rankings*, they cannot be solely used to confirm the absence (and hence stability) of *absolute* change (either mean or variance variable levels). As a result, the sole reliance on test–retest correlations should not be used to reliably infer the existence or absence of any dispositional effects (Newton and Keenan, 1991; Wright et al., 1993). Newton and Keenan further noted that test–retest correlational analysis should *always* be supplemented with an assessment of possible changes in mean variable levels to infer the presence or absence of a dispositional or trait component to the variable of interest, in this case, PWB.

In response to these insights, I suggest the need to extend Newton and Keenan's argument and test for the equality of *both* variable means *and* variances. A finding of equal means will satisfy the definition of a parallel measurement model, while a finding of equal means *and* variances will satisfy the definition of a strictly parallel measurement model (Kristof, 1963). Support for the parallel and strictly parallel models would strongly validate the view that the variable in question, say PWB, is a disposition or trait and provide further insight regarding the POB (situational or state) versus POB (dispositional or trait) distinction emerging in the positive organizational movement. Distressingly, a preliminary literature review of organizational research (whether positive-based or not) published in the top empirical management journals (e.g. ASQ, AMJ, JAP, JOM, JOB, *Personnel Psychology*) over the last several years revealed only one article (Wright and Staw, 1999) testing for parallel and strictly parallel measurement models. A brief review of Wright and Staw's findings is particularly illustrative of the potential merits of this methodological approach.

Wright and Staw reported the results of two independent, longitudinal field studies. In Study 1, the two-year test–retest correlation was an impressive .74 (p < .0001). In Study 2, the one-year test–retest correlation was an equally impressive .77 (p< .0001). Tests for the equality of correlated means found that the means were not significantly different for either Study 1 (t = 1.28, p = 0.21) or Study 2 (t = 1.22, p = 0.23). In addition, tests for the equality of correlated variances did not reveal any differences for either Study 1 (t = −1.36, p = 0.18) or Study 2 (t = −0.62, p = 0.54). Taken together, these findings clearly demonstrate that PWB satisfies the methodologically rigorous definition of a strictly parallel measurement model (Kristof, 1963). More specifically, unlike other research purporting to investigate whether a variable is best considered as a state or trait, Wright and Staw (1999) presented strong evidence of *both* rank-order (test–retest correlational analysis) *and* absolute (tests for the equality of variable means and variance) stability for their measure of well-being.

PWB example summary

Despite the wide use of conceptualizing such positive-based variables as PWB as traits, time or variable timing has not played a significant 'main effect' role in organizational research (Ancona and Chong, 1996). This is especially evident in the positive organizational movement where the predictive value of such dispositionally based variables as PWB has been discounted. Certainly a major reason for this lack of confidence has been the failure of prior research to specifically include the variable time (e.g. Davis-Blake and Pfeffer, 1989; Newton and Keenan, 1991). Wright and

Staw's (1999) consideration of the 'main effect' influences of time by controlling for both relative and absolute stability allowed them to state with confidence that their measure of well-being is a trait and, thus, best included in the domain of POS research. I turn next to my second methodological challenge for positive organizational scholars: how best to examine the potentially positive role of cardiovascular health indicators.

The role of cardiovascular health in positive organizational research

Employee indicators of physical health are important topics in the positive organizational movements. As with indicators of employee psychological health, while the ill effects of cardiovascular disease have long been recognized, the possible beneficial or positive effects of cardiovascular research for individual psychological betterment and physical health have been much less widely recognized in applied research (Wright and Diamond, 2006). One especially promising avenue to adopting a more positive approach to cardiovascular research in organizational settings may lie in the actual manner by which cardiovascular health indicators are measured. As will be shown, the need for a more positive-based approach to cardiovascular research has never been greater than it is today.

Currently, over 65 million Americans, and countless tens of millions around the world, suffer from high blood pressure (American Heart Association, 2005). The American Heart Association (2005) estimated the aggregated cost of cardiovascular disease and stroke in the United States in 2004 alone at almost $370 billion! Of special interest to organizational scholars, roughly 40 percent of the aggregated costs are attributable to lost productivity on the job (Wright and Diamond, 2006). Keying in once again on the negative, the typical organizational research study has been one focused on the potential cardiovascular health problems resulting from employee hypertension (Wright and Sweeney, 1990). My suggestion for positive scholars is twofold in nature. First, I propose that positive research consciously focus on the positive benefits of cardiovascular activity. Relatedly, as I will elaborate shortly, positive-focused scholars will also greatly benefit from expanding the methodology of cardiovascular research, from one concerned with the sole reliance on measuring pulse rate, systolic and diastolic blood pressure, to one including such composite cardiovascular measures as pulse product and pulse pressure. To emphasize the possible positive benefits of research focused on employee cardiovascular activity, I now will briefly examine recent research endeavors suggesting that many differences between happy and unhappy people have not only a psychological but also a physiological basis as well. For those interested in pursuing this fascinating topic further, Staw and his colleagues (see Staw, 2004; Staw and Cohen-Charash, 2005) provide a more detailed review of this line of research.

It has long been recognized that feelings of sadness (unhappiness), fear and anxiety arouse people's autonomic nervous systems, producing pronounced increases in blood pressure, heart rate and vasoconstriction (Fredrickson and Levenson, 1998; Gross et al., 1994). Alternatively, more positive, happier feelings may be beneficial in helping to quell potentially harmful surges in cardiovascular activity (Fredrickson and Losada, 2005). Furthermore, positive feelings provide additional benefits. For example, positive feelings have been shown to produce faster returns to baseline levels of cardiovascular activation following negative emotional arousal (Fredrickson and Levenson, 1998; Fredrickson et al., 2003), lower levels of cortisol (Steptoe et al., 2005) and reductions in subsequent-day physical pain (Gil et al., 2004). Interestingly, and highly germane to my discussion, the most typically used measures of cardiovascular activity, pulse rate, systolic and diastolic blood pressure, might not be the best indicators of positive-based cardiovascular activity. Fortunately, two long recognized, but seldom currently used, composite cardiovascular measures, pulse pressure and pulse product, offer interested positive researchers the opportunity to better link employee cardiovascular activity to indicators of both individual efficiency and organizational effectiveness.

Lovekin (1930) was perhaps the first applied researcher to recognize a possible cardiovascular link to both individual efficiency and organizational effectiveness (Wright and Diamond, 2006). Building upon Cannon's (1915, 1932) seminal work on steady state equilibrium or homeostasis, Lovekin (1930) applied the composite cardiovascular measure, pulse product, to the workplace human efficiency equation. Lovekin's measure of pulse product was defined as the difference between systolic and diastolic blood pressure, multiplied by the pulse rate, and divided by 100. A second composite measure, pulse pressure, currently gaining popularity in the medical sciences, is defined as simply the difference between systolic and diastolic blood pressure.[1]

Foreshadowing this current interest of medical research on the composite cardiovascular measure, pulse pressure, Lovekin (1930) found pulse product to be a very useful index of the level of worker energy expenditure. Based upon the premise that high levels of employee efficiency, a very positive occurrence, is a function of both output and physical energy (input) used, Lovekin (1930: 167) concluded that 'the height and fluctuations of the pulse product, combined with the production records, can be used to distinguish variations in efficiency when comparing departments, workers, or different periods in the day'. In other words, the very basis for pulse product, measurement of an individual's steady state equilibrium or homeostasis, forms the core framework for a positive-based cardiovascular approach.

Recognizing its potential workplace benefits, Mayo (1933) and Roethlisberger and Dickson (1939) later adopted pulse product for use in the famous Hawthorne experiments at the Western Electric plant (Roethlisberger and Dickson, 1939). In particular, pulse product measurements were obtained from the 'famous five' operators in the Relay Assembly Test Room study each hour of the work day over three working days during the spring and fall of 1928 (Wright and Diamond, 2006). Later, during the spring of 1929, similar on-the-job readings were obtained from the five operators in the Mica Splitting Test Room study. In reporting their observations on the role of pulse product in the determination of employee output, fatigue and efficiency, Roethlisberger and Dickson (1939: 120) found 'all operators were working well within their physical capacities'.

Equally important, and consistent with the findings of such pioneering scholars as Addis (1922) and Lovekin (1930), a number of other scholars proposed that composite cardiovascular measures, such as pulse pressure and pulse product, were capable of demonstrating more accurate levels of worker physical energy expenditure than were the more typically used measures of systolic and diastolic blood pressure (e.g. Roethlisberger and Dickson, 1939). In turn, and based upon a definition of efficiency considered in terms of output per unit of energy, Roethlisberger and Dickson concluded that pulse product could be instrumental in the determination of two key research interests of the current positive organizational movement: employee health and productivity.

Despite these promising beginnings, roughly 75 years later, the use of cardiovascular measures in general and pulse product in particular has all but vanished from mainstream organizational research. Nonetheless, incorporating all three indicators, pulse rate, diastolic and systolic blood pressure, the composite measure of pulse product appears especially well-suited for scholars more interested in identifying the positive, as opposed to the negative, consequences of employee cardiovascular activity. Unlike systolic and diastolic blood pressure, the fundamental purpose of composite cardiovascular measures like pulse product is to assess the level of employee organic balance, or steady-state homeostasis. Consider the following hypothetical example involving three employees and assuming that each is currently equally productive.

Employee A has a pulse rate of 80 beats per minute, with systolic and diastolic blood pressure readings of 120 and 70, respectively. This pulse product equals 40 or $[80 \times 120 - 70]/100$. Employee B has a pulse rate of 100 beats per minute (this individual smokes), with systolic and diastolic blood pressure readings of 140 and 90, respectively. Employee B's pulse product equals 50 or $[100 \times 140 - 90]/100$. Finally, employee C has a pulse of 80 beats per minute, with systolic and diastolic blood pressure readings of 135 and 55, respectively. Employee C's pulse product equals 64 or $[80 \times 135 - 55]/100$. Again, I make the assumption that each employee is currently producing at the same level. However, according to the steady-state or homeostasis model (Cannon, 1932), employee A is currently at a much more efficient level than either employee B or C.

Although each employee's contribution to organizational effectiveness is currently the same, one can predict that employee C's (and possibly employee B as well) productivity (and certainly their physical health as well will eventually decline as a result of this inefficient use of their cardiovascular system. As a consequence, if left unattended, the effectiveness of the organization will sooner or later be adversely affected. Interestingly, the customary and sole reliance of previous research on systolic and diastolic blood pressure readings would not signal employee C's cardiovascular reading as problematic. However, recent research confirms that this traditional approach may be erroneous, especially when considering the changing demographics of our rapidly aging workforce.

Consistent with the view presented here, a number of medical researchers are now suggesting that the most accurate measure of heart disease risk, especially for an organization with an aging workforce, may be the composite cardiovascular measure, pulse pressure. Using data from the Framingham Heart Study, Franklin et al. (1999) called into question the wisdom of relying solely on measures of diastolic and systolic blood pressure to predict CHD. In fact, contradicting conventional wisdom, which long assumed that both systolic and diastolic blood pressure were positively related to CHD, Franklin et al. (1999) found that diastolic blood pressure was *negatively* related to CHD. Organizations with a graying workforce should be very interested in these conclusions (Wright and Diamond, 2006). As shown by Franklin et al. (1999), as employees age, systolic pressure will typically rise (a condition known as isolated systolic hypertension), while diastolic pressure tends to fall for many during the aging process. Thus, focusing on only the diastolic reading can result in a masking of the potential risk of CHD for individuals 50 years old or older!

In more practical terms, what these results suggest is that while pulse pressure differences of up to 50 mm Hg are fairly normal for aging employees, differences of 60 mm Hg or more may be problematic for one's health (our employee C), irrespective of the diastolic reading. I suggest that organizations in general, but especially those with a significant number of employees over 50, would greatly benefit from encouraging their age at-risk employees to be aware of the potential cardiovascular health challenges resulting from isolated systolic hypertension (Saunders, 2001; Wright and Diamond, 2006).

Concluding thoughts

Positive organizational research faces a number of challenges in the quest for legitimacy within the organizational sciences. In this chapter, I discussed two methodological challenges faced by scholars in the positive movements. By design, one challenge was concerned with a psychological variable, employee PWB, of interest to the positive organizational movement; the other was concerned with the physiological or cardiovascular dimension. In addition, I expressed my strong belief that the conceptual ambiguity surrounding just what constitutes the temporal domain of POB vs. POS may severely cloud the overriding proactive message of the positive organizational movement for both the scholarly and lay audience alike. Heeding the sage advice from our opening quote from Heisenberg, one suggestion to help keep the message clear necessitates that the temporal domains of state vs. trait be more clearly articulated. To that end, through the use of example, the benefits of supplementing the customary methodological basis for distinguishing state from trait (e.g. test–retest correlational analysis) with tests for parallel (equal means) and strictly parallel (equal variances) measurement models (Kristof, 1963) were presented. Finally, the positive benefits of considering the steady-state and homeostatic capabilities of the composite cardiovascular measure, pulse product, were similarly introduced.

Note

1 Blood pressure readings are composed of two numbers, i.e. 110/70. The top number, or systolic pressure, measures the heart at work – the amount of pressure during the heart's pumping phase, or systole. The bottom number, or diastolic pressure, measures the heart during the resting phase between heartbeats, or diastole (Saunders, 2001: 3). Traditionally, hypertension has been defined as having systolic measures in excess of 140 mm Hg or a diastolic measure of 90 mm Hg or more. Blood pressure is measured as mm Hg because traditionally the device used to measure blood pressure, a *sphygmomanometer*, uses a glass column filled with mercury (Hg) and calibrated in millimeters (mm) (Saunders, 2001: 3). More recently, some medical researchers have proposed reducing the qualifying numbers for high blood pressure below the 140/90 standard (Wright and Diamond, 2006).

References

Addis, T. (1922) 'Blood pressure and pulse rate reactions', *Archives of Internal Medicine*, 30, 246.

Allen, B.P. and Potkay, C.R. (1981) 'On the arbitrary distinction between states and traits', *Journal of Personality and Social Psychology*, 41, 916–28.

Alpert, S. (1995) 'Towards a theory of timing: An archival study of timing decisions in the Persian Gulf War', in L.L. Cummings and B.M. Staw (eds) *Research in Organizational Behavior* (vol. 17, pp. 1–70). Greenwich, CT: JAI Press.

American Heart Association (2005) 'Cardiovascular disease cost'. Retrieved 28 February 2005, from http://www/americanheart.org/presenter,jhtml?identifier=4475.

Ancona, D. and Chong, C.-L. (1996) 'Entrainment: Pace, cycle, and rhythm in organizational behavior', in B.M. Staw and L.L. Cummings (eds) *Research in Organizational Behavior* (vol. 18, pp. 251–84). Greenwich, CT: JAI Press.

Arvey, R.D., Bouchard, T.J., Segal, N.L. and Abraham, L.M. (1989) 'Job satisfaction: Environmental and genetic components', *Journal of Applied Psychology*, 74, 187–92.

Cameron, K.S., Dutton, J.E. and Quinn, R.E. (2003) *Positive Organizational Scholarship: Foundations of a New Discipline*. San Francisco: Berrett-Koehler.

Cannon, W.B. (1915) *Bodily Changes in Pain, Hunger, Fear and Rage*. New York: Appleton.

Cannon, W.B. (1932). *The Wisdom of the Body*. New York: Norton.

Chamberlain, K. and Zita, S. (1992) 'Stability and change in subjective well-being over short time periods', *Social Indicators Research*, 20, 101–17.

Cropanzano, R. and Wright, T.A. (1999) 'A five-year study of change in the relationship between well-being and job performance', *Consulting Psychology Journal: Practice and Research*, 51, 252–65.

Davis-Blake, A. and Pfeffer, J. (1989) 'Just a mirage: the search for dispositional effects in organizational research', *Academy of Management Review*, 14, 385–400.

Diener, E. (1984) 'Subjective well-being', *Psychological Bulletin*, 95, 542–75.

Franklin, S.S., Khan., S.A., Wong N.D., Larson, M.G. and Levy, D. (1999) 'Is pulse pressure useful in predicting risk for coronary heart disease?', The Framingham Study. *Circulation*, 100, 354–60.

Fredrickson, B.L. and Levenson, R.W. (1998) 'Positive emotions speed recovery from the cardiovascular sequalae of negative emotions', *Cognition and Emotion*, 12, 191–220.

Frederickson, B.L. and Losàda, M.F. (2005) 'Positive affect and the complex dynamics of human flourishing', *American Psychologist*, 60, 678–86.

Fredrickson, B.L., Tugade, M.M., Waugh, C.E. and Larkin., G.R. (2003) 'What good are positive emotions in crises? A prospective study of resilience and emotions following the terrorist attacks on the United States on September 11th, 2001', *Journal of Personality and Social Psychology*, 84, 365–76.

George, J. (1991) 'State or trait: Effects of positive mood on prosocial behaviors at work', *Journal of Applied Psychology*, 76, 299–307.

George, J.M. (1992) 'The role of personality in organizational life: Issues and evidence', *Journal of Management*, 18, 185–213.

Gerhart, B. (1987) 'How important are dispositional factors as determinants of job satisfaction? Implications for job design and other personnel programs', *Journal of Applied Psychology*, 72, 366–73.

Gil, K.M., Carson, J.W., Porter, L.S., Scipio, C., Bediako, S.M. and Orringer, E. (2004) 'Daily moods and stress predict pain, health care use, and work activity in African American adults with sickle cell disease', *Health Psychology*, 23, 267–74.

Gross, J.J., Fredrickson, B.L. and Levenson, R.W. (1994) 'The psychophysiology of crying', *Psychophysiology*, 31, 460–8.

Headley, B. and Wearing, A. (1989) 'Personality, life events, and subjective well-being: Toward a dynamic equilibrium model', *Journal of Personality and Social Psychology*, 57, 731–39.

Helmreich, R.L., Sawin, L.L. and Carsrud, A.L. (1986) 'The honeymoon effect in job performance: Temporal increases in the predictive power of achievement motivation', *Journal of Applied Psychology*, 76, 185–8.

Kristoff, W. (1963) 'The statistical theory of stepped-up reliability coefficients when a test has been divided into several equivalent parts', *Psychometrika*, 28, 121–38.

Lovekin, O.S. (1930) 'The quantitative measurement of human efficiency under factory conditions', *Journal of Industrial Hygiene*, 12, 99–120, 163–7.

Luthans, F. (2002a) 'The need for and meaning of positive organizational behavior', *Journal of Organizational Behavior*, 23, 695–706.

Luthans, F. (2002b) 'Positive organizational behavior: Developing and maintaining psychological strengths', *Academy of Management Executive*, 15, 57–72.

Luthans, F. (2003) 'Positive organizational behavior: Implications for leadership and HR development and motivation', in L.W. Porter, G.A. Bigley and R.M. Steers (eds) *Motivation and Work Behavior* (pp. 178–5). New York: McGraw-Hill/Irwin.

Luthans, F. and Avolio, B. (2003) 'Authentic leadership development', in K.S. Cameron, J.E. Dutton and R.E. Quinn (eds) *Positive Organizational Scholarship: Foundations of a New Discipline* (pp. 241–58). San Francisco: Berrett-Koehler.

Mayo, E. (1933) *The Human Problems of an Industrial Civilization*. New York: Viking.

McGrath, J.E. and Rotchford, N.L. (1983) 'Time and behavior in organizations', in L.L. Cummings and B.M. Staw (eds) *Research in Organizational Behavior* (Vol. 5, pp. 57–101). Greenwich, CT: JAI Press.

Newton, T. and Keenan, T. (1991) 'Further analyses of the dispositional argument in organizational behavior', *Journal of Applied Psychology*, 76, 781–7.

Pervin, L.A. (1989) *Personality, Theory, and Research*. New York: Wiley.

Pratt, M.G. and Ashforth, B.E. (2003) 'Fostering positive meaningfulness at work', in K.S. Cameron, J.E. Dutton and R.E. Quinn (eds) *Positive Organizational Scholarship: Foundations of a New Discipline* (pp. 309–27). New York: McGraw-Hill.

Roethlisberger, F.J. and Dickson, W.J. (1939) *Management and the Worker*. Cambridge, MA: Harvard University Press.

Ross, J. and Staw, B.M. (1986) 'Expo 86: An escalation prototype', *Administrative Science Quarterly*, 31, 274–97.

Saunders, C. (2001) *Hypertension: Controlling the Silent Killer*. Boston, MA: Harvard Health Publications.

Staw, B.M. (2004) 'The dispositional approach to job attitudes: An empirical and conceptual review', in B. Schneider and B. Smitt (eds) *Personality in Organizations* (pp. 163–91). Mahwah, NJ: Erlbaum.

Staw, B.M. and Cohen-Charash, Y. (2005) 'The dispositional approach to job satisfaction: More than a mirage, but not yet an oasis', *Journal of Organizational Behavior*, 26, 59–78.

Staw, B.M. and Ross, J. (1985) 'Stability in the midst of change: A dispositional approach to job attitudes', *Journal of Applied Psychology*, 70, 469–80.

Staw, B.M. and Ross, J. (1987) 'Behavior in escalation situations: Antecedents, prototypes, and solutions', in L.L. Cummings and B.M. Staw (eds) *Research in Organizational Behavior* (Vol. 9, pp. 39–78). Greenwich, CT: JAI Press.

Staw, B.M., Bell, N.E. and Clausen, J.A. (1986) 'The dispositional approach to job attitudes: A lifetime longitudinal test', *Administrative Science Quarterly*, 31, 56–77.

Steptoe, A., Wardle, J. and Marmot, M. (2005) 'Positive affect and health-related neuroendocrine, cardiovascular, and inflammatory responses', *Proceedings of the National Academy of Sciences*, USA, 102, 6508–12.

Warr, P. (1987) *Work, Employment, and Mental Health*. New York: New York University Press.

Warr, P. (1990) 'The measurement of well-being and other aspects of mental health', *Journal of Occupational Psychology*, 63, 193–210.

Watson, D., Clark, L.A. and Tellegen, A. (1988) 'Development and validation of brief measures of positive and negative affect: The PANAS scale', *Journal of Personality and Social Psychology*, 54, 1063–70.

Wright, T.A. (1997) 'Time revisited in organizational behavior', *Journal of Organizational Behavior*, 18, 201–4.

Wright, T.A. (2003) 'Positive organizational behavior: An idea whose time has truly come', *Journal of Organizational Behavior*, 24, 437–42.

Wright, T.A. (2005) 'The role of "happiness" in organizational research: Past, present and future directions', in P.L. Perrewé and D.C. Ganster (eds) *Research in Occupational Stress and Well-being* (Vol. 4, pp. 221–64). Amsterdam: JAI Press.

Wright, T.A. and Cropanzano, R. (2000) 'Psychological well-being and job satisfaction as predictors of job performance', *Journal of Occupational Health Psychology*, 5, 84–94.

Wright, T.A. and Diamond, W.J. (2006) 'Getting the "pulse" of your employees: The use of cardiovascular research in better understanding behavior in organizations', *Journal of Organizational Behavior*, 27, 395–401.

Wright, T.A. and Staw, B.M. (1999) 'Affect and favorable work outcomes: Two longitudinal tests of the happy/productive worker thesis', *Journal of Organizational Behavior*, 20, 1–23.

Wright, T.A. and Sweeney, D. (1990) 'Correctional institution workers' coping strategies and their effect on diastolic blood pressure', *Journal of Criminal Justice*, 18, 161–9.

Wright, T.A., Bonett, D.G. and Sweeney, D.A. (1993) 'Mental health and work performance: Results of a longitudinal field study', *Journal of Occupational and Organizational Psychology*, 66, 277–84.

14

Positive Psychological Capital: Has Positivity Clouded Measurement Rigor?

Laura M. Little, Janaki Gooty, and Debra L. Nelson

Drawing upon recent research in positive psychology, a research stream entitled Positive Organizational Behavior (POB) has recently received much attention. POB has been defined by Luthans (2002a, 2002b) as 'the study and application of positively oriented human resource strengths and psychological capacities that can be measured, developed, and effectively managed for performance improvement in today's workplace' (2002b: 59). Although this definition seems to support the study and application of a multitude of constructs already in existence in organizational behavior (e.g. conscientiousness, generalized self-efficacy, extraversion), Luthans (2002b) proposed that constructs must meet certain, specific, well-defined operational criteria to qualify as a POB construct. The most basic of these criteria is that the construct should reflect a capacity for positive outcomes (e.g. greater happiness in life, life satisfaction, well-being, and most importantly better performance). Further, the construct should be *measurable*, state-like, and malleable. Based upon these criteria, Luthans proposed four core constructs: hope, optimism, resiliency and self-efficacy, each reflecting a positive psychological capacity (PsyCap).

Most researchers would agree that these four constructs do indeed meet the criteria for a positive psychological capacity; however, rigorous academic debate has centered on the measurability of these constructs (Lazarus, 2003). The measurability condition stated above necessitates valid and reliable measures, which in turn are central for corroboration of the construct's predictive power. Interestingly, few studies have addressed the validity and reliability of these measures and even fewer have done so in organizational settings. In order for POB to truly attain the status of a solid scientific endeavor, the psychometric properties of the PsyCap measures must be thoroughly investigated. In line with these concerns, we examine the convergent, discriminant and predictive validities for the PsyCap measures. First, we present an overview of the PsyCap constructs' theoretical definitions, followed by a discussion concerning the need for validation of these measures. Next we describe the methods and results of two studies. Finally, we offer a discussion of our results and conclusions with some suggestions for future research.

Conceptual definitions

Of the four PsyCap constructs, self-efficacy is fairly well supported within organizational literature in the form of Bandura's self-efficacy (Bandura, 1982, 1997). Hope, optimism and resiliency, on the other hand, are comparatively newer to research in organizational behavior. Conceptual definitions for each of the PsyCap constructs are presented below.

Hope. Hope has been commonly associated with one's positive expectancy toward the future. Hope derives its scholarly roots from clinical psychology, and has been defined as a positive motivational state that is derived from the combination of successful agency (willpower) and pathways (waypower) (Snyder et al., 1991). Individuals who are hopeful believe in their ability to set goals and accomplish them.

Optimism. Optimism (Tiger, 1971) is defined as a cognitive process directed at positive outcomes or expectancies concerning the social or material future, a future that is seen as both socially desirable and advantageous.

Resiliency. Resiliency is an individual's capability to successfully cope with change, adversity or risk (Stewart et al., 1997). Luthans (2002a) noted that it is the ability to deal with a variety of circumstances, including adversity, uncertainty, conflict, change (positive or negative), and increased responsibility.

Self-efficacy. Self-efficacy is familiar in organizational behavior as Bandura's (1982, 1997) self-efficacy. Luthans (Stajkovic and Luthans, 1998) emphasized the context specificity of self-efficacy in that 'self-efficacy refers to an individual's conviction about his or her abilities to mobilize the motivation, cognitive resources, and courses of action needed to successfully execute a specific task within a given context' (2002b: 60). Alternately, state self-efficacy is a cognitive evaluation that an individual make regarding his/her abilities to perform a specific task in a specific context.

Research rationale

Conceptual and empirical investigations of the construct validity of the PsyCap measures had typically been conducted outside of the field of organizational behavior, at the time of the scale development. Most of the PsyCap scales were developed for a wide variety of populations and settings, not specifically for use in organizational research. Thus, to support using these scales to study organizational behavior and organizational outcomes, it is imperative that these scales be examined for face validity as per Luthan's definitions of the PsyCap constructs as well as underlying factor structures that meet these definitions. Further critics of the POB and/or positive psychology movement have criticized the development and measurement of these constructs particularly in relation to construct validity. Thus, our research seeks to answer a very critical question in POB research: are the measures of PsyCap valid and reliable?

Few studies have looked at discriminant validity amongst PsyCap constructs, and thus positively-oriented constructs have drawn severe criticism citing the lack of methodological rigor (Lazarus, 2003). Several prominent psychologists have called for more measurement level studies aimed at validating measures for these constructs (Lopez and Snyder, 2003), and empirical support for validation of the PsyCap constructs outside of the authors' scale development validation studies are hard to come by.

Moderate to high correlations between some of the PsyCap constructs and similar constructs further supports the need for discriminant validity tests. The state hope scales are reported to correlate (.48–.65 range) with positive and negative affect and dispositional hope was correlated with dispositional optimism in the range of .5–.6 (Snyder et al., 1991). Optimism shares significant conceptual space not only with hope, but also with generalized self-efficacy. This begs the question: are the PsyCap constructs empirically different? Or are they multiple indicators of the same underlying construct? This study examines the distinctiveness of these constructs in relation to one another through multivariate statistical techniques.

One of the main criteria for validation of a new construct is its ability to explain or predict significant variance in other constructs of interest. Such findings help design interventions aimed at performance improvement. This research examines the predictive validity of the PsyCap constructs with respect to several pertinent work related outcomes: subjective well being in Study 1, motivation, satisfaction, turnover intentions, and performance in Study 2.

Subjective well-being. Subjective well-being (SWB) refers to an evaluation by an individual of his/her overall quality of life, pleasures and pains (Diener, 1984; Diener et al., 2003). Emotional well-being, a subset of SWB, has been linked to higher performance ratings (Wright and Cropanzano, 2000). Further, organizations with employees who report greater well-being have been shown to perform better on a number of financial indicators (cf. Keyes and Magyar-Moe, 2003). An individual's hope, optimism, resiliency and self-efficacy classify as strengths that lead to healthy life choices and thus to SWB.

Against this backdrop and potential effects on organizational performance as well as individual performance, our first study explores the predictive power of the PsyCap constructs in regards to SWB. Put differently, does having higher levels of hope, optimism, resiliency and self-efficacy lead to greater subjective well-being? Our second study focuses on more frequently studied outcomes in organizational research: motivation and satisfaction (Hackman and Oldham, 1975), turnover intentions and performance.

Study 1

Participants were 236 undergraduate students from a large Midwestern university. The students received extra credit in an undergraduate management class for participation in the study. The sample was fairly evenly split by gender (42 per cent female and 58 per cent male). Eighty-six per cent of the population were under 25, 11 percent were between the ages of 25 and 34 and 3.4 percent were over 35. Sixty-one percent of the sample had between 1 and 5 years of work experience, 25 percent had between 6 and 10 years of work experience and 5.9 percent had no work experience.

Measures

One measure for each PsyCap construct was used along with measures for state positive affect and subjective well-being. State positive affect is a conceptually similar construct and was used along with the PsyCap constructs to test for discriminant and incremental validity. Subjective well-being was measured as an outcome variable in order to test for incremental validity. As mentioned previously, PsyCap constructs are psychological states rather than dispositions or traits. Consistent with previous studies measuring states, participants were instructed to answer all of the items in accordance to how they were feeling 'right now'.

Hope. The Adult State Hope Scale (Snyder et al., 1996) is a 6-item scale tapping successful agency and pathway. Although the scale was not developed specifically for organizational studies, it has been widely used as a situational assessment of goal-related activities involving academics, sports and work (e.g. Simmons et al., 2003). It contains items such as 'If I should find myself in a jam, I could think of many ways to get out of it' and 'At the present time, I am energetically pursuing my goals'.

Optimism measure. The Life Orientation (or Optimism) Test (LOT) (Scheier, and Carver, 1985) is an 8-item scale designed to measure optimism in relation to dealing with daily life as well as one's ability and belief that one can cope. It contains items such as 'I enjoy dealing with new and unusual situations' and reverse scored 'If something can go wrong for me, it will'.

Resiliency measure. Block and Kremen's (1996) Ego-Resiliency Scale is a 12-item scale that measures the presence of a personality resource that allows individuals to adaptively encounter, function in and shape their environmental contexts and contains items such as 'I enjoy dealing with new and unusual situations' and 'I like new and difficult things'.

Self-efficacy measure. Self-efficacy has been found to have three dimensions: strength, magnitude and generality (Bandura, 1977). Strength refers to efficacy in spite of obstacles, magnitude refers to efficacy over difficult levels of performance and generality refers to a general sense of competence. Because this study is focused on state measures, three strength and magnitude items from the Sherer (1982) Self-Efficacy Scale only were used in this study and contained items such as 'If something looks too complicated at work or school, I will not even bother to try it' and 'When I decide to do something at work, I go right to work or school on it'.

State positive affect. Brief et al.'s (1988) Job Affect Scale (JAS) was used to measure state positive affect. The JAS is a 20-item scale measuring high and low activation of both positive and negative mood. It contains 10 positive affect items (e.g. elated, peppy, enthusiastic) and 10 negative affect items (e.g. distressed, scornful, dull). Respondents are asked to indicate to the extent to which they had experienced these moods and/or emotions over the past week. Consistent with Burke et al.'s (1989) suggestion that unipolar affect scales are likely to provide greater explanatory power, the six high activation positive items were used for the state positive affect variable.

Subjective well-being. Subjective well-being was measured with Deiner's (1984) 4-item scale tapping an individual's evaluation of his/her overall quality of life, pleasures and pains.

Results

Our analysis for both studies consisted of exploratory and confirmatory factor analyses as well as structural equation modeling using the maximum likelihood estimation method. Means, standard deviations and correlations and squared correlations (in parentheses) between factors are presented in Table 14.1.

Measurement model

To test for construct and discriminant validity, an exploratory factor analysis (using principal axis factoring with oblique rotation) was run for each of the PsyCap constructs. Results showed the factors that emerged were consistent with their conceptual definitions as well as generally consistent with previous research. As in previous studies, hope loaded on two factors, agency and pathway. These factors were reasonably intercorrelated (0.38) and the items displayed no significant cross loadings. Self-efficacy had two underlying factors: strength and magnitude. Strength and magnitude were also reasonably intercorrelated (0.40) and demonstrated no significant cross loadings. Previous research using the LOT measure consistently yielded two factors. The presence of two factors has been attributed to both the positive or negative wording of the item (Scheier and Carver, 1985) and to separate factors labeled general optimism and success expectancy (Carifio and Rhodes, 2002). In the present study, two factors were found based on the positive or negative wording of the item.

The factor analysis of resiliency yielded four factors. This is consistent with previous findings (e.g. Kluemper, 2005); however, it is *inconsistent* with the unidimensional conceptual definition of resiliency. Furthermore,

Table 14.1 *Means, standard deviations, and correlations and squared correlations among factors (in parentheses)*

Factor	Means[a]	SD	1	2	3	4	5	6	7
1. Agency	3.85	0.65							
2. Pathway			0.64**						
	3.83	0.70	(0.41)						
3. Optimism			0.71**	0.70**					
	3.81	0.78	(0.50)	(0.49)					
4. Reverse-scored optimism			0.60**	0.51**	0.76**				
	3.60	0.73	(0.36)	(0.26)	(0.58)				
5. Self-efficacy strength			0.47**	0.35**	0.39**	0.54**			
	4.12	0.74	(0.22)	(0.12)	(0.15)	(0.29)			
6. Self-efficacy magnitude			0.49**	0.67**	0.56**	0.34**	0.45**		
	3.89	0.72	(0.24)	(0.45)	(0.28)	(0.12)	(0.18)		
7. State positive affect			0.68**	0.58**	0.65**	0.51**	0.28**	0.37**	
	3.23	0.63	(0.26)	(0.34)	(0.42)	(0.26)	(0.08)	(0.14)	
8. SWB			0.64**	0.52**	0.80**	0.56**	0.22**	0.21*	0.63**
	3.96	0.74	(0.41)	(0.27)	(0.64)	(0.31)	(0.05)	(0.04)	(0.40)

[a] all variables were assessed on a 5-point scale.
* $p < .05$
** $p < .01$

Block and Kremen's scale contains items such as 'Most of the people I meet are likeable' and 'I usually think carefully about something before acting' that do not align with the definition of resiliency as an individual capability to successfully cope with change, adversity or risk. In the light of the factor analytic results, as well as concerns about the face validity, the construct validity of resiliency was not well supported in this study and, thus, was not used in subsequent analysis.

An additional exploratory factor analysis including all items for hope, optimism, self-efficacy, state positive affect, and subjective well-being indicated that each measure was fairly distinct from each of the other constructs' measures. Furthermore, the PsyCap measures did not load with the conceptually similar measures, state positive affect and with subjective well-being. It should be noted that state positive affect loaded on two factors, a finding inconsistent with previous studies. Despite this, no state positive affect item loaded with the PsyCap constructs.

Next, a confirmatory factor analysis was conducted with the PsyCap constructs (the pathway and agency dimensions of hope, positively and negatively worded dimensions of optimism, and the magnitude and strength dimensions of self-efficacy), state positive affect and subjective well-being. Results of the CFA indicate good overall fit (CFI = 0.94 and RMSEA = 0.058, chi square = 690.3, df = 377). Additionally, as can be seen in Table 14.1, all factor loadings were significant at the .05 level. However, the composite reliabilities (CRs) for hope agency, self-efficacy magnitude and state positive affect fell well below the commonly accepted 0.70 threshold, also indicated in Table 14.1 (Netemeyer et al., 1990). This signifies that these measures have low reliability in this sample. Additionally, the average variance explained (AVE) for all the PsyCap variables and state positive affect fell well below the generally accepted 0.50 level (Netemeyer et al., 1990). Furthermore, a chi-square difference test comparing a two factor solution (df = 377; χ^2= 690.3) between hope agency and optimism with a one factor solution (df = 384; χ^2 = 703.8) was not significant, indicating lack of discriminant validity between these factors.

Fornell and Larcker (1981) stated that in order to adequately support discriminant validity, each construct's AVE should be greater than the squared correlation between those constructs. As can be seen in a comparison between Tables 14.1 and 14.2, the AVE for both variables was less than the constructs' squared correlations (in parentheses) for the following pairs of constructs: agency and pathway, pathway and optimism, agency and state positive affect, agency and optimism, pathway and self-efficacy magnitude, optimism and state positive affect, optimism and subjective well-being. One construct's AVE was less than the squared correlation for the following pairs: agency and optimism, agency and self-efficacy magnitude, agency and state positive affect and reversed scored optimism and state positive affect. This result calls into question the discriminant validity of these measures.

Structural model

Structural equation modeling using Lisrel 8.72 was used to analyze the effect of the PsyCap constructs on the outcome subjective well-being. Results indicated good fit (CFI = 0.94; RMSEA = 0.058). The PsyCap constructs explained a large portion of variance (0.77) in subjective well-being; however, the only significant relationships between the PsyCap constructs and subjective well-being was the positive effect of positively worded optimism (βs = 0.97, p < .01, see Figure 14.1) and the negative effect of self-efficacy magnitude (standardized gamma = −0.44). These results are interpreted with caution due to the unreliability of some of the measures as well as the possible lack of discriminant validity.

Summary

Construct, discriminant and incremental validity were not well supported for any of the PsyCap constructs in this study. Block and Kremen's resiliency measure was initially found to have four factors and, after deletion of items lacking face validity and/or content validity, three factors emerged. The factors that emerged do not represent resiliency as defined by Luthans. The low CRs and AVEs for the remaining PsyCap scales do not support construct nor discriminant validity. A conclusion as to the

Table 14.2   *Study 1 measurement properties*

Fit Statistics CFI = 0.94; RMSEA = 0.058; Chi-Square = 690.3; df = 377

All scales	Standardized loading	Composite reliability	Average variance extracted
Agency		0.47	0.23
If I should find myself in a jam, I could think of many ways to get out of it.	0.42		
There are lots of ways around any problem that I am facing now.	0.45		
I can think of many ways to reach my current goals.	0.57		
Pathway		0.68	0.42
At the present time, I am energetically pursuing my goals.	0.64		
Right now, I see myself as being pretty successful.	0.63		
At this time, I am meeting the goals I have set for myself.	0.67		
Optimism		0.67	0.34
In uncertain times, I usually expect the best.	0.57		
I always look on the bright side of things.	0.62		
Right now I'm optimistic about the future.	0.60		
I'm a believer in the idea that 'every cloud has a silver lining'.	0.53		
Reverse scored optimism		0.76	0.45
If something can go wrong for me, it will.	0.55		
I hardly ever expect things to go my way.	0.77		
Things never work out the way I want them to.	0.68		
I rarely count on good things happening to me.	0.66		
Self-efficacy strength		0.76	0.45
If something looks too complicated at work, I will not even bother to try it.	0.81		
I avoid trying to learn new things at work when they look too difficult for me.	0.54		
When trying to learn something new at work, I soon give up if I am not initially successful.	0.48		
I give up on things at work before completing them.	0.80		
Self-efficacy magnitude		0.48	0.32
When I decide to do something at work, I go right to work on it.	0.62		
When I have something unpleasant to do at work, I stick to it until I finish it.	0.63		
State positive affect		0.41	0.20
Active	0.45		
Strong	0.25		
Peppy	0.66		
Excited	0.51		
Enthusiastic	0.25		

Table 14.2   *(Continued)*

Fit Statistics CFI = 0.94; RMSEA = 0.058; Chi-Square = 690.3; df = 377

All scales	Standardized loading	Composite reliability	Average variance extracted
Subjective well-being		.85	.58
In general I consider myself: not a very happy person – a very happy person.	0.89		
Compared to most of my peers, I consider myself: less happy – more happy.	0.80		
Some people are very happy. They enjoy life regardless of what is going on, getting the most out of everything. To what extent does this characterization describe you? Not at all – A great deal.	0.74		
Some people are not very happy. Although they are not depressed they never seem as happy as they might be. To what extent does this characterization describe you?: Not at all – A great deal	0.59		

All factor loadings are significant at the *p* < .05 level.

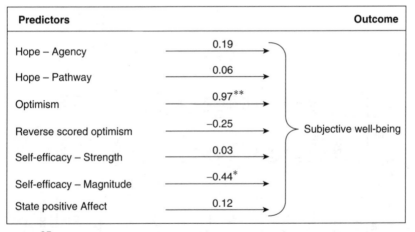

*p < .05
**p < .01

Figure 14.1   *Study 1 Model – CFI = 0.94; RMSEA = 0.058; Chi-Square = 690.30;
df = 377*

construct, discriminant, and predictive validity of resiliency cannot be made until a more appropriate measure is developed. Conclusions as to the predictive validity of these constructs are inappropriate in this sample. Without adequate reliabilities and discriminant validity, predictive validity cannot be determined.

Table 14.3 Means, standard deviations, and correlations and squared correlations among factors (in parentheses)

	Means[a]	SD	1	2	3	4	5	6	7	8	9	10	11
1. Agency	3.89	0.65											
2. Pathway	3.63	0.92	0.79** (0.62)										
3. Optimism	3.73	0.67	0.82** (0.67)	0.63** (0.40)									
4. Reverse scored optimism	4.07	0.75	0.46** (0.21)	0.46** (0.21)	0.63** (0.40)								
5. Self-efficacy strength	4.50	0.61	0.24 (0.06)	0.33** (0.11)	0.25* (0.06)	0.40** (0.16)							
6. Self-efficacy magnitude	3.86	0.90	0.48** (0.23)	0.29** (0.08)	0.43** (0.18)	0.18 (0.03)	0.15 (0.02)						
7. Resiliency	3.76	0.63	0.50** (0.25)	0.54** (0.29)	0.34** (0.12)	0.59** (0.35)	0.57** (0.32)	0.16 (0.03)					
8. State positive affect	3.31	0.76	0.43** (0.18)	0.53** (0.28)	0.32** (0.10)	0.35** (0.12)	0.12 (0.01)	0.01 (0.00)	0.28* (0.08)				
9. Motivation	3.95	0.62	0.34** (0.12)	0.25* (0.06)	0.31* (0.10)	0.22 (0.05)	0.18 (0.03)	0.33** (0.11)	0.47** (0.22)	0.57** (0.32)			
10. General satisfaction	3.81	0.76	0.01 (0.00)	0.35** (0.12)	0.13 (0.02)	0.18 (0.03)	0.21 (0.04)	0.03 (0.00)	0.30** (0.09)	0.51** (0.26)	0.42** (0.18)		
11. Turnover intentions	2.21	1.28	−0.11 (−0.01)	−0.26* (−0.07)	0.02 (0.00)	−0.28 (−0.08)	−0.32 (−0.10)	−0.03 (0.00)	−0.39** (−0.15)	−0.48** (−0.23)	−0.28* (−0.08)	−0.57** (−0.32)	
12. Performance	3.35	0.81	0.05 (0.00)	0.28* (0.08)	0.01 (0.00)	0.09 (0.01)	0.21 (0.04)	−0.11 (−0.01)	0.18 (0.03)	0.23 (0.05)	0.09 (0.01)	0.19 (0.04)	−0.21 (−0.04)

[a] all variables were assessed on a 5-point scale.

* p < .05

** p < .01

Study 2

Undergraduate students from a large Midwestern university were asked to recruit three employees and their manager to participate in an online survey. The students received extra credit for an undergraduate management class for participation in the study. Managers were asked to assign their employees an employee identification number. These numbers allowed the researchers to associate employee survey with manager survey while still ensuring the autonomy of the employee. Each of the employees was given an online survey with the PsyCap measures, state positive affect and outcome variables, general satisfaction, motivation and turnover intentions. The manager was asked to submit an online survey for each of his/her three employees, assessing their performance. The final sample consisted of 97 working professionals from a variety of industries (48 percent maintenance, service or sales; 25 percent clerical; 13 per cent technical; 6 percent administrative; and 6 percent other). The sample was fairly evenly split by gender (42 percent female and 58 percent male), their average age was 33.8 years (S.D. 12.5), and their average tenure was 3.74 years (S.D. 4.28).

Measures

Hope, optimism and self-efficacy were measured using the same scales as indicated in Study 1. Resiliency was measured using a 5-item measure developed by Kluemper (2005). It contains items such as 'Recently, I have been able to adapt to setbacks at work' and 'Lately, I have been able to rebound from unpredictability on the job'. The outcome measures assessed in Study 2 were chosen because of their relevance in the workplace. General satisfaction was measured using Hackman and Oldham's (1975) Job Diagnostic Survey. This 3-item measure taps the degree to which the employee is happy on the job. Motivation was also measured using the Job Diagnostic Survey (Hackman and Oldham, 1975). This 4-item measure taps the degree to which an employee is self-motivated to perform effectively on the job. Turnover intention was measured using a 1-item measure in which employees were asked the frequency with which they thought about quitting. Performance was measured using a 3-item measure in which managers were asked to assess the employee's ability to solve problems, his or her promotability, and his or her overall performance.

Results

Means, standard deviations and correlations and squared correlations (in parentheses) between factors are presented in Table 14.3.

Measurement model

Confirmatory factor analyses using Lisrel 8.72 and the maximum likelihood estimation method indicated marginal to poor overall fit (CFI = 0.86

Table 14.4   *Study 2 confirmatory factor analysis*

Fit Statistics CFI = 0.86; RMSEA = 0.08; Chi-Square = 1136.41; df = 675

All scales	Standardized loading	Composite reliability	Average variance extracted
Agency		0.62	0.36
If I should find myself in a jam, I could think of many ways to get out of it.	0.47		
There are lots of ways around any problem that I am facing now.	0.53		
I can think of many ways to reach my current goals.	0.76		
Pathway		0.85	0.66
At the present time, I am energetically pursuing my goals.	0.82		
Right now, I see myself as being pretty successful.	0.80		
At this time, I am meeting the goals I have set for myself.	0.86		
Optimism		0.74	0.43
In uncertain times, I usually expect the best.	0.52		
I always look on the bright side of things.	0.64		
Right now I'm optimistic about the future.	0.83		
I'm a believer in the idea that 'every cloud has a silver lining'.	0.59		
Reverse scored optimism		0.80	0.51
If something can go wrong for me, it will. (R)	0.50		
I hardly ever expect things to go my way. (R)	0.92		
Things never work out the way I want them to. (R)	0.77		
I rarely count on good things happening to me.(R)	0.59		
Self-efficacy strength		0.82	0.70
If something looks too complicated at work, I will not even bother to try it. (R)	0.59		
I avoid trying to learn new things at work when they look too difficult for me. (R)	0.79		
When trying to learn something new at work, I soon give up if I am not initially successful. (R)	0.71		
I give up on things at work before completing them. (R)	0.60		
Self-efficacy magnitude		0.82	0.70
When I decide to do something at work, I go right to work on it.	0.74		
When I have something unpleasant to do at work, I stick to it until I finish it.	0.92		
Resiliency		0.71	0.33
Recently, I have been able to adapt to setbacks at work.	0.64		
I have not easily bounced back from recent hardships at my company. (R)	0.47		
Lately, I have been able to rebound from unpredictability on the job.	0.51		

Table 14.4   *(Continued)*

Fit Statistics CFI = 0.86; RMSEA = 0.08; Chi-Square = 1136.41; df = 675

All scales	Standardized loading	Composite reliability	Average variance extracted
Despite recent conflicts at work I have been able to adapt.	0.54		
Adjusting to changes at work is currently difficult for me. (R)	0.69		
State positive affect		0.76	0.39
Active	0.49		
Strong	0.56		
Peppy	0.61		
Excited	0.69		
Enthusiastic	0.74		
Motivation		0.69	0.38
My opinion of myself goes up when I do this job well.	0.74		
I feel a great sense of personal satisfaction when I do this job well.	0.80		
I feel bad and unhappy when I discover that I have performed poorly on this job. (R)	0.30		
My own feelings generally are not affected much one way or the other by how well I do on this job.	0.50		
Satisfaction		0.73	0.64
Generally speaking, I am very satisfied with this job.	1.08		
I am generally satisfied with the kind of work I do in this job.	0.33		
Performance		0.87	0.69
His or her ability to solve problems: Very Poor – Very Good	0.75		
His or her potential for promotion: Very Poor – Very Good	0.81		
His or her overall performance: Very Poor – Very Good	0.89		

All factor loadings are significant at the $p < .05$ level.

(R) = reverse scored.

and RMSEA = 0.08, chi-square = 1136.41, df = 675). All factor loadings were significant at the .05 level (see Table 14.3). Additionally, all of the CRs were above the .70 cutoff with the exception of two (agency = 0.62 and motivation = .69). Thus, the reliability issues in Study 1 may have been sample specific. However, the AVEs for hope agency, optimism, and resiliency still fell below the 0.50 cutoff. Chi square difference tests between the factors were all significant supporting discriminant validity. As can be seen in a comparison between Tables 14.3 and 14.4, the AVEs for both variables is less than the constructs' squared correlations (in parentheses) for hope agency and optimism and one construct's AVE is less than the squared correlation for the following pairs: agency and pathway

Predictors		Outcome
Hope – Pathway	−1.29	
Hope – Agency	0.51	
Optimism	0.67	
Reverse scored optimism	−0.37	
Resiliency	0.41	General satisfaction
Self-efficacy – Strength	−0.05	
Self-efficacy – Magnitude	0.20	
State positive Affect	0.51*	

*p < .05
**p < .01

Figure 14.2   *Model 1 – CFI =0.85; RMSEA =0.09 ; Chi-Square = 770.40; df = 428*

and reversed scored optimism and resiliency. These results replicate a lack of discriminant validity between hope and optimism in Study 1 as well as indicate a lack of discriminant validity between optimism and resiliency.

Structural model

Four structural equation models were run in Lisrel 8.72 to look at the incremental effects of the PsyCap constructs over state positive affect on each of the four outcomes variables (Model 1 – Satisfaction; Model 2 – Motivation; Model 3 – Turnover Intentions; Model 4 – Performance).

Results from Model 1 indicate marginal to poor fit (CFI = 0.85; RMSEA =0.09; Chi-Square = 770.40; df = 428). The PsyCap constructs and state positive affect explained 47 percent of the variance in satisfaction, however, the only significant relationship was the positive effect of state positive affect (βs = 0.51, p < .05; see Figure 14.2). It is important to note that the standardized gamma between hope agency and satisfaction is greater than one. This is most likely due to the high correlation between hope and optimism and is further indication of the lack of discriminant validity between these constructs.

Results from Model 2 indicate marginal to poor fit (CFI = 0.86 ; RMSEA = 0.08; Chi-Square = 842.36; df = 491). The PsyCap constructs and state positive affect explained 86 percent of the variance in motivation, however, the only significant relationship was the positive effect of state positive affect (βs = 0.83, p < .01; see Figure 14.3).

Results from Model 3 indicate marginal to poor fit (CFI = 0.87; RMSEA = 0.09; Chi-Square = 713.14; df = 399). The PsyCap constructs and state positive affect explained 42 percent of the variance in turnover

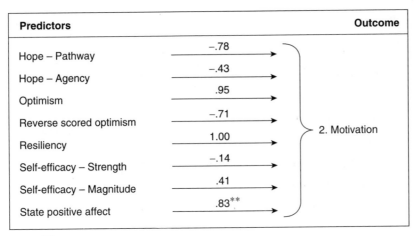

*p < .05
**p < .01

Figure 14.3   *Model 2 CFI = 0.86 ; RMSEA = 0.08; Chi-Square = 842.36; df = 491*

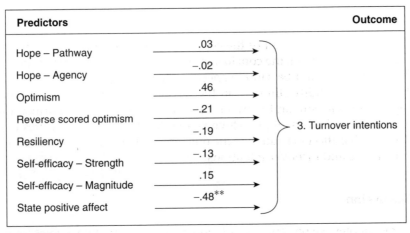

*p < .05
**p < .01

Figure 14.4   *Model 3 CFI = 0.87; RMSEA = 0.09; Chi-Square = 713.14; df = 399*

intentions, however, the only significant relationship was the negative effect of state positive affect ($\beta s = 0.48$, p < .01; see Figure 14.4).

Results from Model 4 indicate marginal to poor fit (CFI = 0.86; RMSEA = 0.09; Chi-Square = 808.66; df = 459). The PsyCap constructs and state positive affect explained 21 percent of the variance in performance however, none of the factors were significantly related to performance (see Figure 14.5).

Figure 14.5   *Model 4 CFI = 0.86; RMSEA = 0.09; Chi-Square = 808.66; df = 459*

Summary

The CRs and AVEs for all of the constructs were much improved in this sample. This supports the conclusion that some of the problems found in the first study could be sample specific. However, indications of lack of discriminant validity still exist in the second study, specifically between hope and optimism, and between optimism and resiliency. Further, this study indicated a lack of predictive validity of the PsyCap measures over state positive affect in relation to the outcome variables general satisfaction, motivation, and turnover intentions.

Discussion

In this chapter, we presented validation evidence across two studies for the psychometric properties of the four suggested PsyCap measures (Luthans, 2002a, 2002b). Such validation is an important step towards the scientific progression of POB research. From Study 1, we concluded that although the PsyCap measures seem to hold up to exploratory analysis techniques, they raise serious concerns when subjected to more rigorous psychometric evaluation using structural equation modeling. Construct, discriminant and incremental validity were not well supported for any of the PsyCap measures in our first study. Block and Kremen's (1996) resiliency measure, for example, did not display the factor structure hypothesized a priori. The low CRs and AVEs across all measures raise doubts regarding their construct validity. The most troubling aspect of our results is the lack of discriminant validity between hope (agency) and optimism. Given these concerns regarding construct, discriminant validity, and reliability, predictive validity cannot be ascertained.

Study 2 included an organizational sample and data from multiple sources. It seems encouraging to see higher CRs and AVEs in this sample; however, concerns regarding construct, discriminant and predictive validity still abound. In fact, this study replicated our finding that state hope and state optimism share considerable conceptual and empirical space as indicated by the lack of discriminating power between these two constructs. The same held true for resiliency and optimism. The most pertinent result with regard to work performance is that none of the PsyCap constructs and state positive affect was found to relate to performance. Moreover, the predictive power of the PsyCap constructs disappeared when state positive affect was accounted for with regard to motivation, satisfaction and turnover intentions. This indeed has been one of the main criticisms of the positive movement (cf. Lazarus, 2003).

Taking a step back from empirical findings across both studies, we need to ask the question: what do our results mean for POB scholarship? Is the study of PsyCap worthy of scientific scrutiny or is it as yet several steps away from attaining the status of a scientific endeavor? Those questions were indeed the motivation of our research. It is important to note that our findings indicate that the two most commonly used measures of PsyCap – hope (Snyder et al., 1996) and optimism (Scheier and Carver, 1985) – did not tap empirically distinct constructs because of shared significant conceptual and empirical space.

We may need to rethink inclusion of hope and optimism as separate constructs. It might be more fruitful to theorize an overarching construct that encompasses both hope and optimism. The more straightforward alternative is measurement development for hope and optimism that more accurately reflect their construct space in organizational settings. Thus, while hope and optimism are theoretically rich in the promise they offer in positive human functioning, at the present time they cannot be fully supported as reliable and valid scientific constructs in organizational settings. The caveat is that this conclusion is based upon research conducted using the specific measures we adopted in this chapter.

Next, for a construct to truly attain some level of significance it has to contribute to additional explanatory power over and above that of similar constructs in that particular nomological net. None of the PsyCap constructs did so over and above the effects of state positive affect. As such, these measures do not offer a value added over state positive affect. It is possible that state positive affect itself constitutes a malleable positive psychological capacity. Management research might be better served by developing interventions that induce state positive affect among employees specifically given its influence on motivation, turnover intentions and satisfaction.

The main limitation of our first study is the use of student samples and potential lack of external validity (Gordon et al., 1987). All the measures used here are self-report instruments; however, as Lopez and Snyder

(2003) posit, these constructs are an individual's perceptions of his/her psychological strengths. Hence, self-reports in this case may be appropriate. Moreover, this study might suffer from common method bias. The results reported with respect to SWB and general optimism should be interpreted with caution. Although the statistical inferences regarding the distinctiveness of the two constructs and thus a large amount of shared variance makes intuitive sense, it is cause for concern. Further, there could be other constructs that share conceptual space with the PsyCap constructs and if so, future research should delve into the distinctiveness of those constructs and PsyCap.

Our second study sought to alleviate the limitations of our first study by using an organizational sample and collection of data from multiple sources. As such, we are more confident in our findings from the second study. However, this study was cross-sectional and a true assessment of states might be more accurate through longitudinal designs. Future research should replicate our study with longitudinal designs to investigate the stability and state-like nature of key POB constructs. Moreover, our choice of measures across both studies followed the most frequently used measures in both organizational literature (newly emerging) and other related disciplines.

In sum, we need rigorous theoretical development concerning what constitutes positive psychological capacities. Other constructs emphasized in our literature such as emotional intelligence, interdependent attachment styles, eustress, vigor and core self-evaluations reflect positive psychological capacities even though they may be more stable (yet changeable) over the life span.

References

Bandura, A. (1977) 'Self-efficacy: Toward a unifying theory of behavioral change', *Psychological Review*, 84, 191–215.

Bandura, A. (1982) 'Self-efficacy mechanism in human agency', *American Psychologist*, 37, 122–47.

Bandura, A. (1997) *Self-efficacy: The Exercise of Control*. New York: Freeman.

Block, J. and Kremen, A.M. (1996) 'IQ and ego-resiliency: Conceptual and empirical connections and separateness', *Journal of Personality and Social Psychology*, 70, 349–61.

Brief, A.P, Burke, M.J., George, J.M., Robinson, B.S. and Webster, J. (1988) 'Should negative affectivity remain an unmeasured variable in the study of job stress?', *Journal of Applied Psychology*, 73, 193–8.

Burke, M.J., Brief, A.P., George, J.M., Robinson, B.S. and Webster, J. (1989) 'Measuring affect at work: Confirmatory analyses of competing mood structures with conceptual linkage to cortical regulatory systems', *Journal of Personality and Social Psychology*, 57, 1091–1102.

Carifio, J. and Rhodes, L. (2002) 'Construct validities and the empirical relationships between optimism, hope, self-efficacy, and locus of control', *Work: Journal of Prevention, Assessment and Rehabilitation*, 19, 125–36.

Diener, E. (1984) 'Subjective well being', *Psychological Bulletin*, 95, 542–75.

Diener, E., Oishi, S. and Lucas, R.E. (2003) 'Personality, culture and subjective well-being: Emotional and cognitive evaluations of life', *Annual Review of Psychology*, 54, 403–25.

Fornell, C. and Larcker, D.F. (1981) 'Evaluating structural equation models with observable variables and measurement error', *Journal of Marketing Research*, 19, 39–50.

Gordon, M.E., Slade, L.A. and Schmitt, N. (1987) 'Student guinea pigs: Porcine predictors and particularistic phenomena', *Academy of Management Review*, 12, 160–3.

Hackman, J.R. and Oldham, G.R. (1975) 'Development of the job diagnostic survey', *Journal of Applied Psychology*, 60, 159–70.

Keyes, C.L. and Magyar-Moe, J.L. (2003) 'The measurement and utility of adult subjective well-being', in S.J. Lopez and C.R. Snyder (eds) *Positive Psychological Assessment: A Handbook of Models and Measures* (pp. 411–25). Washington, DC: American Psychological Association.

Kluemper, D. (2005) 'State resiliency: Development of a measure'. Working paper, Spears School of Business, Oklahoma State University.

Lazarus, R.S. (2003) 'Does the Positive Psychology Movement have legs?', *Psychological Inquiry*, 14, 93–109.

Lopez, S.J and Snyder, C.R. (2003) 'The future of positive psychological assessment', in S.J. Lopez and C.R. Snyder (eds) *Positive Psychological Assessment: A Handbook of Models and Measures*. Washington, DC: American Psychological Association.

Luthans, F. (2002a) 'The need for and meaning of positive organizational behavior', *Journal of Organizational Behavior*, 23, 695–706.

Luthans, F. (2002b) 'Positive organizational behavior: Developing and managing psychological strengths', *Academy of Management Executive*, 16, 57–72.

Netemeyer, R.G., Johnston, M.W. and Burton, S. (1990) 'Analysis of role conflict and role ambiguity in a structural equations framework', *Journal of Applied Psychology*, 75, 148–57.

Scheier, M.F. and Carver, C.S. (1985) 'Optimism, coping, and health: Assessment and implications of generalized outcome expectancies', *Health Psychology*, 4, 219–47.

Sherer, M. (1982) 'The self-efficacy scale: Construction and validation', *Psychological Reports*, 51, 663–71

Simmons, B.L., Nelson, D.L. and Quick, J.C. (2003) 'Health for the hopeful: A study of attachment behavior in home health care nurses', *International Journal of Stress Management*, 10, 361–75.

Snyder, C.R., Harris, C., Anderson, J.R., Holleran, S.A., Irving, L.M., Sigmon, S.T., Yoshingobu, L., Gibb, J., Langelle, C. and Harney, P. (1991) 'The will and the ways', *Journal of Personality and Social Psychology*, 60, 570–85.

Snyder, C.R., Sympson, S.C., Ybasco, F.C., Borders, T.F., Babyak, M.A. and Higgins, R.L. (1996) 'Development and validation of the state hope scale', *Journal of Personality and Social Psychology*, 70, 321–35.

Stajkovic, A.D. and Luthans, F. (1998) 'Self-efficacy and work-related performance: A meta-analysis', *Psychological Bulletin*, 124, 240–61.

Stewart, M., Reid, G. and Mangham, C. (1997) 'Fostering children's resilience', *Journal of Pediatric Nursing*, 12, 21–31.

Tiger, L. (1971) *Optimism: The Biology of Hope*. New York: Simon & Schuster.

Wright, T.A. and Cropanzano, R. (2000) 'Psychological well-being and job satisfaction as predictors of job performance', *Journal of Occupational Health Psychology*, 5, 84–94.

Index

Note
f = figure
t = tables